I0764008

THE

CONSTITUTIONAL TEXT-BOOK:

A

PRACTICAL AND FAMILIAR EXPOSITION

OF THE

Constitution of the United States,

AND

OF PORTIONS OF THE PUBLIC AND ADMINISTRATIVE LAW OF THE FEDERAL GOVERNMENT.

By FURMAN SHEPPARD.

"It is of infinite moment that you should properly estimate the immense value of your National Union to your collective and individual happiness: that you should cherish a cordial, habitual, and immovable attachment to it: accustoming yourselves to think and speak of it as of the palladium of your political safety and prosperity."

WASHINGTON'S *Farewell Address to the People of the United States.*

PHILADELPHIA:
SOWER, POTTS & CO.,
530 MARKET ST., AND 523 MINOR ST.

PREFACE.

PROFESSIONAL treatises and judicial decisions must doubtless continue to be our chief original sources of constitutional exposition; yet, after all, it is from that humbler class of books in which the results of the learned investigations of jurists and statesmen are embodied in a cheap, plain, and popular form, that the great mass of the community derive their information concerning our political institutions. Judge Story was himself sensible of this, when he condensed the substance of his extensive commentaries into a small volume "designed for the use of school libraries and general readers." It is an important addition, however, to the usefulness of such a manual, that it should pass beyond a formal disquisition upon the mere text of the Constitution, and enter into the practical administrative details and the public law of the government, so as to exhibit to some extent its actual workings. An acquaintance with the machinery by which the Constitution is applied and enforced, is no less important than an understanding of the written instrument.

Our object has accordingly been, not only to present in familiar language a brief outline of the generally-received interpretation of each clause, but to illustrate it by a reference to such facts and to such legislation by Congress as seemed necessary to its proper elucidation. Long trains of reasoning and abstract discourses upon political topics have been studiously avoided, as interfering with our plan. Principles have been stated briefly, and sometimes in the very language of judicial decisions, legal treatises, or public documents. There is no attempt to decide unsettled questions, or to deal with disputed points in the manner of a controversialist or a partisan.

The sole aim of the author has been to furnish an elementary manual of the Constitution, which might possibly be instrumental in extending a knowledge of its meaning, and consequently of increasing our attachment to it as the great charter of our national renown.

TABLE OF CONTENTS.

CHAPTER VIII.

CHAPTER IX.

CHAPTER X.

CHAPTER XI.

CHAPTER XII.

CHAPTER XIII.

CHAPTER XIV.

CHAPTER XV.

CHAPTER XVI.

THE

CONSTITUTIONAL TEXT-BOOK.

CHAPTER I.

THE DISCOVERY AND SETTLEMENT OF THE COLONIES OF NORTH AMERICA.

§ 1. In March, 1496, Henry the Seventh, King of England, commissioned John Cabot and his three sons, Sebastian, Lewis, and Sanctius, to set forth on a voyage of discovery, and to conquer and occupy any lands not already in the possession of a Christian nation. Under this commission, Cabot and his son Sebastian departed in May, 1497; and, after discovering the islands of Newfoundland and St. Johns, sailed along the coast of the mainland north and south, and claimed for the English king the territory from the Gulf of Mexico to an indefinite extent on the north, without, however, attempting either settlement or conquest.

§ 2. From this discovery by Cabot, originated the title by which England claimed North America. That title depended upon the first discovery of the continent, and was called the Right of Discovery. It was a principle adopted in the practice of the nations of Europe, that the first discovery of unknown countries gave to the government, whose subjects had made the discovery, a title to the possession of such newly-found lands.

§ 3. Under this title the original inhabitants were permitted to remain in the territory; but they were restrained from selling or granting its soil, except to the sovereign by whose subjects it had been discovered, who claimed for himself the sole right to dispose of it; consequently, no other persons could acquire a title from the natives, either by purchase or by conquest.

§ 4. There does not seem to be any just reason why the first discovery of a country should give a right to the possession of it, especially where it is inhabited, as North America was. The rule was probably adopted in order to prevent conflicting claims by different governments to the same territory.

§ 5. Uninhabited countries cannot be said to belong to any particular nation, for no nation has taken possession of them. Whenever, therefore, a nation first discovers uninhabited lands, it has a right to take possession of them, and its title will be regarded by other nations as good, provided the discovery is followed up by an actual settlement, or by colonizing it within a reasonable time, or by making other use of it; but, if some one of these things is not done, the title is considered to be incomplete and abandoned, and the land will be open to fresh occupants.

§ 6. Although the titles derived from discovery may not originally have been very just, their validity, after a lapse of several centuries, cannot now be overthrown. By successive transfers they have become vested in the several States and in the United States, and they have been recognised and acceded to by the Supreme Court of the United States. We still hold this country under the title by which it was originally acquired, and we claim that that title has, by treaties or by grants, descended to us.

§ 7. In the settlement of a new country, there is a distinction in regard to the laws which become of force there. If the country be uninhabited, the laws of the nation to which the settlers belong, spring immediately into operation, so far as they are applicable to the situation and local circumstances of the settlers, who would otherwise be without laws to govern them. If the country be inhabited, and acquired by treaty, conquest, or purchase, the general rule is, that the laws already existing remain in force until altered or repealed, unless they be contrary to religion or morality.

§ 8. Although North America was inhabited at the time it was colonized, the colonists disregarded the occupancy and claims of the Indian tribes, and considered themselves as settling an unoccupied country. We must, therefore, regard them as bringing with them to the new world the laws of England, so far as they were applicable to their situation, and it was so resolved by the Continental Congress in the Declaration of Rights.

§ 9. In fact, the charters under which the colonies were settled (except that of Pennsylvania) expressly declared that all subjects of the king, and their children, inhabiting therein, should be deemed natural-born subjects, and should enjoy all the privileges and immunities thereof.

The colonies were not affected by acts of Parliament passed after the date of their settlement, unless they were expressly named therein.

§ 10. The names of the thirteen original colonies were Virginia, Massachusetts, New Hampshire, Connecticut, Rhode Island, New York, New Jersey, Pennsylvania, Delaware, Maryland, North Carolina, South Carolina, and

Georgia. These colonies have, with reference to their form of government, been divided into three classes, as follows:

(1.) Provincial or Royal Governments.

(2.) Proprietary Governments.

(3.) Charter Governments.

§ 11. Under the Provincial governments, a governor was appointed by the king, as his deputy, to rule according to his instructions. The king also appointed a council to assist the governor and aid in making laws. The governor established courts and raised military forces. He had power to call together legislative assemblies of freeholders and others, in which the council formed an upper house, he himself exercising a negative upon their proceedings, as well as the right to adjourn them for a time, or to dissolve them. These assemblies made local laws, which had to be submitted to the king for his approval or disapproval.

New Hampshire, New York, New Jersey, Virginia, North and South Carolina, and Georgia, were provincial colonies.

§ 12. In the Proprietary governments, the king granted his rights and privileges to certain individuals, who became proprietaries of the colony, and held it as if it were a feudal principality. These proprietaries appointed the governor, directed the calling together of the legislative assemblies, and exercised all those acts of authority which in the provincial governments were exercised by the king.

At the time of the Revolution there were but three colonies of this description: Maryland, of which Lord Baltimore was proprietary, and Pennsylvania and Delaware, of which William Penn was proprietary. The Carolinas and New Jersey, which had been proprietary governments, became Royal governments before the Revolution.

§ 13. In the Charter governments, the powers and rights were vested by a charter from the king in the colonists generally, and were placed upon a more free and democratic foundation. In Connecticut and Rhode Island, the governor, council, and the assembly, were chosen every year by the freemen of the colony. But by the charter granted by William and Mary, in 1691, to the colony of Massachusetts, the governor was appointed by the king, the council chosen annually by the general assembly, and the house of representatives chosen by the people, though in other respects the charter was quite liberal in its provisions.

At the Revolution, Massachusetts, Rhode Island, and Connecticut were the only charter governments existing.

§ 14. Notwithstanding these diversities in the form of their government, the situation and circumstances of the colonists were similar in several very important particulars. They were entitled to the rights and liberties of English subjects, and to the advantages of the laws of England. They were mostly a sober, industrious, and persevering people. They established provincial legislatures to regulate their local affairs. They did not hold their lands by any burdensome feudal tenures. The governments were administered upon popular principles, and generally marked by a liberal policy.

§ 15. Many of the settlers in the colonies emigrated from England at a time of great religious and political excitement, and were filled with the spirit of liberty, of free inquiry, and of opposition to the prerogatives of the crown and to an establishe l church, which such excitement had produced. Schools and colleges were founded, and religion, education, and printing encouraged. The great distance of the colonies from the mother-country weakened her power over them, so that a love of freedom was gradually enabled to grow up almost unperceived by the English government.

In Pennsylvania soon after its settlement, in Maryland, and in New England, (except Rhode Island,) the English law of primogeniture (that is, the right of the eldest son and his descendants to succeed to the inheritance of the ancestor) was abolished, and the estates of a decedent were divided among all his descendants, which tended to equalize property, increase the number of landholders, and encourage habits of industry.

§ 16. The colonies, nevertheless, had no political connection with each other. They had no right to form treaties or alliances among themselves, or enter into any connection with foreign powers. The law of nations did not recognise them as sovereign states, but only as dependencies on the crown of England. They could not make treaties, declare war, or send or receive ambassadors. Each colonist, however, had the full rights of a British subject in every other colony.

CHAPTER II.

THE ARTICLES OF CONFEDERATION.

§ 17. ALTHOUGH the colonies were politically distinct, yet, in consequence of the similarity of their laws, religion, institutions, interests, and situation generally, they were frequently led to unite together for the purpose of advancing their common welfare. The New England colonies often joined to defend themselves against the hostilities of the Indian tribes.

§ 18. For instance, in 1643, the colonies of Massachusetts, Connecticut, Plymouth, and New Haven, for the purpose of protection against the Indians and Dutch, formed an alliance by the name of the United Colonies of New England.

§ 19. So also in 1754, upon the suggestion of a branch of the British government, delegates from New Hampshire, Massachusetts, Rhode Island, Connecticut, New York, Pennsylvania, and Maryland, assembled to deliberate upon the best means of defending themselves in case of a war with France, which was then likely to occur.

§ 20. When England began to oppress the colonies, they were thus naturally led again to form a union for their common protection. In 1765, upon the recommendation of Massachusetts, a congress of delegates from nine colonies assembled at New York, and published a bill of rights, in which they asserted that the sole power of taxation resided in the colonies.

§ 21. The first Continental Congress, composed of delegates from almost all the colonies, assembled at Philadelphia, September 5, 1774, and chose Peyton Randolph president, and Charles Thomson secretary. They styled themselves "the delegates appointed by the good people of these colonies," and continued in session till October 26 of the same year. This Congress, among several other valuable state papers, published a Declaration of Rights, which is important as fully setting forth the natural and constitutional rights to which the colonists believed themselves entitled. It is, therefore, included in the Appendix.

§ 22. A second Continental Congress assembled in Philadelphia May 10, 1775. This last-mentioned Congress continued its sittings during the Revolutionary war, and until the Articles of Confederation went into effect. In both Congresses the votes were taken by colonies, the delegation from each colony having one vote, which was determined by a majority of the delegates: for instance, if a colony had seven delegates in Congress, they would cast but one vote, which was determined by a majority of the seven delegates. If the delegates of a colony were equally divided, no vote could be given.

§ 23. The Declaration of Independence, passed July 4, 1776, wholly dissolved the political connection between England and the colonies, the latter being therein styled, for the first time, THE UNITED STATES OF AMERICA, a title which was afterward retained by the Articles of Confederation, and has been since continued. It then became necessary that the States should unite for the effectual prosecution of the war and the formation of alliances with foreign countries.

§ 24. On the 11th of June, 1776, the same day on which a committee was appointed by Congress for preparing a declaration of independence, it was resolved to appoint another committee to prepare and digest the form of a confederation to be entered into between the colonies. This committee, on the 12th of July following, reported a plan of a confederacy, consisting of twenty articles.

§ 25. This draft was considered and debated at various times; but was finally adopted by Congress, November, 15, 1777. These Articles of Confederation were ratified in July, 1778, by the delegates from all the States, except New Jersey, Delaware, and Maryland. But they were subsequently signed on the part of New Jersey, November 25, 1778, and were ratified on the part of Delaware, February 22, 1779. The delegates from Maryland did not sign the articles until March 1, 1781, though in the mean time she had zealously united with the other States in the prosecution of the war. The ratification of the articles was, therefore, completed March 1, 1781, and, on the second day of March, 1781, Congress assembled under the Confederation.

§ 26. These articles are printed at length in the Appendix. They formed the thirteen States, by the style of "The United States of America," into a firm league of friendship with each other, for their defence, the security of their liberties, and their mutual and general welfare, binding themselves to assist each other against all force offered to, or attacks made upon them, or any of them, on account of religion, sovereignty, trade, or any pretence whatever. (Art. III.)

§ 27. Each State retained its own sovereignty, and all powers not expressly delegated to the United States in congress assembled. Delegates were to be chosen every year by each State, not less than three, nor more than seven in number, to meet in congress. Each State was to support the expenses of its own delegates. In deciding questions, the votes were taken by States, each State having a single vote.

§ 28. All the expenses of the war and for the general welfare were to be supplied by the several States, in proportion to the value of the lands and improvements thereon in each State, surveyed for or granted to any person.

§ 29. Congress was authorized to appoint a committee, consisting of one delegate from each State, to sit during the recess of Congress, called a committee of the States. The committee of the States, or any nine of its members, were authorized to execute, in the recess of Congress, such of the powers of that body, as Congress, with the consent of nine States, should think fit to invest them with; but no power was to be delegated to the committee, the exercise of which required nine States in Congress.

§ 30. Congress could not engage in war, grant letters of marque and reprisal, enter into treaties or alliances, coin money or regulate its value, determine the sums necessary for the use of the United States, emit bills of credit, borrow or appropriate money, designate the size of the army and navy, or appoint a commander-in-chief of the army or navy, without the assent of nine States; nor could a question upon any other point, except adjournment from day to day, be determined unless by the votes of the majority of the States in Congress.

§ 31. This Confederation was intended to be perpetual; nor was any alteration in the articles to be made, unless agreed to in Congress and afterward confirmed by the legislature of every State.

§ 32. Down to the time of the final ratification of the Articles of Confederation in 1781, the direction of the Revolutionary war devolved upon the Continental Congress

There was no settled form of government. The powers of the Congress were not defined; but were altogether vague and uncertain. In fact, the government was of a revolutionary or provisional character, exercising such authority as the necessities of the times required.

§ 33. It was soon found that the plan detailed in the Articles of Confederation was impracticable. It gave to Congress no means of enforcing its laws upon the States, and the States disregarded the recommendations of Congress with impunity. The Congress had no power to lay taxes or collect a revenue for the public service; nor could it regulate commerce, either with foreign nations or among the several States. The public debt incurred by the war was very great, and the Articles of Confederation in no way provided effectual means for its payment.

§ 34. It became evident in a short time that distress and ruin would overspread the country, unless some different and more vigorous form of government were adopted. This discouraging state of affairs led to the proceedings which finally terminated in the formation and adoption of the present federal constitution.

§ 35. It has been said that the government of the United States has passed through the three following forms:

(1.) The Revolutionary.

(2.) The Confederate.

(3.) The Constitutional.

§ 36. The Revolutionary government extended from the time of the meeting of the first Continental Congress, March 5, 1774, down to the final ratification of the Articles of Confederation, March 1, 1781.

The Confederate government extended from the ratification of the Articles of Confederation down to the time when the Constitution went into operation, March 4, 1789.

The Constitutional government is that which has existed under the Constitution, and to it we are now about to direct our attention.

CHAPTER III.

ADOPTION OF THE CONSTITUTION.

§ 37. In 1785, the legislatures of Virginia and Maryland appointed commissioners to form a compact relative to the navigation of the Chesapeake bay and the rivers Potomac and Pocomoke. They met, but felt that larger powers were necessary, and referred the subject to their respective States.

§ 38. Accordingly, in January, 1786, the legislature of Virginia appointed several gentlemen "to meet such commissioners as were, or might be, appointed by the other States in the Union, at such time and place as should be agreed upon by the said commissioners, to take into consideration the trade and commerce of the United States; to consider how far a uniform system, in their commercial intercourse and regulations, might be necessary to their common interest and permanent harmony; and to report to the several States such an act relative to this great object, as, when unanimously ratified by them, would enable the United States in congress assembled effectually to provide for the same."

§ 39. It was afterward agreed that this meeting should be held at Annapolis, in Maryland, in September of the same year. The resolutions were communicated to the States, and the meeting was held at the time and place appointed. Commissioners from the States of Virginia, Delaware, Pennsylvania, New Jersey, and New York attended. Delegates were appointed by New Hampshire, Massachusetts, Rhode Island, and North Carolina, but did not attend.

§ 40. So small was the number of States represented, that the delegates did not think proper to proceed to the important business which had brought them together. They were also satisfied that they ought to be intrusted with more ample powers, embracing other objects in addition to the mere regulation of trade and commerce.

§ 41. They, therefore, prepared an address and a report to be submitted to Congress and all the States, in which they recommended the States to concur "in the appointment of commissioners to meet at Philadelphia on the second Monday in May, 1787, to take into consideration the situation of the United States, to devise such further provisions as should appear to them necessary to render the constitution of the federal government adequate to the exigencies of the Union, and to report such an act for that purpose to the United States in congress assembled, as, when agreed to by them, and afterward confirmed by the legislature of every State, will effectively provide for the same."

§ 42. Virginia first appointed delegates. The legislature of New York instructed its delegates in Congress to bring the subject before that body; and in February, 1787, Congress, by a resolution, declared that it was expedient "that a convention of delegates, who shall have been appointed by the several States, be held at Philadelphia, for the sole and express purpose of revising the Articles of

Confederation and reporting to Congress and the several legislatures such alterations and provisions therein as shall, when agreed to in Congress and confirmed by the States, render the federal constitution adequate to the exigencies of the government and the preservation of the Union."

§ 43. In consequence of these proceedings, delegates to the convention were appointed from all the States except Rhode Island, and the convention met at the State-House in Philadelphia, on the 14th day (the second Monday) of May, 1787, the time designated; but a majority of the States not being represented, the members present adjourned from day to day until Friday, May 25. Upon, organizing, George Washington, who was a delegate from Virginia, was unanimously elected to preside over their deliberations. Among the delegates were many of the most eminent men of the States.

§ 44. It will be seen from the proceedings mentioned above, that the object of calling the convention was to revise the Articles of Confederation. So weak and defective, however, was the old form of government, that a majority of the delegates determined to form an entirely new one.

§ 45. After much discussion, the present Constitution was finally adopted, as the result of their labours, on the 17th of September, 1787, and was signed by the members of the convention. There were great difficulties in its formation, arising out of jealousies among the States, and the difference in their extent, wealth, population, habits, religion, education, and political views: nothing but a wise and patriotic spirit of mutual concession and of moderation could have overcome such obstacles.

§ 46. The convention directed the new Constitution to be

laid before Congress, and proposed that it should afterward be submitted to a convention of delegates chosen in each State by the people thereof, under a recommendation of its legislature, for their assent and ratification; also, that as soon as nine States had thus ratified it, Congress should take measures for the election of a President, and fix the time and place for commencing proceedings under it. The convention also transmitted to Congress the resolutions and letters which we have appended to the Constitution. According to this recommendation, Congress, on the 28th of September, 1787, transmitted the plan of the Constitution and the letter of the convention, to the several legislatures of the States, in order to be submitted to a convention of delegates chosen in each State by the people thereof.

§ 47. Conventions assembled in the different States in 1787 and 1788, and the new system was discussed with great learning and zeal amid many conflicting opinions; but was at last adopted, though not without much opposition.

§ 48. On the 17th of September, 1788, Congress, having received ratifications of the Constitution from the conventions of all the States, except North Carolina and Rhode Island, resolved that the first Wednesday in January, 1789, should be the day for appointing electors in the several States which may have ratified the Constitution before that day; that the first Wednesday of the following February should be the day for the electors to assemble and vote for a President; and that the first Wednesday in the following March should be the time for commencing operations under the Constitution at New York, then the seat of government.

§ 49. Accordingly, elections were held in the several

States for electors; and the electors thus appointed met and voted for President and Vice-President. There were sixty-nine electoral votes cast, of which George Washington received the whole number, and was therefore unanimously elected President, and John Adams received thirty-four, the next greatest number of votes, and was therefore elected Vice-President.

§ 50. The States having also elected their senators and representatives, the first constitutional Congress, composed of representatives from the eleven States, which had then ratified the Constitution, assembled on Wednesday, the 4th day of March, 1789, and on that day the new Constitution of the United States went into legal operation, and proceedings were commenced under it. A quorum of members, however, did not appear until April 1, and Congress then entered upon the transaction of business

§ 51. On the 6th of April, the electoral votes were counted in the presence of the Senate and House of Representatives by the President of the Senate, elected for that purpose, and the result appeared as above stated.

On Thursday, April 30, George Washington took the oath required by the Constitution, which was administered to him by the Chancellor of the State of New York, and delivered his inaugural address. John Adams entered upon his duties as President of the Senate, on Tuesday, April 21.

§ 52. The ratification of North Carolina was not received by Congress until January, 1790, and that of Rhode Island, until June of the same year. In the mean time, those States had been regarded, in many respects, as foreign States.

§ 53. The following are the dates of the ratification of the Constitution by each of the original thirteen States:—

(1.) Delaware, December 7, 1787.
(2.) Pennsylvania, December 12, 1787.
(3.) New Jersey, December 18, 1787.
(4.) Georgia, January 2, 1788.
(5.) Connecticut, January 9, 1788.
(6.) Massachusetts, February 6, 1788.
(7.) Maryland, April, 28, 1788.
(8.) South Carolina, May 23, 1788.
(9.) New Hampshire, June 21, 1788.
(10.) Virginia, June 26, 1788.
(11.) New York, July 26, 1788.
(12.) North Carolina, November 21, 1789.
(13.) Rhode Island, May 29, 1790.

THE

CONSTITUTION

OF THE

United States of America.

We the People of the United States, in order to form a more perfect Union, establish Justice, insure domestic Tranquillity, provide for the common defence, promote the general Welfare, and secure the Blessings of Liberty to ourselves and our Posterity, do ordain and establish this CONSTITUTION for the United States of America.

ARTICLE. I.

SECTION. 1. All legislative Powers herein granted shall be vested in a Congress of the United States, which shall consist of a Senate and House of Representatives.

SECTION. 2. [1] The House of Representatives shall be composed of Members chosen every second Year by the People of the several States, and the Electors in each State shall have the Qualifications requisite for Electors of the most numerous Branch of the State Legislature.

[NOTE.—The small figures in brackets are not in the original, but have been added subsequently, to mark the different clauses in a section.]

[2] No Person shall be a Representative who shall not have attained to the Age of twenty five Years, and been seven Years a Citizen of the United States, and who shall not, when elected, be an Inhabitant of that State in which he shall be chosen.

[3] Representatives and direct Taxes shall be apportioned among the several States which may be included within this Union, according to their respective Numbers, which shall be determined by adding to the whole Number of free Persons, including those bound to Service for a Term of Years, and excluding Indians not taxed, three fifths of all other Persons. The actual Enumeration shall be made within three Years after the first Meeting of the Congress of the United States, and within every subsequent Term of ten Years, in such Manner as they shall by Law direct. The Number of Representatives shall not exceed one for every thirty Thousand, but each State shall have at Least one Representative; and until such enumeration shall be made, the State of New Hampshire shall be entitled to chuse three, Massachusetts eight, Rhode-Island and Providence Plantations one, Connecticut five, New-York six, New Jersey four, Pennsylvania eight, Delaware one, Maryland six, Virginia ten, North Carolina five, South Carolina five, and Georgia three.

[4] When vacancies happen in the Representation from any State, the Executive Authority thereof shall issue Writs of Election to fill such Vacancies.

[5] The House of Representatives shall chuse their

Speaker and other officers; and shall have the sole Power of Impeachment.

SECTION. 3. [1] The Senate of the United States shall be composed of two Senators from each State, chosen by the Legislature thereof, for six Years; and each Senator shall have one Vote.

[2] Immediately after they shall be assembled in Consequence of the first Election, they shall be divided as equally as may be into three Classes. The Seats of the Senators of the first Class shall be vacated at the Expiration of the second Year, of the second Class at the Expiration of the fourth Year, and of the third class at the Expiration of the sixth Year, so that one-third may be chosen every second Year; and if Vacancies happen by Resignation, or otherwise, during the Recess of the Legislature of any State, the Executive thereof may make temporary Appointments until the next Meeting of the Legislature, which shall then fill such Vacancies.

[3] No person shall be a Senator who shall not have attained to the Age of thirty Years, and been nine Years a Citizen of the United States, and who shall not, when elected, be an Inhabitant of that State for which he shall be chosen.

[4] The Vice President of the United States shall be President of the Senate, but shall have no Vote, unless they be equally divided.

[5] The Senate shall chuse their other Officers, and also a President pro tempore, in the Absence of the Vice Pre-

sident, or when he shall exercise the Office of President of the United States.

[6] The Senate shall have the sole Power to try all Impeachments. When sitting for that Purpose, they shall be on Oath or Affirmation. When the President of the United States is tried, the Chief Justice shall preside: And no Person shall be convicted without the Concurrence of two thirds of the Members present.

[7] Judgment in Cases of Impeachment shall not extend further than to removal from Office, and Disqualification to hold and enjoy any Office of honour, Trust or Profit under the United States: but the Party convicted shall nevertheless be liable and subject to Indictment, Trial, Judgment and Punishment, according to Law.

SECTION. 4. [1] The Times, Places and Manner of holding Elections for Senators and Representatives, shall be prescribed in each State by the Legislature thereof; but the Congress may at any time by Law make or alter such Regulations, except as to the places of chusing Senators.

[2] The Congress shall assemble at least once in every Year, and such Meeting shall be on the first Monday in December, unless they shall by Law appoint a different Day.

SECTION. 5. [1] Each House shall be the Judge of the Elections, Returns and Qualifications of its own Members, and a Majority of each shall constitute a Quorum to do Business; but a smaller Number may adjourn from day to day, and may be authorized to compel the Attendance of absent Members, in such Manner, and under such Penalties as each House may provide.

[2] Each House may determine the Rules of its Proceedings, punish its Members for disorderly Behaviour, and, with the Concurrence of two thirds, expel a Member.

[3] Each House shall keep a Journal of its Proceedings, and from time to time publish the same, excepting such Parts as may in their Judgment require Secrecy; and the Yeas and Nays of the Members of either House on any question shall, at the Desire of one fifth of those Present, be entered on the Journal.

[4] Neither House, during the Session of Congress, shall, without the Consent of the other, adjourn for more than three days, nor to any other Place than that in which the two Houses shall be sitting.

SECTION. 6. [1] The Senators and Representatives shall receive a Compensation for their Services, to be ascertained by Law, and paid out of the Treasury of the United States. They shall in all Cases, except Treason, Felony and Breach of the Peace, be privileged from Arrest during their Attendance at the Session of their respective Houses, and in going to and returning from the same; and for any speech or debate in either House, they shall not be questioned in any other Place.

[2] No Senator or Representative shall, during the Time for which he was elected, be appointed to any civil Office under the Authority of the United States, which shall have been created, or the Emoluments whereof shall have been

encreased during such time; and no Person holding any Office under the United States, shall be a Member of either House during his Continuance in Office.

SECTION. 7. [1] All Bills for raising Revenue shall originate in the House of Representatives; but the Senate may propose or concur with Amendments as on other Bills.

[2] Every Bill which shall have passed the House of Representatives and the Senate, shall, before it become a Law, be presented to the President of the United States; If he approve he shall sign it, but if not he shall return it, with his Objections to that House in which it shall have originated, who shall enter the Objections at large on their Journal, and proceed to reconsider it. If after such Reconsideration two thirds of that House shall agree to pass the Bill, it shall be sent, together with the Objections, to the other House, by which it shall likewise be reconsidered, and if approved by two thirds of that House, it shall become a Law. But in all such Cases the Votes of both Houses shall be determined by yeas and Nays, and the Names of the Persons voting for and against the Bill shall be entered on the Journal of each House respectively. If any Bill shall not be returned by the President within ten Days (Sundays excepted) after it shall have been presented to him, the same shall be a law, in like Manner as if he had signed it, unless the Congress by their Adjournment prevent its Return, in which Case it shall not be a Law.

[3] Every Order, Resolution, or Vote to which the Concurrence of the Senate and House of Representatives may be necessary (except on a question of Adjournment) shall be presented to the President of the United States; and before the Same shall take Effect, shall be approved by him, or being disapproved by him, shall be repassed by two thirds of the Senate and House of Representatives, according to the Rules and Limitations prescribed in the Case of a Bill.

SECTION. 8. The Congress shall have Power

[1] To lay and collect Taxes, Duties, Imposts and Excises, to pay the Debts and provide for the common Defence and general Welfare of the United States; but all Duties, Imposts and Excises shall be uniform throughout the United States;

[2] To borrow Money on the credit of the United States;

[3] To regulate Commerce with foreign Nations, and among the several States, and with the Indian Tribes;

[4] To establish an uniform Rule of Naturalization, and uniform Laws on the subject of Bankruptcies throughout the United States;

[5] To coin Money, regulate the Value thereof, and of foreign Coin, and fix the Standard of Weights and Measures;

[6] To provide for the Punishment of counterfeiting the Securities and current Coin of the United States;

[7] To establish Post Offices and post Roads;

[8] To promote the progress of Science and useful Arts,

by securing for limited Times to Authors and Inventors the exclusive Right to their respective Writings and Discoveries;

[9] To constitute Tribunals inferior to the supreme Court;

[10] To define and punish Piracies and Felonies committed on the high Seas, and Offences against the Law of Nations;

[11] To declare War, grant Letters of Marque and Reprisal, and make Rules concerning Captures on Land and Water;

[12] To raise and support Armies, but no Appropriation of Money to that Use shall be for a longer Term than two Years;

[13] To provide and maintain a Navy;

[14] To make Rules for the Government and Regulation of the land and naval Forces;

[15] To provide for calling forth the Militia to execute the Laws of the Union, suppress Insurrections and repel Invasions;

[16] To provide for organizing, arming, and disciplining, the Militia, and for governing such Part of them as may be employed in the Service of the United States, reserving to the States respectively, the Appointment of the Officers, and the Authority of training the Militia according to the Discipline prescribed by Congress;

[17] To exercise exclusive Legislation in all Cases whatsoever, over such District (not exceeding ten Miles square)

as may, by Cession of particular States, and the Acceptance of Congress, become the Seat of the Government of the United States, and to exercise like Authority over all Places purchased by the Consent of the Legislature of the State in which the Same shall be, for the Erection of Forts, Magazines, Arsenals, Dock-Yards, and other needful Buildings;—And

[18] To make all Laws which shall be necessary and proper for carrying into Execution the foregoing Powers, and all other Powers vested by this Constitution in the Government of the United States, or in any Department or Officer thereof.

SECTION. 9. [1] The Migration or Importation of such Persons as any of the States now existing shall think proper to admit, shall not be prohibited by the Congress prior to the Year one thousand eight hundred and eight, but a Tax or Duty may be imposed on such Importation, not exceeding ten dollars for each Person.

[2] The Privilege of the Writ of Habeas Corpus shall not be suspended, unless when in Cases of Rebellion or Invasion the public Safety may require it.

[3] No Bill of Attainder or ex post facto Law shall be passed.

[4] No Capitation, or other direct, Tax shall be laid, unless in Proportion to the Census or Enumeration herein before directed to be taken.

[5] No Tax or Duty shall be laid on Articles exported from any State.

[6] No Preference shall be given by any Regulation of Commerce or Revenue to the Ports of one State over those of another: nor shall Vessels bound to, or from, one State, be obliged to enter, clear, or pay Duties in another.

[7] No Money shall be drawn from the Treasury, but in Consequence of Appropriations made by Law; and a regular Statement and Account of the Receipts and Expenditures of all public Money shall be published from time to time.

[8] No Title of Nobility shall be granted by the United States: And no Person holding any Office of Profit or Trust under them, shall, without the Consent of the Congress, accept of any present, Emolument, Office, or Title, of any kind whatever, from any King, Prince, or foreign State.

SECTION. 10. [1] No State shall enter into any Treaty, Alliance, or Confederation; grant Letters of Marque and Reprisal; coin Money; emit Bills of Credit; make any Thing but gold and silver Coin a Tender in Payment of Debts; pass any Bill of Attainder, ex post facto Law, or Law impairing the Obligation of Contracts, or grant any Title of Nobility.

[2] No State shall, without the consent of the Congress, lay any Imposts or Duties on Imports or Exports, except what may be absolutely necessary for executing it's inspection Laws: and the net Produce of all Duties and Imposts, laid by any State on Imports or Exports, shall

be for the Use of the Treasury of the United States and all such Laws shall be subject to the Revision and Controul of the Congress.

[3] No State shall, without the Consent of Congress, lay any Duty of Tonnage, keep Troops, or Ships of War in time of Peace, enter into any Agreement or Compact with another State, or with a foreign Power, or engage in War, unless actually invaded, or in such imminent Danger as will not admit of Delay.

ARTICLE. II.

SECTION. 1. [1] The executive Power shall be vested in a President of the United States of America. He shall hold his Office during the Term of four Years, and, together with the Vice President, chosen for the same Term, be elected, as follows

[2] Each State shall appoint, in such Manner as the Legislature thereof may direct, a Number of Electors, equal to the whole Number of Senators and Representatives to which the State may be entitled in the Congress: but no Senator or Representative, or Person holding an Office of Trust or Profit under the United States, shall be appointed an Elector.

*[3] The Electors shall meet in their respective States, and vote by Ballot for two Persons, of whom one at least shall not be an Inhabitant of the same State with themselves.

---

* This clause has been supplied by the 12th amendment, on page 51.

And they shall make a List of all the Persons voted for, and of the Number of Votes for each; which List they shall sign and certify, and transmit sealed to the Seat of the Government of the United States, directed to the President of the Senate. The President of the Senate shall, in the Presence of the Senate and House of Representatives, open all the Certificates, and the Votes shall then be counted. The Person having the greatest Number of Votes shall be the President, if such Number be a Majority of the whole Number of Electors appointed; and if there be more than one who have such Majority and have an equal number of Votes, then the House of Representatives shall immediately chuse by Ballot one of them for President; and if no Person have a Majority, then from the five highest on the List the said House shall in like Manner chuse the President. But in chusing the President, the Votes shall be taken by States, the Representation from each State having one Vote; a Quorum for this Purpose shall consist of a Member or Members from two thirds of the States, and a Majority of all the States shall be necessary to a Choice. In every Case, after the Choice of the President, the Person having the greatest Number of Votes of the Electors shall be the Vice President. But if there should remain two or more who have equal Votes, the Senate shall chuse from them by Ballot the Vice President.

[4] The Congress may determine the Time of chusing the Electors, and the Day on which they shall give their

Votes; which Day shall be the same throughout the United States.

[5] No Person except a natural born Citizen, or a Citizen of the United States, at the time of the Adoption of this Constitution, shall be eligible to the Office of President; neither shall any Person be eligible to that Office who shall not have attained to the Age of thirty five Years, and been fourteen Years a Resident within the United States.

[6] In Case of the Removal of the President from Office, or of his Death, Resignation, or Inability to discharge the Powers and Duties of the said office, the same shall devolve on the Vice President, and the Congress may by Law provide for the Case of Removal, Death, Resignation, or Inability, both of the President and Vice President, declaring what Officer shall then act as President, and such Officer shall act accordingly, until the Disability be removed, or a President shall be elected.

[7] The President shall, at stated Times, receive for his Services, a Compensation, which shall neither be encreased nor diminished during the Period for which he shall have been elected, and he shall not receive within that Period any other Emolument from the United States, or any of them.

[8] Before he enter on the Execution of his Office, he shall take the following Oath or Affirmation:—

"I do solemly swear (or affirm) that I will faithfully "execute the Office of President of the United States, and "will to the best of my Ability, preserve, protect and "defend the Constitution of the United States."

SECTION. 2. [1] The President shall be Commander in Chief of the Army and Navy of the United States, and of the Militia of the several States, when called into the actual Service of the United States; he may require the Opinion, in writing, of the principal Officer in each of the executive Departments, upon any Subject relating to the Duties of their respective Offices, and he shall have Power to grant Reprieves and Pardons for Offences against the United States, except in Cases of Impeachment.

[2] He shall have Power, by and with the Advice and Consent of the Senate, to make Treaties, provided two thirds of the Senators present concur; and he shall nominate, and by and with the Advice and Consent of the Senate, shall appoint Ambassadors, other public Ministers and Consuls, Judges of the supreme Court, and all other Officers of the United States, whose Appointments are not herein otherwise provided for, and which shall be established by Law: but the Congress may by Law vest the Appointment of such inferior Officers, as they think proper, in the President alone, in the Courts of Law, or in the Heads of Departments.

[3] The President shall have Power to fill up all Vacancies that may happen during the Recess of the Senate, by granting Commissions which shall expire at the End of their next Session.

SECTION. 3. He shall from time to time give to the

Congress Information of the State of the Union, and recommend to their Consideration such Measures as he shall judge necessary and expedient; he may, on extraordinary Occasions, convene both Houses, or either of them, and in Case of Disagreement between them, with Respect to the time of Adjournment, he may adjourn them to such Time as he shall think proper; he shall receive Ambassadors and other public Ministers; he shall take Care that the Laws be faithfully executed, and shall Commission all the officers of the United States.

SECTION. 4. The President, Vice President and all civil Officers of the United States, shall be removed from Office on Impeachment for, and Conviction of, Treason, Bribery, or other high Crimes and Misdemeanors.

ARTICLE III.

SECTION. 1. The judicial Power of the United States, shall be vested in one supreme Court, and in such inferior Courts as the Congress may from time to time ordain and establish. The Judges, both of the supreme and inferior Courts, shall hold their Offices during good Behavior, and shall, at stated Times, receive for their Services, a Compensation which shall not be diminished during their Continuance in Office.

SECTION. 2. [1] The judicial Power shall extend to all Cases, in Law and Equity, arising under this Constitution, the Laws of the United States, and Treaties made, or which shall be made, under their Authority;—to all Cases affecting Ambassadors, other public Ministers and Consuls;—to all Cases of admiralty and maritime Jurisdiction;—to Controversies to which the United States shall be a Party;—to Controversies between two or more States;—between a State and Citizens of another State; —between Citizens of different States,—between Citizens of the same State claiming Lands under Grants of different States, and between a State, or the Citizens thereof, and foreign States, Citizens or Subjects.

[2] In all Cases affecting Ambassadors, other public Ministers and Consuls, and those in which a State shall be Party, the supreme Court shall have original Jurisdiction. In all the other Cases before mentioned, the supreme Court shall have appellate Jurisdiction, both as to Law and Fact, with such Exceptions, and under such Regulations as the Congress shall make.

[3] The Trial of all Crimes, except in Cases of Impeachment, shall be by Jury; and such Trial shall be held in the State where the said Crimes shall have been committed; but when not committed within any State, the Trial shall be at such Place or Places as the Congress may by Law have directed.

SECTION. 3. [1] Treason against the United States, shall consist only in levying War against them, or in adhering to their Enemies, giving them Aid and Comfort. No Person shall be convicted of Treason unless on the Testimony of two Witnesses to the same overt Act, or on Confession in open Court.

[2] The Congress shall have Power to declare the Punishment of Treason, but no Attainder of Treason shall work Corruption of Blood, or Forfeiture except during the Life of the Person attainted.

ARTICLE. IV.

SECTION. 1. Full Faith and Credit shall be given in each State to the public Acts, Records, and judicial Proceedings of every other State. And the Congress may by general Laws prescribe the Manner in which such Acts, Records and Proceedings shall be proved, and the Effect thereof.

SECTION. 2. [1] The Citizens of each State shall be entitled to all Privileges and Immunities of Citizens in the several States.

[2] A Person charged in any State with Treason, Felony, or other Crime, who shall flee from Justice, and be found in another State, shall on Demand of the executive Authority of the State from which he fled, be delivered up, to be removed to the State having Jurisdiction of the Crime.

[3] No Person held to Service or Labour in one State, under the Laws thereof, escaping into another, shall, in Consequence of any Law or Regulation therein, be discharged from such Service or Labour, but shall be delivered up on Claim of the Party to whom such Service or Labour may be due.

SECTION. 3. [1] New States may be admitted by the Congress into this Union; but no new State shall be formed or erected within the Jurisdiction of any other State; nor any State be formed by the Junction of two or more States, or Parts of States, without the Consent of the Legislatures of the States concerned as well as of the Congress.

[2] The Congress shall have Power to dispose of and make all needful Rules and Regulations respecting the Territory or other Property belonging to the United States; and nothing in this Constitution shall be so construed as to Prejudice any Claims of the United States, or of any particular State.

SECTION. 4. The United States shall guarantee to every State in this Union a Republican Form of Government, and shall protect each of them against Invasion, and on Application of the Legislature, or of the Executive (when the Legislature cannot be convened) against domestic Violence.

ARTICLE V.

The Congress, whenever two thirds of both Houses shall deem it necessary, shall propose Amendments to this Constitution, or, on the Application of the Legislatures of two thirds of the several States, shall call a Convention for proposing Amendments, which, in either Case, shall be valid to all Intents and Purposes, as Part of this Constitution, when ratified by the Legislatures of three fourths of the several States, or by Conventions in three fourths thereof, as the one or the other Mode of Ratification may be proposed by the Congress; Provided that no Amendment which may be made prior to the Year one thousand eight hundred and eight shall in any Manner affect the first and fourth Clauses in the Ninth Section of the first Article; and that no State, without its Consent, shall be deprived of its equal Suffrage in the Senate.

ARTICLE. VI.

[1] All Debts contracted and Engagements entered into, before the Adoption of this Constitution, shall be as valid against the United States under this Constitution, as under the Confederation.

[2] This Constitution, and the Laws of the United States which shall be made in Pursuance thereof; and all Treaties made, or which shall be made, under the authority of the United States, shall be the supreme Law of the Land; and the Judges in every State shall be bound thereby, any Thing in the Constitution or Laws of any State to the Contrary notwithstanding.

[3] The Senators and Representatives before mentioned, and the Members of the several State Legislatures, and all executive and judicial Officers, both of the United States and of the several States, shall be bound by Oath or Affirmation, to support this Constitution; but no religious Test shall ever be required as a Qualification to any Office or public Trust under the United States.

ARTICLE. VII.

The Ratification of the Conventions of nine States, shall be sufficient for the Establishment of this Constitution between the States so ratifying the Same.

DONE in Convention by the Unanimous Consent of the States present the Seventeenth Day of September in the Year of our Lord one thousand seven hundred and Eighty seven and of the Independance of the United States of America the Twelfth. **In Witness** whereof We have hereunto subscribed our Names,

Go WASHINGTON—
Presidt and deputy from Virginia

NEW HAMPSHIRE.

JOHN LANGDON — NICHOLAS GILMAN

MASSACHUSETTS.

NATHANIEL GORHAM — RUFUS KING

CONNECTICUT.

WM SAML JOHNSON — ROGER SHERMAN

NEW YORK.

ALEXANDER HAMILTON

NEW JERSEY.

WIL LIVINGSTON — DAVID BREARLEY
WM PATERSON — JONA DAYTON

PENNSYLVANIA.

B FRANKLIN — THOMAS MIFFLIN
ROBT MORRIS — GEO CLYMER
THO FITZSIMONS — JARED INGERSOLL
JAMES WILSON — GOUV MORRIS

DELAWARE.

Geo Read — Gunning Bedford, Jun'r
John Dickinson — Richard Bassett
Jaco Broom

MARYLAND.

James M'Henry — Dan of St Thos Jenifer
Danl Carroll

VIRGINIA.

John Blair — James Madison, Jr

NORTH CAROLINA.

Wm Blount — Rich'd Dobbs Spaight,
Hu Williamson

SOUTH CAROLINA.

J Rutledge — Charles Cotesworth Pinckney
Charles Pinckney — Pierce Butler

GEORGIA.

William Few — Abr Baldwin

Attest: WILLIAM JACKSON, *Secretary.*

§ 54. The following are the proceedings of the convention, containing the resolutions and letter which were transmitted to Congress together with the Constitution:—

IN CONVENTION, MONDAY, SEPTEMBER 17, 1787.

Present: The States of New Hampshire, Massachusetts, Connecticut, Mr. Hamilton from New York, New Jersey, Pennsylvania, Delaware, Maryland, Virginia, North Carolina, South Carolina, and Georgia.

Resolved, That the preceding Constitution be laid before the United States in Congress assembled, and that it is the opinion of this convention that it should afterwards be submitted to a convention of delegates, chosen in each State by the people thereof, under the recommendation of its legislature, for their assent and ratification; and that each convention, assenting to and ratifying the same, should give notice thereof, to the United States in Congress assembled.

Resolved, That it is the opinion of this convention, that as soon as the conventions of nine States shall have ratified this Constitution, the United States in Congress assembled should fix a day on which electors should be appointed by the States which shall have ratified the same, and a day on which the electors should assemble to vote for the President, and the time and place for commencing proceedings under this Constitution. That after such publication the electors should be appointed, and the Senators and Representatives elected; that the electors should meet on the day fixed for the election of the President, and should transmit their votes certified, signed, sealed, and directed as the Constitution requires, to the Secretary of the United States in Congress assembled; that the Senators and Representatives should convene at the time and place assigned; that the Senators should appoint a president of the Senate, for the sole purpose of receiving, opening, and counting the votes for President; and that, after he shall be chosen, the Congress, together with the President, should, without delay, proceed to execute this Constitution.

By the unanimous order of the convention.

GEORGE WASHINGTON, *President.*

WILLIAM JACKSON, *Secretary.*

IN CONVENTION, SEPTEMBER 17, 1787.

SIR. We have now the honour to submit to the consideration of the United States in Congress assembled, that constitution which has appeared to us the most advisable.

The friends of our country have long seen and desired that the power of making war, peace, and treaties, that of levying money and regulating commerce, and the correspondent executive and judicial authorities, should be fully and effectually vested in the General Government of the Union; but the impropriety of delegating such extensive trust to one body of men is evident: hence results the necessity of a different organization.

It is obviously impracticable, in the Federal Government of these States, to secure all rights of independent sovereignty to each, and yet provide for the interest and safety of all. Individuals entering into society must give up a share of liberty to preserve the rest. The magnitude of the sacrifice must depend as well on situation and circumstance as on the object to be obtained. It is at all times difficult to draw with precision the line between those rights which must be surrendered and those which may be reserved; and on the present occasion this difficulty was increased by a difference among the several States as to their situation, extent, habits, and particular interests.

In all our deliberations on this subject, we kept steadily in our view that which appears to us the greatest interest of every true American—the consolidation of our Union—in which is involved our prosperity, felicity, safety, perhaps our national existence. This important consideration, seriously and deeply impressed on our minds, led each State in the convention to be less rigid on points of inferior magnitude than might have been otherwise expected; and thus the Constitution which we now present is the result of a spirit of amity, and of that mutual deference and concession which the peculiarity of our political situation rendered indispensable.

That it will meet the full and entire approbation of every State, is not, perhaps, to be expected; but each will doubtless consider that, had her interest been alone consulted, the consequences might have been particularly disagreeable or injurious to others; that it is liable to as few exceptions as could reasonably have been expected, we hope and believe; that it may promote the lasting welfare of that country so dear to us all, and secure her freedom and happiness, is our most ardent wish.

With great respect, we have the honour to be, sir, your excellency's most obedient, humble servants.

By unanimous order of the convention.

GEORGE WASHINGTON, *President.*

His excellency the PRESIDENT OF CONGRESS.

ARTICLES

IN ADDITION TO, AND AMENDMENT OF,

THE CONSTITUTION

OF THE

United States of America,

Proposed by Congress, and ratified by the Legislatures of the several States, pursuant to the fifth article of the original Constitution.

(ARTICLE I.)

Congress shall make no law respecting an establishment of religion, or prohibiting the free exercise thereof; or abridging the freedom of speech, or of the press; or the right of the people peaceably to assemble, and to petition the Government for a redress of grievances.

(ARTICLE II.)

A well regulated Militia, being necessary to the security of a free State, the right of the people to keep and bear Arms, shall not be infringed.

(ARTICLE III.)

No Soldier shall, in time of peace be quartered in any house, without the consent of the Owner, nor in time of war, but in a manner to be prescribed by law.

(ARTICLE IV)

The right of the people to be secure in their persons, houses, papers, and effects, against unreasonable searches and seizures, shall not be violated, and no Warrants shall issue, but upon probable cause, supported by Oath or affirmation, and particularly describing the place to be searched, and the persons or things to be seized.

(ARTICLE V.)

No person shall be held to answer for a capital, or otherwise infamous crime, unless on a presentment or indictment of a Grand Jury, except in cases arising in the land or naval forces, or in the Militia, when in actual service in time of War or public danger; nor shall any person be subject for the same offence to be twice put in jeopardy of life or limb; nor shall be compelled in any Criminal Case to be a witness against himself, nor be deprived of life, liberty, or property, without due process of law; nor shall private property be taken for public use, without just compensation.

(ARTICLE VI.)

In all criminal prosecutions, the accused shall enjoy the right to a speedy and public trial, by an impartial jury of the State and district wherein the crime shall have been committed, which district shall have been previously ascertained by law, and to be informed of the nature and cause of the accusation; to be confronted with the witnesses against him; to have Compulsory process for obtaining Witnesses in his favour, and to have the Assistance of Counsel for his defence.

(ARTICLE VII.)

In Suits at common law, where the value in controversy shall exceed twenty dollars, the right of trial by jury shall be preserved, and no fact tried by a jury shall be otherwise re-examined in any Court of the United States, than according to the rules of the common law

(ARTICLE VIII.)

Excessive bail shall not be required, nor excessive fines imposed, nor cruel and unusual punishments inflicted.

(ARTICLE IX.)

The enumeration in the Constitution, of certain rights, shall not be construed to deny or disparage others retained by the people.

(ARTICLE X.)

The powers not delegated to the United States by the Constitution, nor prohibited by it to the States, are reserved to the States respectively, or to the people.

(ARTICLE XI.)

The Judicial power of the United States shall not be construed to extend to any suit in law or equity, commenced or prosecuted against one of the United States by Citizens of another State, or by Citizens or Subjects of any Foreign State.

(ARTICLE XII.)

The Electors shall meet in their respective states, and vote by ballot for President and Vice President, one of whom, at least, shall not be an inhabitant of the same state with themselves; they shall name in their ballots the person voted for as President, and in distinct ballots the person voted for as Vice-President, and they shall make distinct lists of all persons voted for as President, and of all persons voted for as Vice-President, and of the number of votes for each, which lists they shall sign and certify, and transmit sealed to the seat of the government of the United States, directed to the President of the Senate;—The President of the Senate shall, in presence of the Senate and House of Representatives, open all the certificates and the votes shall then be counted;—The person having the greatest number of votes for President, shall be the President, if such number be a majority of the whole number of Electors appointed; and if no person have such majority, then from the persons having the highest numbers not exceeding three on the list of those voted for as President, the House of Representatives shall choose immediately, by ballot, the President. But in choosing the President, the votes shall be taken by states, the representation from each state having one vote; a quorum for this purpose shall consist of a member or members from two-thirds of the states, and a majority of all the states shall be necessary to a choice. And if the House of Representatives shall not choose a President whenever the right of choice shall devolve upon them, before the fourth day of March next following, then the Vice-President shall act as President, as in the case of the death or other constitutional disability of the President.—The person having the greatest number of votes as Vice-President, shall be the Vice-President, if such number be a majority of the whole number of Electors appointed, and if no person have a majority, then from the two highest numbers on the list, the Senate shall choose the Vice-President; a quorum for the purpose shall consist of two-thirds of the whole number of Senators, and a majority of the whole number shall be necessary to a choice. But no person constitutionally ineligible to the office of President shall be eligible to that of Vice-President of the United States.

(ARTICLE XIII.)

SECTION 1. Neither slavery nor involuntary servitude, except as a punishment for crime whereof the party shall have been duly convicted, shall exist within the United States, or any place subject to their jurisdiction.

SECTION 2. Congress shall have power to enforce this article by appropriate legislation.

(ARTICLE XIV.)

SECTION 1. All persons born or naturalized in the United States, and subject to the jurisdiction thereof, are citizens of the United States and of the State wherein they reside. No State shall make or enforce any law which shall abridge the privileges or immunities of citizens of the United States: nor shall any State deprive any person of life, liberty, or property, without due process of law, nor deny to any person within its jurisdiction the equal protection of the laws.

SECTION 2. Representatives shall be apportioned among the several States according to their respective numbers, counting the whole number of persons in each State, excluding Indians not taxed. But when the right to vote at any election for the choice of electors for President and Vice-President of the United States, representatives in Congress, the executive or judicial officers of a State, or the members of the Legislature thereof, is denied to any of the male inhabitants of such State, being twenty-one years of age, and citizens of the United States, or in any way abridged, except for participation in rebellion or other crime, the basis of representation therein shall be reduced in the proportion which the number of such male citizens shall bear to the whole number of male citizens twenty-one years of age in such State.

SECTION 3. No person shall be a senator or representative in Congress, or elector of President or Vice-President, or hold any office, civil or military, under the United States, or under any State, who, having previously taken an oath as a member of Congress, or as an officer of the United States, or as a member of any State Legislature, or as an executive or judicial officer of any State, to support the Constitution of the United States, shall have engaged in insurrection or rebellion against the same, or given aid or comfort to the enemies thereof. But Congress may, by a vote of two-thirds of each House, remove such disability.

SECTION 4. The validity of the public debt of the United States, authorized by law, including debts incurred for payment of pensions and bounties for services in suppressing insurrection or rebellion, shall not be questioned. But neither the United States nor any State shall assume or pay any debt or obligation incurred in aid of insurrection or rebellion against the United States, or any claim for the loss or emancipation of any slave; but all such debts, obligations and claims shall be held illegal and void.

SECTION 5. Congress shall have power to enforce, by appropriate legislation, the provisions of this article.

(ARTICLE XV.)

SECTION 1. The right of the citizens of the United States to vote shall not be denied or abridged by the United States, or by any State, on account of race, color or previous condition of servitude.

SECTION 2. The Congress shall have power to enforce this article by appropriate legislation.

CHAPTER IV.

THE PREAMBLE—DISTRIBUTION OF LEGISLATIVE POWERS—THE HOUSE OF REPRESENTATIVES.

§ 55. A CONSTITUTION is the fundamental law of a country, setting forth the principles upon which the government is founded, the political and individual rights of the citizens, and the manner in which the sovereign powers are organized, distributed, and administered.

§ 56. This fundamental law in some countries is contained in a single written instrument, generally called the Constitution.

In other countries it is to be collected from ancient usages, legislative acts, royal grants, judicial decisions, and other sources.

§ 57. The Government of the United States is an illustration of the first case. Here there is a written constitution, and every act of Congress contrary thereto is unconstitutional, and therefore void.

§ 58. England is an illustration of the second case. There we find no written constitution; but the fundamental law is said to be contained in ancient usages, acts of Parliament, and decisions of the courts. No act of Parliament can, therefore, be, in a strict sense, and in our meaning of the term, unconstitutional, or can be declared to be such by the courts, for the general power of Parliament to make laws is unlimited.

§ 59. The Constitution commences with the following declaration:—

"We the People of the United States, in order to form a more perfect Union, establish Justice, insure domestic Tranquillity, provide for the common defence, promote the general Welfare, and secure the Blessings of liberty to ourselves and our Posterity, do ordain and establish this CONSTITUTION for the United States of America."

§ 60. This part of the Constitution has been termed the Preamble, though it was not so named by its framers. A preamble is the commencement of a statute, which declares the design or motives of the legislature in passing it. In the present instance it refers to some of the evils existing under the Articles of Confederation, and sets forth the benefits sought to be attained by the establishment of the new form of government.

§ 61. The objects which the people of the United States had in view in establishing the present Constitution, are briefly stated to be six in number, as follow:—

(1.) To form a more perfect union.

(2.) To establish justice.

(3.) To insure domestic tranquillity.

(4.) To provide for the common defence.

(5.) To promote the general welfare.

(6.) To secure the blessings of liberty to themselves and their posterity.

§ 62. The preamble is not an enacting part of the Constitution, but is in the nature of a recital. It does not grant any powers, nor does it enlarge or lessen any of the powers clearly given in the body of the Constitution. Its only purpose is to explain the objects or motives of the framers of the Constitution.

§ 63. There are three great departments of government:
(1.) The Legislative.
(2.) The Judicial.
(3.) The Executive.

The Legislative enacts laws; the Judicial interprets and applies them; the Executive enforces them.

§ 64. The Constitution of the United States separates these three departments, makes each one independent of the others, and places them in different hands. The Constitutions of the States have also done so; for experience has shown that the separation of these powers is far more favourable to liberty than is their union in the same person. The first article of the Constitution treats of the legislative department; the second article, of the executive department; the third article, of the judicial.

ARTICLE I.

The first article treats of the legislative department of the government.

"SECTION 1. All legislative powers herein granted shall be vested in a Congress of the United States, which shall consist of a Senate and House of Representatives."

§ 65. By the Articles of Confederation, the legislature consisted of only one body. Instances of a single legislative body are also found in the first Constitution of Georgia, and of Pennsylvania, and in the Constitution of Vermont prior to the amendments of 1828; but in the constitutional convention, all the States, except Pennsylvania, were in favour of dividing Congress into two distinct bodies—a Senate and a House of Representatives.

§ 66. In England, the Parliament consists not only of

the House of Lords and the House of Commons, but of the king in his political capacity. With us, Congress means the Senate and House of Representatives, and does not include the President.

§ 67. The advantages of vesting the legislative powers in two branches are chiefly the following. It is more apt to check hasty legislation and temporary excitement by delaying the final passage of a proposed law until there shall have been ample time for reflection and inquiry. It makes it less likely that laws will be passed from private and personal influence, for in a single assembly of men it generally happens that there are a few leaders who exercise great control over the others. It increases the probability that good laws will be passed, because they may be altered, and must be revised and concurred in, by a separate and independent body.

"SECTION 2. [Clause 1.] The House of Representatives shall be composed of Members chosen every second Year by the People of the several States, and the Electors in each State shall have the Qualifications requisite for Electors of the most numerous Branch of the State Legislature."

§ 68. Under the Articles of Confederation, the delegates to Congress were appointed for one year, in such manner as the State legislatures should direct, with power reserved to the States to recall their delegates within the year, and send others in their place for the remainder of the year. (Art. V. § 1.) The delegates were, in fact, chosen by the State legislatures, except in Rhode Island and Connecticut, where they were chosen by the people. The Constitution changed this system by requiring the representatives to be elected by the people of the several States, and by extending the term of service to two years.

§ 69. The Constitution does not prescribe uniform qualifications for those who may vote for representatives. The differences in the qualifications of voters in the several States were so great, and each State was so strongly attached to its own provisions on the subject, that an attempt to introduce uniformity of qualifications throughout all the States might have resulted in a rejection of the whole Constitution.

§ 70. This clause avoids the difficulty by declaring that all who are qualified to vote for members of the most numerous branch of the State legislature, shall be qualified to vote for representatives in Congress. If, therefore, we wish to ascertain what persons in a particular State are qualified to vote for members of Congress, we must consult the Constitution or laws of that State, and ascertain who are qualified to vote for members of the most numerous branch of the State legislature; the Constitution of the United States declares that the qualifications of the voters shall be the same in both cases.

§ 71. If popular elections take place at long intervals, they do not properly represent the will of the people; if they are too frequent, society is kept in a state of excitement, and public measures become uncertain and fluctuating; besides, much inconvenience is thus occasioned to communities spread over a large extent of territory, and expense is incurred and time lost in travelling to and from the place of voting.

§ 72. The period of service in the legislature should not be so long that members will begin to lose their feeling of responsibility to the people who have elected them; nor should it be so short as to expire just at the time they have acquired a practical knowledge of public affairs and the details of business. A proper medium is to be selected between those two extremes.

§ 73. The framers of the Constitution thought that elections for representatives once in two years were sufficiently frequent; hence it is provided by this section that representatives shall be chosen every second year. In England, members of Parliament occupy their seats for seven years, which is the duration of each Parliament, unless dissolved sooner by the king. By the Articles of Confederation, the delegates to Congress were chosen every year. The Constitution went into operation, March 4, 1789, and the term of service in the House of Representatives consequently commenced at that time, and continued for two years. On the fourth day of March, therefore, in every other year, there is said to be a new Congress.*

* As in public documents and official proceedings, the Congresses are frequently referred to by their successive numbers, as the first, second, third, fourth, &c., it has been thought that the following table, showing the commencement of the first session of each Congress, will be found useful for reference:

	Assembled.		Assembled.
1st Congress	March 4, 1789.	18th Congress	Dec. 1, 1823.
2d Congress	Oct. 24, 1791.	19th Congress	Dec. 5, 1825.
3d Congress	Dec. 2, 1793.	20th Congress	Dec. 3, 1827.
4th Congress	Dec. 7, 1795.	21st Congress	Dec. 7, 1829.
5th Congress	May 15, 1797.	22d Congress	Dec. 5, 1831.
6th Congress	Dec. 2, 1799.	23d Congress	Dec. 2, 1833.
7th Congress	March 4, 1801.	24th Congress	Dec. 7, 1835.
8th Congress	Oct 17, 1803.	25th Congress	Sept. 4, 1837.
9th Congress	Dec. 2, 1805.	26th Congress	Dec. 2, 1839.
10th Congress	Oct. 26, 1807.	27th Congress	May 31, 1841.
11th Congress	May 22, 1809.	28th Congress	Dec. 4, 1843.
12th Congress	Nov. 4, 1811.	29th Congress	Dec. 1, 1845.
13th Congress	May 24, 1813.	30th Congress	Dec. 6, 1847.
14th Congress	Dec. 4, 1815.	31st Congress	Dec. 3, 1849
15th Congress	Dec. 1, 1817.	32d Congress	Dec. 1, 1851.
16th Congress	Dec. 6, 1819.	33d Congress	Dec. 5, 1853
17th Congress	Dec. 3, 1821.		

[Clause 2.] "No Person shall be a Representative who shall not have attained to the Age of twenty five Years, and been seven Years a Citizen of the United States, and who shall not, when elected, be an Inhabitant of that State in which he shall be chosen."

§ 74. The qualifications of a representative consist of these three particulars:—

(1.) He must be not less than twenty-five years of age.

(2.) He must have been a citizen of the United States for seven years.

(3.) He must be an inhabitant of the State in which he shall be chosen.

These are the only qualifications established by the Constitution, and the better opinion is that the States have no right to require other or different qualifications.

§ 75. A representative is not required to be a citizen of the United States by birth. If a foreigner by birth, he may become a citizen by naturalization, and then becomes eligible as a representative after a citizenship of seven years.

§ 76. At the time of the adoption of the federal Constitution, many of the inhabitants of the colonies, and many who had fought bravely in the Revolutionary war, were emigrants from Europe, and it was deemed just that they should be entitled to share in the offices and honours of the new government which they had aided in establishing. They were, therefore, made eligible as representatives, though the limitation of a previous seven years' citizenship was thought necessary, lest such representatives might be disposed to favour their native country in managing the foreign affairs and other subjects of legislation. An alien must reside here five years before he becomes a citizen; this, added to the seven years of citizenship which the above clause requires, amounts, in all, to twelve years of previous residence before he is eligible as a representative.

§ 77. The representative must be an inhabitant of the State in which he is chosen. It is not required that he should be a resident of the particular district from which he has been chosen, nor that he should have resided either in the district or the State for any definite length of time before his election. Nor is it said that he shall lose his seat if he remove from his State or district during the two years. It is not necessary that he should possess a certain amount of property, or profess any particular form of religious belief.

[Clause 3.] "Representatives and direct Taxes shall be apportioned among the several States which may be included within this Union, according to their respective Numbers, which shall be determined by adding to the whole Number of free Persons, including those bound to Service for a Term of Years, and excluding Indians not taxed, three fifths of all other Persons. The actual Enumeration shall be made within three Years after the first Meeting of the Congress of the United States, and within every subsequent Term of Ten Years, in such Manner as they shall by Law direct. The Number of Representatives shall not exceed one for every thirty Thousand, but each state shall have at Least one Representative; and until such enumeration shall be made, the State of New Hampshire shall be entitled to chuse three, Massachusetts eight, Rhode Island and Providence Plantations one, Con necticut five, New York six, New Jersey four, Pennsylvania eight, Delaware one, Maryland six, Virginia ten, North Carolina five, South Carolina five, and Georgia three."

§ 78. A tax is a duty laid by government for its service, on the person, property, or income, of individuals. Taxes are of two kinds, direct and indirect. A direct tax is laid directly on the income or property itself; for instance, on lands or houses. An indirect tax is one laid on articles of production or consumption.

Direct taxes are seldom levied, except when other sources of income fail. The only instances of them under the Constitution, were in 1798, 1813, and 1815.

This clause requires that direct taxes shall be apportioned among the States, according to their population respectively. The subject of taxation will be considered more fully hereafter.

§ 79. By the Articles of Confederation, (Art. 8,) the expenses of the United States for the common defence and general welfare, were to be paid by each State in proportion to the value of land surveyed to individuals, together with the improvements and buildings thereon. This placed the liability of a State to direct taxation upon the basis of property, whereas the Constitution places it upon the basis of population.

§ 80. The representative population of the States, that is, their population for the purposes of representation, is ascertained by taking the whole number of free persons, including those bound to service for a term of years, and adding thereto three fifths of all other persons.

The Indians that remain in the States are included in the number of free persons if they are taxed.

The representative population, as thus estimated, will

consequently be less than the total population. By the census of 1850, the representative population of the United States was computed at 21,767,673 persons; while the total population was returned as 23,191,876.

§ 81. The words "other persons" are generally supposed to refer to slaves. Some of the States were in favour of, and others opposed to, including that class in the estimate of the population of a State, so as to increase the number of its representatives. Conflicting opinions existed which were maintained with great bitterness. There were slaves in all the States when the Constitution was adopted, though some contained a much greater number than others.

§ 82. This clause was finally adopted as a compromise; and it was agreed, not that all, but only three-fifths of the slaves should be included in the representative population of the States, and that direct taxes should be apportioned in the same manner. Thus the States in which there was a large number of slaves, while they were allowed an increase of representatives on account of the slave population, were also subjected in like proportion to an increased burden of direct taxation.

§ 83. In order to ascertain the population of the States, so as to apportion the representatives and direct taxes, a general enumeration of the inhabitants of all the States is directed to be taken within three years after the first meeting of Congress, and within every subsequent term of ten years, in such manner as Congress may direct. This enumeration is called the census. In ancient Rome (from whose language the word is derived) the census was an enumeration of the number of Roman citizens, including a valuation of each one's property, and a registration of his tribe, family, children, and servants.

§ 84. The census of the United States has been taken seven times, namely, in 1790, 1800, 1810, 1820, 1830, 1840, and 1850. The duty of taking the census has been intrusted chiefly to the marshals of the United States, (who are the executive officers of the federal courts, corresponding to the sheriffs in the States,) and to assistants appointed by them.

§ 85. According to the act of Congress regulating this subject, each marshal divides his district into smaller divisions, not exceeding twenty thousand persons in each, and appoints an assistant for each subdivision. Each assistant then visits personally every dwelling-house and family in his subdivision, and makes the inquiries of some member of the family which are required by the act of Congress. These inquiries must be answered, or a penalty of thirty dollars is forfeited to the use of the United States. The expense of taking the last census was $1,318,027.53.

§ 86. The census has not been restricted to a mere enumeration of the inhabitants of the States; but has included a collection of interesting and valuable statistics and facts relating to agriculture, commerce, mines, manufactures, education, and other subjects, so as to exhibit a full view of the pursuits, industry, resources, and productions of the country. The general results of the census are then printed and published under the authority of Congress.

§ 87. The following diagram shows the comparative total population of the several States and territories of the Union during successive periods of ten years each, or at each census, since 1790. In the first column, the States are arranged in the order of their relative rank at that time—Virginia being first, Massachusetts the second, and Tennessee the least populous of all the States of

6 *

which the Union was then composed.* In the last column, the States are arranged in the order of their rank, as determined by the census of 1850, New York having become the first, Virginia the fourth, Massachusetts the sixth, and Tennessee the fifth.

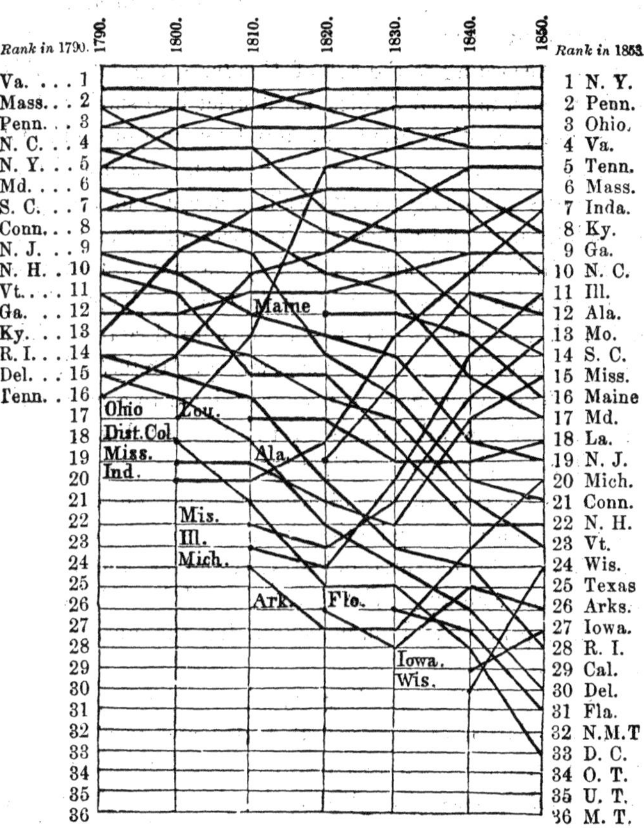

* This diagram was prepared by Professor Gillespie of Union College, who has obligingly assented to its publication here.

§ 88. The heavy lines extending in a zigzag course from the first to the last column exhibit the rise or fall of the States in each period of ten years. Thus Kentucky, which stood thirteenth in 1790, rose to be ninth during the first period, to be seventh during the second period, to be sixth during the third period, and continued to hold that rank for two periods, until 1840, when she began to decline, and in 1850 she appears as the eighth State. Michigan, which stood twenty-fourth in 1810, was twenty-seventh in 1820 and in 1830, twenty-third in 1840, and twentieth in 1850. Thus, by following the line of each State, we may trace its comparative rise and fall at each successive census.

§ 89. The clause under consideration provides that there shall be one representative for every thirty thousand inhabitants. If the population of a State does not reach that number, it is, nevertheless, entitled to one representative. The first apportionment of representatives among the several States was merely temporary, and intended to exist only until the first census. As the population of the country has increased, the number of representatives has been increased by various acts of Congress.

§ 90. The first House of Representatives consisted of 65 members, which was one for every 30,000 inhabitants. By the census of 1790, there were constituted 106 representatives—one for every 33,000 inhabitants. By that of 1800, 142 representatives—one for every 33,000 inhabitants. By that of 1810, 183 representatives—one for every 35,000 inhabitants. By that of 1820, 213 representatives—one for every 40,000 inhabitants. By that of 1830, 242 representatives—one for every 47,700 inhabitants. By that of 1840, 223 representatives—one for every 70,680 inhabitants. By the act of May 23, 1850, the number of representatives was increased to 233 members from the States, which is one for every 93,423 inhabitants. Subsequently an additional member was allowed to California, making the whole number of representatives 234.

Under the census of 1860, one representative was apportioned to every 124,183 inhabitants; and by act of March 4, 1862, eight more representatives were added, making 242.

Every territory, in which a regularly organized territorial government has been established by act of Congress, is entitled to have one representative in Congress, who may participate in the debates, but cannot vote. Such territories are generally called organized territories.

§ 91. An act of Congress of May 23, 1850, directs the Secretary of the Interior, after each enumeration of the inhabitants of the States, to ascertain the entire representative population of the United States, by adding to the whole number of free persons in all the States, including those bound to service for a term of years, and excluding Indians not taxed, three-fifths of all other persons. He is then to divide the aggregate population as thus ascertained, by 233, the number of representatives fixed by the act, and the result of that division, rejecting any fractions or remainders which may be left, shall be the ratio or rule of apportionment of representatives among the several States. He then divides the representative population of each State by the ratio thus determined, and the result of this last division gives the number of representatives apportioned to such State. The aggregate of representatives ascertained in this way is less than 233.

§ 92. The loss in the number of members is caused by the fractions remaining in the several States on the division of their population by the ratio, and is compensated by assigning to so many States having the largest fraction, one additional member each, for its fraction, as may be necessary to make the whole number of representatives amount to 233. When the apportionment is completed, the Secretary of the Interior sends a certificate thereof to the House of Representatives, and to the Executive of each State a certificate of the number of representatives apportioned to such State.

§ 93. Thus, by dividing the aggregate representative population of the States, which by the census of 1850 was ascertained to be 21,767,673, by 233, the number of representatives established, as we have seen, by law, a quotient of 93,423 is obtained as the ratio of representation; this ratio, being divided into the representative population of each State respectively, gives a total of 219 representatives; California, Delaware, and Florida each, returned in the census as having a population less than the ratio, are, nevertheless, by the clause we are now considering, each entitled to one representative, which increases the total number to 222. This still leaves eleven representatives, who, by the act above mentioned, are to be assigned to the eleven States having the highest fractions.

§ 94. By a special act of July 30, 1852, an additional representative is allowed to California until a new apportionment, in consequence of the defectiveness of the census returns for that State; and, until such new apportionment, the whole number of representatives from the States was increased to 234.

§ 95. As the House of Representatives is at present constituted, there are four modes in which a State may be entitled to a representative:

(1.) By the ratio of representation.

(2.) By its large fraction.

(3.) By the constitutional provision that "each State shall have at least one representative."

(4.) By special law.

§ 96. The following table shows how the representatives were distributed among the States by the census of 1860, according to the above modes:

	By ratio and large fraction.	By provision of the Constitution.	By special law.	Total.
Alabama	6	...	...	6
Arkansas	3	...	...	3
California	3	...	...	3
Connecticut	4	...	...	4
Delaware	...	1	...	1
Florida	1	...	...	1
Georgia	7	...	...	7
Illinois	13	...	1	14
Indiana	11	...	...	11
Iowa	5	...	1	6
Kansas	...	1	...	1
Kentucky	8	...	1	9
Louisiana	5	...	...	5
Maine	5	...	...	5
Maryland	5	...	...	5
Massachusetts	10	...	...	10
Michigan	6	...	...	6
Mississippi	5	...	...	5
Missouri	9	...	...	9
Minnesota	1	...	1	2
Nevada	...	1	...	1
New Hampshire	3	...	...	3
New Jersey	5	...	...	5
New York	31	...	...	31
North Carolina	7	...	...	7
Ohio	18	...	1	19
Oregon	...	1	...	1
Pennsylvania	23	...	1	24
Rhode Island	1	...	1	2
South Carolina	4	...	...	4
Tennessee	8	...	...	8
Texas	4	...	...	4
Vermont	2	...	1	3
Virginia } *West Virginia }	11	...	...	11
Wisconsin	6	...	...	6
Total	230	4	8	242

[Clause 4.] "When vacancies happen in the Representation from any State, the Executive Authority

* By the act of Dec. 31, 1862, West Virginia was erected into a separate State, and was given three representatives until the next census; but the act does not say whether they shall be deducted from the apportionment to Virginia or not.

thereof shall issue Writs of Election to fill such Vacancies."

§ 97. This clause provides that when vacancies occur in the representation from any State, the governor thereof may issue writs for a special election to fill the vacancy. Those who are elected in pursuance of such writs are not elected for a full term, but only for the unexpired portion of the term which has become vacant.

[Clause 5.] "The House of Representatives shall chuse their Speaker and other officers; and shall have the sole Power of Impeachment."

§ 98. The House of Representatives at the commencement of each session elects a Speaker, who is the presiding officer of the house.

In England, the Speaker of the House of Commons is chosen by the house; but he must be approved by the king. The king's approbation is now always taken for granted, though formerly it was necessary that it should be expressly given.

§ 99. The officers of the House of Representatives, in addition to the Speaker, are—a clerk, who, with his assistants, keeps the records and journals of the proceedings of the house; a sergeant-at-arms, who executes the commands of the house; a doorkeeper; and a postmaster, who superintends the post-office kept in the Capitol for the accommodation of the members. The clerk is required to take an oath or affirmation to discharge truly and faithfully his duties to the best of his knowledge and ability. He also gives security to account for all public money coming into his hands. The sergeant-at-arms and door keeper are sworn to keep the secrets of the house. A clergyman is also usually chosen, every session, to act as chaplain, who offers prayer at the opening of each morning session, and performs such other religious services as may be required.

The subject of impeachment will be spoken of hereafter.

CHAPTER V.

THE SENATE.

SECTION 3. [Clause 1.] "The Senate of the United States shall be composed of two Senators from each State, chosen by the Legislature thereof, for six Years; and each Senator shall have one Vote."

§ 100. The Senate constitutes the other branch of the legislative power. Senators are elected, not directly by the people, as representatives are, but by the legislatures of the respective States. In the Senate, the States, having each two delegates, are placed upon an equal footing, while in the House they are represented in proportion to their population. In this respect, the Constitution, by giving to each State an equal voice in the Senate, without regard to difference of population, wealth, or dimensions, resembles the old Confederation.

§ 101. The Constitution does not prescribe the mode in which the legislatures are to elect senators. In most of the States the senators are chosen by a joint vote, that is, both branches of the State legislature meet together and vote as if they constituted a single body; but in some of the States each branch votes separately, and both must agree in the choice of the same candidate; this is termed a concurrent vote.

§ 102. Under the Articles of Confederation, the votes in Congress were taken by States, so that each State had but one vote, no matter what was the number of its representatives. The provision in the Constitution that each senator shall have one vote, was intended to introduce a different mode of voting.

§ 103. If all the States, or a majority of them, should refuse to elect senators, the legislative powers of the Senate would be suspended; but if any one State should refuse to elect them, the Senate would not, on that account, be the less capable of performing all its proper business.

[Clause 2.] "Immediately after they shall be assembled in Consequence of the first Election, they shall be divided as equally as may be into three Classes. The Seats of the Senators of the first Class shall be vacated at the Expiration of the second Year, of the second Class at the Expiration of the fourth Year, and of the third class at the Expiration of the sixth Year, so that one-third may be chosen every second Year; and if Vacancies happen by Resignation, or otherwise, during the Recess of the Legislature of any State, the Executive thereof may make temporary Appointments until the next Meeting of the Legislature, which shall then fill such Vacancies."

§ 104. By this clause the Senate is changed gradually, so that, although new members are constantly coming in, there are always in the Senate some of the older and more experienced members. Every two years one-third of the members retire, and are replaced by others. In the original division of the members into classes, the senators from each State were placed in separate classes, in order that their terms of service might expire at different periods, and that there might not be a vacancy at the same time in the seats of both senators from the same State. Senators from new States are placed in the classes by lot, but in such manner as shall keep the classes as nearly equal as may be.

§ 105. In order that a State shall not be unrepresented on account of the death or resignation of its senators, or otherwise, the governor of a State is authorized to fill, by his appointment, vacancies that occur when the legislature of the State is not in session. Such appointments are temporary, and continue only till the meeting of the legislature, when another senator is elected. If the vacancy occurs when the legislature is in session, it is to be filled by an election by that body.

§ 106. It appears to have been decided by the Senate of the United States in 1825, that the governor of a State cannot make an appointment in the recess of a State legislature to fill a vacancy which will happen, but has not happened at the time of the appointment. He must wait until the vacancy has actually occurred before he can constitutionally appoint.

[Clause 3.] "No person shall be a Senator who shall not have attained to the Age of thirty Years, and been nine Years a Citizen of the United States, and who shall not, when elected, be an Inhabitant of that State for which he shall be chosen."

§ 107. The qualifications of a senator consist of these three particulars:

(1.) He must have attained to the age of thirty years.

(2.) He must have been nine years a citizen of the United States.

(3.) He must, when elected, be an inhabitant of the State for which he is chosen.

§ 108. A senator must be at least thirty years of age, because the knowledge and experience of mature life are necessary to qualify him for his duties. He need not be a native born citizen of the United States; but, if an alien, he must have been a citizen for nine years. If sufficient time has not elapsed for him to lose his partiality for the land of his birth, he might be disposed to favour it in advising and consenting to treaties, and in otherwise managing the foreign affairs of our government and the business of legislation.

§ 109. He must, when elected, be an inhabitant of the State for which he is chosen, in order that he may know the wants of those whom he represents. It will be seen, upon comparison, that the qualifications of a senator, as to age and residence, are higher than those of a representative, and the reason is, that his duties are thought to be more honourable and responsible.

§ 110. No qualification as to property, and no profession of a particular form of religious belief, are required of a senator; nor is a previous residence in the State for a definite period of time necessary; nor does he forfeit his seat if he cease to be an inhabitant of the State for which he is chosen; nor can the legislature of his State recall him; nor is he, or a representative, incapable of being re-elected.

[Clause 4.] "The Vice President of the United States shall be President of the Senate, but shall have no Vote, unless they be equally divided."

§ 111. The Speaker of the House of Representatives is a member of that body; but the presiding officer of the Senate is not himself a member of the Senate. If he were, the State he represented might, through him, actually obtain, or from the jealousy of the other States be supposed to obtain, more than its share of influence; and if he were not allowed to vote except when the Senate was equally divided, his vote would be lost to his State; and if he were allowed to vote on all occasions, then, in case of an equal division, there would be no casting vote, unless he were allowed to vote a second time, which would give his State an undue importance. Besides, it was thought the Vice-President would be more impartial, as presiding officer, than a senator would be, because he is not elected by a single State, but by the whole country.

[Clause 5.] "The Senate shall chuse their other Officers, and also a President pro tempore, in the Absence of the Vice President, or when he shall exercise the Office of President of the United States."

§ 112. Although the Vice-President of the United States is, by virtue of his office, the President of the Senate, yet the Senate is authorized to choose its other officers. The Senate may also elect a president *pro tempore* (that is, for a time) in the absence of the Vice-President, or when he shall exercise the office of President of the United States.

§ 113. It is customary for the Vice-President to vacate his chair in the Senate just before the close of each session, and the Senate then elect a President pro tempore, to preside in the Senate in case the Vice-President shall be called upon to exercise the office of President of the United States, in consequence of the death of the President, or otherwise.

[Clause 6.] "The Senate shall have the sole power to try all Impeachments. When sitting for that Purpose, they shall be on Oath or Affirmation. When the President of the United States is tried, the Chief Justice shall preside: And no Person shall be convicted without the Concurrence of two thirds of the Members present."

§ 114. Clause fifth of the preceding section declares that the House of Representatives shall have the sole power of impeachment, that is, of bringing forward or proposing an impeachment; but the power to try all impeachments, after they have been brought forward by the House, is by the present clause vested exclusively in the Senate. The object of this provision is to prevent the same body from being both accusers and judges, which would clearly be unjust.

§ 115. An impeachment is a written accusation charging a civil officer of the United States with treason, bribery, or other high crime or misdemeanor.

In England, the House of Commons, like our House of Representatives, has the sole power of impeachment, and it is tried by the House of Lords, as it is here by the Senate.

§ 116. The convention that formed the Constitution, originally intended to give the trial of impeachments to the Supreme Court of the United States, but afterward adopted the present plan, chiefly because impeachments are applied not altogether to strictly legal offences, but to those of a political nature and extraordinary character, and to misdemeanors in office and violations of public trust, which can scarcely be provided for beforehand, or defined by positive law, or judged by technical rules. Besides, the judges of the Supreme Court are appointed by the President, and if he, or any of his advisers or agents, were on trial, the judges might be biased in favour of the interests of him to whom they owed their elevation to office. A judge of the Supreme Court is himself liable to impeachment, and in such case the other judges would be likely to feel some partiality toward him.

§ 117. In England, when the House of Lords try an impeachment, the lords are not sworn, but give their verdict upon their honour. With us, the senators are required to act under oath or affirmation, just as jurymen are. An affirmation is a solemn declaration made by those who have scruples of conscience against taking an oath. The House of Lords decide the question of guilt or innocence by a simple majority. In the Senate, a majority of two-thirds is requisite for conviction, so that the accused is in less danger of being sacrificed to the excitement usually attending an impeachment.

§ 118. Upon the removal of the President from office, his powers and duties devolve upon the Vice-President of the United States, who is the presiding officer in the Senate. If he presided in the Senate at the trial of an impeachment against the President, he might be inclined to favour his conviction, in order to succeed him in office. It is, therefore, provided that in such case the chief justice of the Supreme Court shall preside.

§ 119. Since the adoption of the Constitution, there have been four trials for impeachment, namely:

(1.) That of William Blount, commenced in 1799. He was then a senator of the United States, and was charged with conspiring, while a senator, to carry on a military expedition against the Spanish territories, and with other misdemeanors. But the Senate decided that he was not a "civil officer' within the meaning of a clause in the Constitution, to be considered hereafter, and therefore not liable to impeachment.

(2.) That of John Pickering in 1803. He was judge of the District Court of the United States for the New Hampshire District, and was charged with various acts of misdemeanor as a judge, found guilty and sentenced to removal from office.

(3.) That of Samuel Chase, commenced November 30, 1804. He was an associate justice of the Supreme Court of the United States, and was charged with official misconduct, but acquitted.

(4.) That of James H. Peck, commenced in 1830. He was judge of the District Court of the United States for the Missouri District, and charged with exercising unlawful authority as a judge, but acquitted.

§ 120. In England, when the person impeached is found guilty, he is sentenced to suffer the whole punishment prescribed by law for the offence. As impeachments are frequently connected with political considerations, and urged on with much zeal, there is danger that the successful party, unless restrained by law, will make an improper use of its triumph, and impose excessive punishments. This is prevented in the United States by the provision that the judgment in cases of impeachment shall extend only to removal from office, and disqualification to hold any office under the United States. The accused still remains liable, nevertheless, to trial and punishment in a court of law, if his offence be such as is punishable by law.

§ 121. Thus, if one were impeached for treason, the judgment pronounced by the Senate, upon conviction, would extend only to removal from office, and future disqualification to hold any office under the United States. He would still be subject to an indictment for treason in a court of law, and if found guilty, would be sentenced to death, the punishment provided by law; if acquitted, the judgment of the Senate upon the impeachment would still stand.

§ 122. When it is proposed to impeach an officer, some member of the House of Representatives moves for the appointment of a committee to report charges against the accused. If the committee report in favour of impeachment, they present a statement of the charges, and a committee is appointed to impeach the offender before the Senate. Then the Senate, by its sergeant-at-arms, summons the accused to appear and answer. When the day for his appearance has arrived, he is furnished with a copy of the charges, and is allowed time to answer them. The House of Representatives replies to the answer when it is put in, declares its readiness to prove its charges, and generally appoints managers to conduct the impeachment.

§ 123. A time is then determined for trial, legal advisers are allowed to the accused, and his witnesses are compelled to attend. The trial proceeds according to the usual rules of courts of justice, and, after it is concluded, the Senate consider the subject. Then each member being called on by name, says whether, in his opinion, the accused is guilty or not guilty. If two-thirds declare him guilty of any or all of the charges, the Senate concludes the proceedings by declaring its judgment.

A subsequent part of the Constitution designates the persons and the offences which may be the subjects of impeachment.

CHAPTER V.

PROVISIONS APPLICABLE BOTH TO THE SENATE AND HOUSE OF REPRESENTATIVES.

SECTION 4. [Clause 1.] "The Times, Places and Manner of holding Elections for Senators and Representatives shall be prescribed in each State by the Legislature thereof; but the Congress may at any time by Law make or alter such Regulations, except as to the places of chusing Senators."

§ 124. The circumstances of the different States were so various, and so liable to change, that it was not deemed practicable to establish, by the Constitution, a general election law. The regulation of the time, place, and manner of congressional elections is, therefore, intrusted to the State legislatures, reserving to Congress the power to make or alter such regulations, except as to the place of choosing senators. Such power in Congress would be useful and absolutely necessary, in case a State should refuse or neglect to provide for the election of members of Congress, or in case it should be deemed expedient to establish a uniform time and manner of holding the elections.

Congress cannot alter the place of choosing senators, because senators are chosen by the State legislatures at the seat of government or capital of the State.

§ 125. Congress has not, as yet, (except as mentioned in the next section,) made any regulations relative to the time, place, or manner of choosing senators or representatives. The States have control of the subject at present, and the modes that have been established in the different States are various. In some States all the representatives from the State were formerly chosen together on one general ticket; in others, they were chosen separately in districts. In some States the successful candidate must have a majority of all the votes; in others, it is sufficient if he have a larger number of votes than any other candidate. In some States the votes have been *viva voce*, (that is, by the living voice;) in others, they are by ballot, that is, by printed or written ticket. Differences in the mode of choosing senators by the State legislatures have already been referred to. (§101.)

§ 126. By an act of Congress, passed June 25, 1842, it is provided that the representatives from a State shall be elected by districts, equal in number to the number of representatives to which the State is entitled, and each of these congressional districts shall elect one representative.

[Clause 2.] "The Congress shall assemble at least once in every Year, and such Meeting shall be on the first Monday in December, unless they shall by Law appoint a different Day."

§ 127. In England, Parliament assembles at the call of the king, and at such time as he designates. This clause requires Congress to assemble at least once a year, on the first Monday of December, unless they shall by law appoint a different day, and it will appear from the table on page 58 that a different day for assembling has frequently been appointed.

§ 128. It seems that, by the ancient statutes and practice

in England, the Parliament assembled annually, or oftener, if there was need. An act passed in the reign of William and Mary declared that there should not be a longer interval than three years between the dissolution of one Parliament and the calling of another. By a subsequent statute in the reign of George I., seven years is made the term for which a Parliament shall exist, unless sooner dissolved by the king.

§ 129. The Constitution does not, in express terms, determine the place where Congress shall meet. It is provided by an act of Congress, that, when on account of the prevalence of a contagious sickness, or for other causes, it would be dangerous to the health of the members to meet at the place to which Congress shall stand adjourned, the President may, by proclamation, convene Congress at such other place as he may deem proper.

SECTION 5. [Clause 1.] "Each House shall be the Judge of the Elections, Returns and Qualifications of its own Members, and a majority of each shall constitute a Quorum to do business; but a smaller Number may adjourn from day to day, and may be authorized to compel the Attendance of absent Members, in such Manner, and under such Penalties as each House may provide."

§ 130. Each house is the judge of the elections, returns, and qualifications of its own members. It is appropriate to the dignity of Congress that it should exercise this right, and it is, perhaps, better qualified to do so than any other tribunal. A similar right belongs to the Parliament of England, and is vested in the legislatures of the several States by their respective constitutions.

§ 131. By an act of Congress, passed February 19,

1851, it is declared that, when any person shall intend to contest an election of any member of the House of Representatives, he shall, within thirty days after the result of the election has been legally determined, give notice in writing to the member whose seat he designs to contest, and in the notice he must specify particularly the grounds upon which he relies. The member who has been returned as elected, within thirty days after the service of the notice upon him, must answer the notice, either admitting or denying the facts alleged, and stating the grounds upon which he rests the validity of his election; and must also serve a copy of his answer upon the contestant.

§ 132. The act further prescribes a mode in which evidence shall be taken in cases of such contested elections. Witnesses may be summoned to give evidence, or to produce papers, before certain classes of judicial officers enumerated in the act, and they incur a penalty for neglecting or refusing to attend or testify, unless prevented by sickness or unavoidable necessity. The questions to the witness and his answers are taken down by writing, in the presence of the parties, and by the officer before whom the examination is had are transmitted immediately, duly certified under his hand and sealed up, to the clerk of the House of Representatives. The House then examines all the evidence, and, after full inquiry and deliberation, adjudges the seat to the party to whom it appears rightfully to belong. The Senate also, in case of a contested election in that body, investigates all the allegations, proofs, and circumstances, and decides between the claimants. The decision of the House or of the Senate is final and conclusive.

§ 133. In order to prevent the passage of laws by a small number of the representatives or the senators, it is declared that no business shall be transacted by either house unless a quorum is present, consisting of a majority of its members. But a smaller number may adjourn from day to day, and compel the attendance of absentees, so that Congress may not be dissolved in consequence of the refusal or neglect of members to attend its sittings.

§ 134. By the rules of the House of Representatives, members who are absent from the house when the roll of names is called, and for whom no sufficient excuses are made, may, by order of those members present, if fifteen in number, be taken into custody as they appear, or may be sent for and taken into custody wherever to be found, by special messengers to be appointed for that purpose. No member can absent himself from the service of the house, unless he have leave, or be sick, or unable to attend. Any fifteen members (including the speaker, if there be one) may compel the attendance of absent members.

The rules of the Senate also provide for enforcing the attendance of absentees.

[Clause 2.] "Each House may determine the Rules of its Proceedings, punish its Members for disorderly Behaviour, and, with the Concurrence of two thirds, expel a Member."

§ 135. The Constitution does not undertake to prescribe the mode of transacting business in Congress, but gives to each house authority to determine the rules of its proceedings. Accordingly, the Senate and House of Representatives have each, from time to time, adopted a number of standing rules, orders, and joint rules, in which the order and manner of conducting their business is set forth with great minuteness.

§ 136. The power given to each house to punish its members for disorderly behaviour, and, with the concurrence of two-thirds, to expel a member, is intended to enable Congress effectually to maintain its usefulness, dignity, and independence.

§ 137. What sort of disorderly conduct may be punished, and what punishment may be inflicted besides expulsion, do not appear to be very clearly settled. The Senate, in 1797, expelled William Blount for an offence which was not committed in his official character, nor during a session of Congress, nor at Washington, nor in violation of any positive law. He was charged with an attempt to entice from his duty an agent of the government among the Indians, and to destroy the confidence of the Indians in the general government.

§ 138. There is no express power given by the Constitution to either house to punish for a breach of its privileges, for disorderly conduct, or for contempt, except when committed by its own members. Yet it has been held that such power exists, because it is essential to the protection, dignity, and existence of the legislative body; also, that Congress is the sole tribunal to determine when it should be exercised, or what punishment should be inflicted.

§ 139. A similar power has been frequently exercised by the legislatures of the States and by the Parliament in England. When imprisonment is a part of the punishment imposed for contempt, such imprisonment, unless limited to a shorter period, terminates with the session of Congress, and no court has a right to inquire directly into the correctness or propriety of the commitment or to discharge the prisoner.

[Clause 3.] "Each House shall keep a Journal of its Proceedings, and from time to time publish the same, excepting such Parts as may in their Judgment require Secrecy; and the Yeas and Nays of the Members of either House on any question shall, at the Desire of one fifth of those Present, be entered on the Journal."

§ 140. The object of a journal is to provide a permanent and accurate record of the proceedings of Congress. The journal of the House is drawn up by the clerk; that of the Senate, by the secretary.

§ 141. The deliberations, votes, and proceedings of the Senate and House of Representatives are generally open to the public. The Senate, however, frequently holds what are termed "executive sessions," in which confidential communications from the President of the United States, nominations to office, treaties, and other matters are considered. It may also hold confidential legislative sessions. When acting on confidential or executive business, the Senate is cleared of all persons except the secretary, the principal clerk, the sergeant-at-arms, and doorkeeper, and sits with closed doors.

§ 142. Thus, too, whenever confidential communications are received by the House of Representatives from the President, the house is cleared of all persons except the members, clerk, sergeant-at-arms, and doorkeeper, and so continues during the reading of such communications, and (unless otherwise directed by the house) during all the debates and proceedings had thereon. Also, when the speaker or any other member shall inform the house that he has communications to make which he conceives ought to be kept secret, the house is in like manner cleared till the communication be made, and it be determined whether the matter requires secrecy.

§ 143. The proceedings of the Senate in executive session, from which the injunction of secrecy has not been removed, and its confidential legislative proceedings, are contained in manuscript records, and are accessible only to the President of the United States, and to the members and the secretary and certain officers of the Senate; but no further extract from those records can be furnished except by special order of the Senate.

§ 144. The journals of the House, and the journals of the legislative proceedings of the Senate, and of such portions of the executive business of the Senate as have been directed to be made public, have been regularly printed and published from the organization of the government, March 4, 1789, down to the present time. The rules of the House of Representatives require the clerk, at the end of each session, to send one of the printed copies of the journal to the executive and to each branch of the legislature of every State.

§ 145. The yeas and nays, or a recorded list of the affirmative and negative votes of the members, shall be taken at the desire of one-fifth of those present. The name of each member is then called, and the manner in which he votes is entered in the journal, and thus becomes known to his constituents and the country. The taking of the yeas and nays requires a great deal of time, and they are often called for by the minority for the sole purpose of embarrassing and delaying the majority. Hence it is that they are not allowed to be taken, except by a vote of one-fifth of the members present.

§ 146. A member of the Senate or House, if he desires to vote on a question, must be present and give his vote in person. He cannot appoint a proxy to vote for him in his absence, although in England a lord in Parliament may, by license obtained from the king, make another lord his proxy to vote for him in his absence; a similar privilege, however, is not extended to members of the House of Commons.

§ 147. By one of the rules of the House of Representatives, no member is allowed to vote on any question in the event of which he is immediately and particularly interested.

By an act of Congress, passed April 21, 1808, no member of Congress is allowed to hold or enjoy any contract or agreement made in behalf of the United States, and, if he shall enter into any such contract, he may be adjudged guilty of a high misdemeanor, and sentenced to pay a large fine, and the contract becomes void. By the same act, penalties are imposed upon any officer of the United States who enters into a public contract with a member of Congress.

[Clause 4.] "Neither House, during the Session of Congress, shall, without the Consent of the other, adjourn for more than three days, nor to any other Place than that in which the two Houses shall be sitting."

§ 148. This clause is intended to secure convenience and despatch in the business of legislation, by preventing the delay and inconvenience which would be occasioned if one branch of the legislature could suspend its sittings for a long period, or could adjourn to a place remote from that in which the other house is sitting.

§ 149. In England, the king has a right to adjourn a Parliament from one session to another, or to put an end to its existence altogether, which renders another election necessary. In this country, the President has no authority to put an end to a session of Congress, and he cannot even adjourn their sittings from one day to another day, unless the two houses disagree with respect to the time of adjournment. (Art. II., sect. 3.)

§ 150. Congress can separate only in two ways: 1st, by adjournment; 2d, by expiration of the two years, which is the limit of the duration of a Congress; for a new Congress commences on the 4th of March in every other year. The number of sessions which a particular Congress may hold, is not fixed by the Constitution; a Congress generally holds two, but sometimes three sessions. All that the Constitution requires, is that Congress shall assemble at least once in every year, and such meeting shall be on the first Monday in December, unless they shall by law appoint a different day. The time when one session of a Congress shall close and the next session commence, is generally determined by a joint resolution of the Senate and House of Representatives. But in every second year Congress must necessarily adjourn on the 3d day of March, because the term for which all the representatives and one-third of the senators are elected expires on that day.

SECTION 6. [Clause 1.] "The Senators and Representatives shall receive a Compensation for their Services, to be ascertained by Law, and paid out of the Treasury of the United States. They shall in all Cases, except Treason, Felony and Breach of the Peace, be privileged from Arrest during their Attendance at the Session of their respective Houses, and in going to and returning from the same; and for any speech or debate in either House, they shall not be questioned in any other Place."

§ 151. The members of Parliament in England do not now receive any compensation, though it was not altogether so in former times. The Constitution provides a compensation to members of Congress, in order that persons of moderate means in life might not be excluded from this branch of the public service on account of the expense attending it, or be led into temptation by their wants while in the national councils.

§ 152. Under the Confederation, the expenses of the delegates were paid by the States they represented. If the members of Congress were paid by the States, or directly by their constituents, there might be great inequalities in the rate of pay—some receiving more, some less, than others; their constituents or the States could at any time withdraw the compensation, and besides, the members would, perhaps, feel themselves less independent and free in their action.

§ 153. Previous to 1816, each member of the Senate and House of Representatives, and each delegate from the territories, was allowed six dollars per day while actually attending in session, and one day's compensation for every twenty miles of travel to and from the seat of government. By an act, passed March 19, 1816, the former acts were repealed, and the compensation of the members was fixed at $1500 per annum, and also the former allowance for travelling expenses.

Since the 4th of March, 1817, the pay of each member of the Senate and House of Representatives has been fixed at eight dollars a day during the period of his attendance in Congress, without deduction in case of sickness; and eight dollars for every twenty miles travelled, in the usual road, in going to and returning from the seat of government. The compensation of the President of the Senate pro tempore in the absence of the Vice-President, and of the Speaker of the House of Representatives, is sixteen dollars a day.

§ 155. By the rules of the House of Representatives, it is made the duty of the sergeant-at-arms to keep the accounts for the pay and mileage of members, to prepare checks, and if required to do so, to draw the money from the treasury on such checks for the members, and pay it over to the member entitled thereto; but the check must be previously signed by the Speaker and endorsed by the member. The mileage to be received by each member is ascertained by a committee appointed for that purpose, and reported by them to the sergeant-at-arms. The sergeant-at-arms is required to give bond with surety to the United States in a sum not less than five nor more than ten thousand dollars, at the discretion of the Speaker, and with such surety as the Speaker shall approve, faithfully to account for the money coming into his hands for the pay of members.

§ 156. In the Senate, the money appropriated for the compensation of members and officers, as well as for the contingent expenses of the Senate, is paid at the treasury on requisitions drawn by the secretary of the Senate, and is kept, disbursed, and accounted for by him. He gives bond in the sum of twenty thousand dollars for the faithful application of such funds.

§ 157. Members of Congress are also, by this clause, entitled to certain personal privileges. They are privileged from arrest in all cases, except treason, felony, and breach of the peace, during their attendance at the session of their respective houses, and in going to and returning therefrom. The reason of this exemption is, that their constituents may not be left unrepresented in the debates and votes. A similar privilege, in favour of the members of the legislatures, exists generally under the State constitutions, and it has long been exercised in England, not only by the members of Parliament, but by their wives and children. Our Constitution limits the privilege to senators and representatives themselves, and does not extend it to their families.

§ 158. This privilege, however, is limited. It does not extend to treason, which is defined in another part of the Constitution; nor to felony, which is a legal term of wide signification, used to denote a class of crimes which, by the ancient common law of England, occasioned a forfeiture of land or goods, and to which the punishment of death was generally attached; nor does it extend to a breach of the peace, which is a violation of the public order or a disturbance of the public peace.

§ 159. No member of Congress can be lawfully questioned in any other place for any speech or debate in either house. The object of this is to secure freedom of speech, independence, and liberty in the discussions. But if a member publish a speech which is libellous, it is said he is not protected by his privilege, and may be proceeded against as in ordinary cases of libel. The debates in Congress have for many years, however, been reported and published at the expense and by the authority of Congress.

[Clause 2.] "No Senator or Representative shall, during the Time for which he was elected, be appointed to any civil Office under the Authority of the United States, which shall have been created, or the Emoluments whereof shall have been encreased during such time; and no Person holding any Office under the United States, shall be a Member of either House during his Continuance in Office."

§ 160. This clause is intended to prevent members of Congress from creating civil offices, or increasing the salary attached to such offices already existing, for the sake of benefiting or advancing themselves. No senator or representative can, during the term for which he has been elected, be appointed to an office which has been created, or to one the emoluments of which have been increased, during such term, although he may be appointed after the expiration of the term.

§ 161. The prohibition in the former part of the clause does not extend to military offices, because they frequently require to be filled immediately, without delay; but no officer under the United States, either civil or military, can be a senator or representative during his continuance in office. A person may hold an office under the United States when elected a member of Congress; but he must resign it before he can take his seat in Congress.

CHAPTER VII.

THE ENACTMENT OF LAWS.

SECTION 7. [Clause 1.] "All Bills for raising Revenue shall originate in the House of Representatives; but the Senate may propose or concur with Amendments as on other Bills.

§ 162. Bills for raising revenue are generally considered to be those only by which taxes are levied, and not such as may incidentally have the effect of creating a revenue.

In England, the House of Commons possesses the sole

power of originating bills for raising revenue, or "money bills," as they are called there; and the Commons will not suffer the House of Lords to make the least alteration or amendment in, or exert any power over, such bills, but that of simply agreeing to or rejecting them.

§ 163. A similar right to originate all bills for raising revenue is granted by the Constitution to the House of Representatives, because that body is more popular in its character, more immediately dependent upon the people, and more directly represents their opinions and wishes, and possesses at the same time more knowledge of the local wants and resources of each part of the country.

§ 164. The Senate is not a permanent and hereditary body, like the House of Lords; but is an elective body, representing the States; and as the States, as such, are interested in the apportionment of direct taxes, there seemed no good reason for excluding the Senate from some control over money bills. They are, therefore, allowed to propose or concur with amendments, as on other bills, but they cannot originate such bills.

[Clause 2.] Every Bill which shall have passed the House of Representatives and the Senate, shall, before it become a Law, be presented to the President of the United States; If he approve he shall sign it, but if not he shall return it, with his Objections to that House in which it shall have originated, who shall enter the Objections at large on their Journal, and proceed to reconsider it. If after such Reconsideration two thirds of that House shall agree to pass the Bill, it shall be sent, together with the Objections, to the other House, by which it shall likewise be reconsidered, and if approved by two thirds of that House, it shall become a Law. But in all such Cases the Votes of both Houses shall be determined by yeas and Nays, and the Names of the Persons voting for and against the Bill shall be entered on the Journal of each House respectively. If any Bill shall not be returned by the President within ten Days (Sundays excepted) after it shall have been presented to him, the same shall be a law, in like Manner as if he had signed it, unless the Congress by their Adjournment prevent its Return, in which Case it shall not be a Law.

§ 165. The Constitution does not prescribe the mode of enacting laws; that is determined by the rules and practice of the Senate and House of Representatives. Bills may originate either in the Senate or the House of Representatives, except they be bills for raising revenue, which, as we have just seen, must originate in the House. The general mode of passing bills in both bodies is quite similar, though not in all respects the same. It will be sufficient, for an understanding of the subject, to refer more particularly, as an illustration of the manner of enacting laws, to the course pursued in the House of Representatives.

§ 166. By the rules of the House, a bill, which is the original form or draft of a law proposed to be enacted, may be introduced into the House in the report of a committee, or upon a motion by a member of the House for leave to introduce it. In the latter case, at least one day's notice of the motion must be given, or a memorandum thereof filed with the clerk and entered on the journal. But the rule in regard to the introduction of bills on leave is rarely practised; nearly all the bills not regularly reported by a committee are introduced with or without consent, as the case may be.

§ 167. By another rule, every bill shall receive three several readings previous to its passage, and no bill can be read twice on the same day without the special order of the House. The first reading is for information, and if opposition is made, which is not usual, however, at the first reading, the question is put, "Shall this bill be rejected?" If no opposition is made, or if the question to reject be negatived, the bill goes to its second reading without any motion for that purpose; and in such cases the actual practice is for the second reading to take place forthwith, immediately after the first reading, it being understood that it is by the special order of the House. The whole bill is not, in point of fact, read, but only its title, for members are informed of the contents of the bill by printed copies of it, which are furnished to them, except in the case of bills introduced on leave, which are never printed until reported back from the committee to which they may have been referred, which is after the second reading, as every bill is read twice before it is referred.

§ 168. Upon the second reading of a bill, it may, according as the House shall determine, be committed, that is, referred, either to a select committee, or a standing committee, or a committee of the whole house; or it may be ordered to be engrossed, that is, copied on paper in a fair round hand, and a day be appointed when it shall be read a third time. According to the uniform practice of the House for many years, whenever a bill is ordered to be engrossed it is immediately read the third time. It is usually engrossed in advance; but whether engrossed or not, it is considered as engrossed, a question as to the fact of engrossment being seldom if ever raised.

§ 169. If the bill be committed, after it has been considered by the committee, it is reported back to the House, either with or without amendments, which are adopted or rejected by the House, as it sees fit. After amendments are disposed of, the bill must be ordered to be engrossed, and is then ready for the third reading, at which the vote is taken on its final passage.

§ 170. After its passage, the bill is signed by the Speaker, and sent to the Senate for concurrence. If the Senate refuse to concur, the bill fails to become a law. Or the Senate may pass the bill with amendments, and it is then returned to the House, where the amendments may be concurred in, and the bill as amended be passed. But if the House refuse to concur in the amendments of the Senate, the bill will then fail.

§ 171. In case, however, of amendments in one body, which are disagreed to in the other, a committee from both is appointed at the request of either, termed a committee of conference, in which the reasons for and against the amendments are freely discussed, and such conference frequently results in a compromise or adjustment of views, which is reported to the Senate and House respectively by its committee of conference.

§ 172. After a bill has passed both bodies, it is enrolled on parchment by the clerk of the House of Representatives, or by the secretary of the Senate, according as the bill may have originated in the one body or the other, and the enrolment is then compared by a joint committee of the Senate and House, with the engrossed bill as passed, for the purpose of correcting errors, if there be any, in the enrolment.

§ 173. After that committee has thus examined the enrolment, and has so reported, the enrolled bill is signed, first by the Speaker of the House of Representatives, and afterward by the President of the Senate; an endorsement is made upon it, certifying whether the bill originated in the Senate or the House of Representatives, and it is then presented by the committee to the President of the United States for his approval, the day of such presentation being entered on the journal both of the Senate and the House.

§ 174. If the President approves it, he signs it; if he does not approve it, he returns it, together with his objections in writing, to the house in which it originated. His power is confined to the approval or rejection of bills; he cannot propose any amendments in them. The power of the President to object to bills and refuse to sign them, is commonly known as the veto power.

§ 175. In ancient Rome there was a body of officers called the Tribunes of the People, whose proper object was the protection of the people against the encroachments of the Senate and Consuls. In the earlier times of their existence, they could not enter the Senate, but had their seats before the door of the Senate-room, where they heard all the deliberations, and could hinder the passage of any decree by the single word *veto*, which is a Latin word, signifying *I forbid*.

§ 176. In England, the king possesses an absolute veto, though it is rarely exercised, which prevents the passage of the law against which it is exerted. The President's veto is not absolute, but qualified. It has no other effect than to cause the legislature to reconsider the proposed law and examine it more carefully, and to suspend or delay its passage until two-thirds of the members of each house agree to pass it.

§ 177. The object of the veto is to enable the President

to protect the executive department of the government against the encroachments of the legislative department, and sc to prevent his constitutional authority from being weakened or taken from him. It is also intended to be used to check the passage of rash, improper, and unconstitutional laws, and laws enacted without due consideration, as in times of temporary political excitement or violent party spirit.

§ 178. The objections of the President are to be entered on the journals of the house in which the bill originated, in order that they may be permanently recorded and preserved. The vote upon the passage of the law is required to be taken by yeas and nays, and the names of the persons voting for and against the bill are entered upon the journals, so that the members may be induced to vote with more care and deliberation.

§ 179. If, upon reconsideration, the bill is passed by a vote of two-thirds of the house in which it originated, it is then to be sent, together with the President's objections, to the other house, where it is also reconsidered, and if approved by two-thirds of that house, it becomes a law without the signature of the President, and notwithstanding his objections.

§ 180. If the President could retain a bill, which had been sent to him, for an indefinite period of time, without affixing his signature, its passage might thus be prevented or delayed. It is, therefore, provided that, if it shall not be returned by him within ten days, (Sundays excepted,) it shall become a law in like manner as if he had signed it, unless he be prevented from returning it by the adjournment of Congress, in which case it shall not become a law.

§ 181. An act of Congress goes into effect the day on

which it is approved by the President, unless the act itself appoint a different time.

The commencement of an act of Congress is as follows: "*Be it enacted by the Senate and House of Representatives of America in Congress assembled*, That," &c.

[Clause 3.] "Every Order, Resolution, or Vote to which the Concurrence of the Senate and House of Representatives may be necessary (except on a question of Adjournment) shall be presented to the President of the United States; and before the Same shall take Effect, shall be approved by him, or being disapproved by him, shall be repassed by two thirds of the Senate and House of Representatives, according to the Rules and Limitations prescribed in the Case of a Bill."

§ 182. Were it not for the above clause, Congress might pass measures in the form of orders or resolutions instead of passing them by bills, and thus evade the President's veto. It is, therefore, provided that orders, resolutions, or votes to which the concurrence or joint assent both of the Senate and House of Representatives is necessary, shall be sent to the President for his signature, and be subject to the same regulations in that respect as if they were bills.

9*

CHAPTER VIII.

THE POWERS VESTED IN CONGRESS.

SECTION 8.

§ 183. THE object of this important section is to enumerate the various powers which have been expressly granted to Congress by the Constitution.

§ 184. The mere grant of a power to Congress by the Constitution does not of itself imply that the States are prohibited from exercising the same power. It is not alone the existence of the power in Congress, but its actual exercise by that body, which restricts the States in the exercise of the same power. For instance, Congress, as we shall see, is authorized to establish uniform laws on the subject of bankruptcies throughout the United States; but it has been held that the States may pass bankrupt laws, provided there be no law on the subject enacted by Congress. It is when the language in which a power is granted to Congress, or the nature of the power, requires that it should be enjoyed by Congress exclusively, that the subject is taken from the legislatures of the States.

Powers which may be exercised both by Congress and the States are termed concurrent powers; those which are exercised by Congress alone are termed exclusive powers.

[Clause 1.] "The Congress shall have Power to lay and collect Taxes, Duties, Imposts and Excises, to pay the

Debts and provide for the common Defence and general Welfare of the United States; but all Duties, Imposts and Excises shall be uniform throughout the United States."

§ 185. It has been a subject of frequent discussion whether the words "to pay the debts and provide for the common defence and general welfare of the United States," grant a separate and independent power to Congress, or whether they are used only to point out the purpose for which the taxes, duties, and imposts are to be collected. The latter opinion is generally received as correct. The clause conveys the power of taxation, yet restrains the purpose to which it is to be exercised—to payment of the debts and provision for the common defence and general welfare of the United States.

§ 186. The constitutional power of Congress to lay taxes is thus limited to three purposes:

(1.) To pay the public debt.

(2.) To provide for the common defence.

(3.) To provide for the general welfare.

These objects refer to the common interests of all the States, and exclude such purposes as are of a local or partial nature, the advantages of which are enjoyed only by one or a few of the individual States.

§ 187. Taxes have been defined in § 78. Duties are charges upon goods and merchandise imported or exported, that is, brought into or taken out of the country. But they are almost wholly confined to charges upon imported goods; for those laid upon exported articles are designed rather to check the exportation of the articles than to raise a revenue. Imposts is a word used in a general sense as similar in meaning to tax or public burden. Excises are inland charges upon articles produced or manufactured within a country, while in the hands of the producer or manufacturer.

§ 188. Under the Articles of Confederation, (Art. 8,) all expenses incurred for the common defence and general welfare were supplied by the several States in proportion to the value of all the land in the State granted to or surveyed for any person, with the buildings and improvements thereon. The taxes for paying the share or proportion of each State were levied and collected by the authority and under the direction of the respective State legislatures. The Continental Congress had no authority to lay a tax directly upon, and collect it from, the inhabitants of the States. It could only make a requisition upon the legislatures of the States for the amount of their contribution to the common treasury, and the States could, at their pleasure, either grant or refuse the sums thus required of them, or pay a less sum. This was one of the most serious evils of the Confederation.

§ 189. This clause, however, gives to Congress the general power of imposing taxes immediately upon the citizens of the States, and declares that duties, imposts, and excises (but not taxes) shall be uniform throughout the United States. Other parts of the Constitution provide for direct taxes.

Art. I. sec. 2, clause 3, requires that direct taxes shall be apportioned among the States, according to their respective numbers as determined by the census; and sec. 9, clause 4, of the same article, prohibits any capitation or other direct tax, unless in proportion to the census. A capitation, or, as it is sometimes called, a poll-tax, is a tax imposed upon each head, or person, of the population.

§ 190. There are two rules, therefore, for the government of Congress in imposing taxes:

(1.) The rule of apportionment.

(2.) The rule of uniformity.

Capitation and other direct taxes are to be laid by the first rule; duties, imposts, excises, and indirect taxes generally, are to be laid by the second rule.

§ 191. The difference between the operation of a direct tax laid according to the rule of apportionment, and an indirect tax laid according to the rule of uniformity, may be thus illustrated:

Suppose Congress were to impose a tax of ten dollars on each carriage, and the number of carriages in the United States were two hundred and thirty-four, which is the number of representatives at present in Congress. The sum derived from the tax would be $2,340. Now, if this were to be regarded as a direct tax, and therefore apportioned among the States according to the number of their representatives in Congress, Rhode Island, having two representatives, would have to pay $\frac{2}{234}$ of the tax, equal to twenty dollars; and Ohio, having twenty-one representatives, would have to pay $\frac{21}{234}$ of the tax, equal to two hundred and ten dollars.

§ 192. If, then, there were in Rhode Island five persons owning a carriage, each would have to pay one-fifth of the tax payable by that State, which would be four dollars; and if in Ohio there were a hundred persons owning carriages, each would have to pay a hundredth part of the tax payable by that State, which would be two dollars and ten cents; so that in the former State the tax upon the owner of a carriage would be nearly twice as much as in the latter State.

§ 193. But if the tax which we have supposed is regarded as an indirect tax, (and such it was decided really to be,) it would be laid according to the rule of uniformity, and then each owner of a carriage would have to pay ten dollars, no matter what was the number of persons in a particular State owning carriages.

§ 194. The power of Congress to lay and collect taxes, duties, imposts, and excises, extends not only to the States, but to the District of Columbia, though it is not represented in Congress, and also to the territories of the United States. But Congress is not bound to extend a direct tax to the district and territories. They are held subject to taxation because they are a part of the Union, and the power of taxation vested by the Constitution in Congress extends over the whole country.

§ 195. The Supreme Court of the United States on one occasion expressed great doubts whether any taxes are direct taxes within the meaning of the Constitution, except capitation taxes and taxes on land; and such seems to be the general opinion.

§ 196. Duties on imports are of two kinds:

(1.) Specific duties.

(2.) *Ad valorem* duties.

A specific duty is a tax of a certain amount on goods, estimating them by weight, bulk, or measure; for instance, a duty of one dollar on every ton of iron, or of one cent on every pound of sugar or yard of calico, would be a specific duty. An *ad valorem* duty is one estimated according to the value or cost of the goods; a duty of five per cent. on iron; that is, five dollars on every one hundred dollars' worth of iron, would be an *ad valorem* duty.

§ 197. Duties are laid on imports and tonnage. By tonnage is meant the cubical contents or burden of a vessel expressed in tons. The duties paid on the tonnage of a ship or vessel, are also called tonnage. By former acts of Congress, vessels of the United States entering from a foreign port, or entering a collection district in one State from a district in another State, were subject to certain tonnage duties. Such duties were also imposed on foreign vessels, but higher than those paid by American vessels.

§ 198. These duties are now, by an act of May 31, 1830, abolished in relation to American vessels, and vessels of the United States are admitted into the ports of the United States free of duty. All tonnage duties on foreign vessels are also abolished, provided the President is satisfied that the corresponding duties of such foreign nation, so far as they operate to the disadvantage of the United States, have been abolished.

§ 199. By Article I. sect. 10, clause 2, the several States are prohibited from laying any imposts or duties on exports or imports, without the consent of Congress, except what may be absolutely necessary for executing their inspection laws, by which are meant laws providing for the examination of commodities, in order to ascertain their quality; and they are also prohibited, by the same clause, from laying any duty on tonnage without the consent of Congress. The object of these provisions is to vest the supervision and control of the whole subject in Congress.

§ 200. The duties charged upon imports or exports are paid by the person who imports or exports the goods. If imported goods are not to be used in the United States, but are to be re-exported, an allowance is made to the importer, and in some cases the whole, in others a part, of the duties is paid back to him. This allowance is called a drawback. The collector of the port at which the goods are entered gives to the importer a certificate, called a debenture, which sets forth the amount due to him by the United States for drawback of duties.

§ 201. The rate of customs and duties payable on merchandise is called a tariff. The list of articles arranged so as to exhibit the various duties, drawbacks, &c., charged or allowed on the importation or exportation of foreign and domestic articles, is also called a tariff.

§ 202. If the importer intends to re-export merchandise, he may deposit it in a public warehouse established by the government, generally termed a bonded warehouse, or, under certain regulations, in a private bonded warehouse, and give bond for the payment of the duties, in case it should not be exported again, but be used in the United States.

§ 203. Where the acts of Congress impose an *ad valorem* rate of duty, it is made the duty of the collector of the port at which the goods are imported, to cause the actual market value at wholesale price of the goods, at the period of their exportation to the United States, in the principal markets of the country whence they have been imported, to be appraised and estimated; to such value are added certain costs and charges, and thus the true value of the goods is ascertained, upon which the duties are assessed.

§ 204. In each of the large ports of the United States, appraisers, and, in some instances, assistant appraisers, are appointed by the President, to perform all the duties in the appraisement of imports and exports, required by the revenue laws. They are the detectors of frauds in invoices.

§ 205. An invoice is an account of goods or merchandise sent by merchants to the purchasers, in which the marks of each package, with their nature, value, charges,

&c., are set forth. Invoices of imported goods must be verified by the oath of the importer, his consignee, or agent. The person from whom goods are shipped is called the consignor; the person to whom they are shipped is termed the consignee.

§ 206. The appraisers are the judges of the quality and cost of goods, and they compare the goods with the invoice, or calculate and fix the value of the goods entered without invoice. The invoices of all goods and merchandise imported from a foreign port are submitted to the appraiser, together with such packages as are ordered for examination. If the packages are found to agree with the invoices in quantity, quality, and manufacture, the facts are noted on the invoice; if they do not so agree, the appraiser makes his return to the collector accordingly.

§ 207. When goods are not supposed to be fraudulently invoiced, but in the judgment of the appraisers are not invoiced at their full value, they add such an amount as will bring them up to their full value. When fraud is suspected, the appraiser reports the facts to the collector, and, if he agree with the appraiser in his suspicions, the goods are ordered to be seized.

§ 208. A manifest is a written instrument containing a true account of the cargo of a ship or commercial vessel. The manifest of ships or vessels belonging in whole or in part to citizens of the United States, in which goods are imported, is required, by act of Congress, to be signed by the master of the vessel, and to set forth the names of the places where the goods were taken on board, and the places in the United States to which they are consigned; also the name, description, and tonnage, of the vessel; a particular account of the goods on board, and the names of the persons to whom they are consigned, together with the names of the passengers on board.

§ 209. The duties and charges upon goods, wares, and merchandise, imported or exported, are collected under the direction of the Treasury department. The States are for this purpose divided into collection districts, in each of which is a collector appointed by the President and Senate for the term of four years, but removable at the pleasure of the President. In each collection district there is established one port for the entry of goods, and one or more ports of delivery, each port of entry being also a port of delivery.

§ 210. The collector receives, at the port of entry within his district, all the documents required by law to be produced when vessels and the goods imported in them are entered. The entry of goods is the submitting to the collector and officers of the customs the goods imported, with a statement or description of them, together with the original invoices.

§ 211. The duties of a collector of customs are to receive all reports, manifests, and documents to be made or exhibited on the entry of any ship or vessel; to record all manifests in books; to receive the entries of all ships or vessels, and the goods, wares, or merchandise imported in them; to estimate, together with the naval officer, where there is one, or alone, where there is none, the amount of duties payable, endorsing the amounts upon the respective entries.

§ 212. He also receives all moneys paid for duties, and takes the bonds for securing their payment, and grants permits for the unlading and delivery of goods. He is authorized, with the approbation of the secretary of the treasury, to employ proper persons as weighers, gaugers, measurers, and inspectors, at the several ports within his district, and to provide storehouses for the safe keeping of goods, and such scales, weights, and measures as may be necessary. The collector does not grant a permit for the unloading and delivery of goods until the duties have been paid, or bonds with sureties have been given for their payment at a certain time.

The official business of the collector is transacted at the custom-house.

§ 213. In some of the more important ports, a naval officer and surveyor are also appointed. An act of Congress makes it the duty of the naval officer to receive copies of manifests and entries, and, together with the collector, estimate the duties on all goods subject to duty, (and no duties shall be received without such estimate,) and to keep a separate record of them; also to countersign all permits, clearances, certificates, debentures, and other documents granted by the collector, and to examine the collector's account of duties, receipts, bonds, and expenditures, and, if found right, to certify them.

§ 214. The naval officer is appointed directly by the President. He is independent of the collector, and is intended to act as a check upon that officer; all entries, therefore, which are commenced in the collector's office, must be continued through the naval office, and are carried through the same forms in both offices.

§ 215. The surveyor has charge of the inspectors, weighers, measurers, and gaugers within his port. He visits and inspects all vessels that arrive, and makes a return to the collector, of the vessels as they arrive. He is an independent officer, appointed by the President.

§ 216. The collector, naval officer, surveyor, or other person specially appointed by them for that purpose, has authority to enter any ship or vessel in which there is reason to suspect that any goods subject to duty are concealed, and to search for and seize such goods: and if they suspect goods are concealed in any store or building, they may, upon application on oath to any justice of the peace, obtain a warrant to enter and search such place, (in the daytime only,) and seize and secure for trial, the goods that may be found there.

§ 217. All such goods on which the duties shall not have been paid, or secured to be paid, are to be forfeited; and all other violations of the revenue laws are punished by severe fines and penalties.

§ 218. There are also small, swift-sailing vessels attached to the more important ports, built by and under the command of the government, called revenue cutters, which are used for pursuing smugglers, that is, those who import or export goods privately and contrary to law, or without paying the duties, and for otherwise enforcing the revenue laws. The revenue cutters are also authorized to aid in enforcing the quarantine and health laws of the States.

§ 219. Congress has at different times passed many acts concerning the navigation, ships, and seamen of the United States, and giving numerous privileges to vessels owned and commanded by our own citizens. Such vessels are entitled to be registered, enrolled, or licensed, according to the nature of the trade in which they are engaged, and are thereupon considered as vessels of the United States, entitled to the benefits and privileges of such ships.

§ 220. The registry of a vessel is a record made in the office of the collector of the district to which the vessel belongs, embracing the measurement of the vessel, her name, the port to which she belongs, her burden, the year, and the name of the place in which she was built, and the names and residences of the owners. A certificate of the registry is given by the collector to the owner or captain of the vessel. Certificates of registry are issued to American vessels engaged in the foreign trade.

§ 221. No owner is compelled to register his vessel; but, unless registered, (with the exception of those enrolled and licensed in the coasting and fishing trades,) she is not entitled to the privileges and benefits of a vessel of the United States, although she be built, owned, and commanded by citizens thereof.

§ 222. In order to obtain a register, oath must be made that the master is a citizen of the United States, and that the vessel has been built in the United States, and is wholly owned by citizens thereof. If the master of a registered vessel is changed, or if the vessel's name be altered, such fact must be endorsed upon the register at the custom-house, or she will cease to be considered a vessel of the United States.

§ 223. The trade carried on between one part of the United States and another, on the sea-coast, or on navigable rivers, is called the coasting trade. All vessels built in the United States and wholly owned by citizens thereof, which are destined to be employed in the coasting and fishing trades, (except those engaged in whaling,) and are above twenty tons burden, in order to become entitled to the privileges of vessels of the United States in those trades, must be both enrolled and licensed; if they are less than twenty tons, they need not be enrolled, but must be licensed. Licenses are valid only for one year after their date, but they may be renewed at any time. The same qualifications and requisites in all respects are demanded, in order to the enrolling and licensing of a vessel, which are required for a registry.

§ 224. Registered vessels may be enrolled and licensed

upon giving up the registry; and enrolled and licensed vessels may be registered on giving up the enrolment and license. Vessels enrolled and licensed for the coasting trade, cannot, under penalty of forfeiture, proceed on a foreign voyage, without giving up their enrolment and license, and receiving a registry.

§ 225. Vessels owned by American citizens and employed in the foreign trade, which, on account of being foreign built, or for other cause, are refused a register, are termed unregistered vessels, and sail under the authority of a sea-letter, certifying such vessel to be the property of a citizen of the United States.

§ 226. Certificates of record are granted to vessels built in the United States, but which belong wholly, or in part, to citizens or subjects of a foreign power.

The certificates of registry, and of enrolment, and licenses, are termed permanent, if the vessel belongs to the port or district where the certificate or license is issued, and temporary, if the vessel belongs to another port or district.

§ 227. Masters of vessels bound to foreign ports, are furnished by the collectors with a list of their crew, distinguishing foreigners from citizens, and with a certificate of citizenship to each citizen seaman, called his protection certificate. The crew-list, as required by acts of Congress and sometimes by treaties, is necessary for the protection of the crew of every vessel in the course of her voyage during a war.

[Clause 2.] "To borrow Money on the credit of the United States."

§ 228. A similar power was granted to the Continental Congress by the Articles of Confederation, (Art. 9, § 5.)

Taxes and duties may not be sufficient at all times to supply the wants of the government. During wars, especially, it is often necessary to borrow money.

[Clause 3.] "To regulate Commerce with foreign Nations, and among the several States, and with the Indian Tribes."

§ 229. Commerce is defined to be an exchange of goods, wares, or property of any kind, between nations or individuals. The word, as used in the Constitution, seems to include not only traffic or barter, but intercourse and navigation.

§ 230. Under the Confederation, commerce was in a very depressed state, chiefly because of the want of power in Congress to establish and enforce regulations on the subject. Congress could, indeed, enter into treaties with foreign nations, but had no means of enforcing the observance of them by the States. Each State made its own regulations with reference to trade and commerce, and naturally sought to favour its own local interests even at the expense of the other States. These hostile restrictions led to measures of retaliation, the tendency of which was to destroy all commercial intercourse.

§ 231. This clause grants to Congress the full power of regulating foreign and domestic commerce, navigation, and intercourse. The power does not extend to internal traffic between individuals in different parts of the same State, but to the trade which may be carried on between the United States and foreign States, and among the several States, and from one State to places within the territory of another State.

§ 232. Congress is authorized to regulate the whole subject of commerce; its power has been decided to be exclusive. A State, therefore, cannot lay a tax on importers or on imported goods, because that would be a restraint upon the sale of imported goods, and the importation of foreign goods is a part of commerce, the regulation of which belongs solely to Congress. In like manner, certain acts of the legislature of New York granting, for a term of years, to Robert R. Livingston and Robert Fulton the exclusive right to navigate the waters within the jurisdiction of that State, with steamboats, were held to be violations of this clause of the Constitution, and therefore void, so far as they prohibited vessels licensed under the laws of the United States to carry on the coasting trade, from navigating the same waters.

§ 233. The authority granted by this clause extends to fisheries along the coast, the government of seamen on board of American ships, to the subject of wrecks, to the enactment of pilotage laws, and of laws regulating quarantine.

Quarantine is a period of time during which a vessel arriving in port, and suspected of being infected with a malignant or contagious disease, is not allowed to communicate with the shore, except under particular restrictions. The object of compelling a vessel to perform quarantine, is to prevent the introduction of disease into the country.

§ 234. This authority extends also to the construction of light-houses and of buoys, to clearing rivers, harbours, and bays of obstructions to navigation, and to constituting ports for the entry of goods; it likewise includes the laying of a temporary embargo, but not of a perpetual embargo, because that would have the effect of destroying, not of regulating, commerce. An embargo is a restraint or prohibition on vessels, to prevent their leaving a port.

§ 235. The laws which exist in many of the States providing for the inspection of certain articles, such as flour, meat, &c., the laws of the States for regulating their internal commerce, and those with respect to turnpike-roads, ferries, &c., are valid, and are not within the power given to Congress to regulate commerce.

§ 236. By the Articles of Confederation, (Art. 9, sec. 4,) Congress was empowered to regulate the trade and manage all affairs with the Indians who were not members of any of the States, provided the legislative right of any State within its own limits was not infringed. The Constitution, however, gives to Congress the power of regulating commerce with the Indian tribes wherever situated, whether they be within or without the limits of a particular State or of the United States. The Indian tribes within a State, or in the national territories, are regarded as domestic nations, exercising the powers of government, but dependant on the United States, and holding their territory only by right of occupancy.

[Clause 4.] "To establish an uniform Rule of Naturalization, and uniform Laws on the subject of Bankruptcies throughout the United States."

§ 237. Naturalization means the act by which an alien, or foreigner, becomes a citizen of the United States.

Under the Confederation, each State possessed the power to naturalize aliens. The regulations upon the subject, and the qualifications required by the different States, were various, which led to confusion and to conflicts; for some States required a short, others a long period, of previous residence.

§ 238. The Articles of Confederation (Art. 4) declared that the free inhabitants of each State were entitled to the privileges of citizens in all other States. A foreigner, by becoming naturalized in a State which required a short period of previous residence, could then remove into a State which required a long period, obtain the privileges of a citizen there, and thus evade the laws of the latter State.

§ 239. To remedy the evils in this respect existing under the Confederation, the Constitution gives Congress the power to establish a rule of naturalization which shall be uniform throughout the whole country. This clause does not in express terms prohibit the States from establishing rules of naturalization; but it has been held that the power of Congress is necessarily exclusive, and operates to restrain the States, because, if each State had power to establish a distinct rule for itself, there would probably be no uniform rule.

§ 240. By an act of Congress, passed in 1790, a foreigner was required to reside two years in the United States before he could become naturalized; in 1795, the period of previous residence was extended to five years; in 1798, it was still farther extended to fourteen years; in 1802, it was again reduced to five years, where it remains at present.

§ 241. Any alien, being a free white person, in order to become a citizen of the United States, must first declare on oath, or affirmation, before some national or State court, at least two years before his application for admission as a citizen, that it is his intention, in good faith, to become a citizen of the United States, and to renounce all allegiance to the government of which he is at the time a subject. This is commonly called his declaration of intention.

§ 242. Afterward, at the time of his application, he must swear to support the Constitution of the United

States, and to renounce all allegiance and fidelity to every foreign prince or State. It is also necessary that he shall have resided in the United States five years at least prior to his application, and in the State or territory where he then resides, at least one year, and that during that time he has behaved as a man of good moral character, attached to the principles of the Constitution of the United States, and well disposed to the good order and happiness of the same. The applicant is not allowed to prove his residence by his own oath; but he must bring forward witnesses to the fact, who are citizens of the United States.

§ 243. Children of persons duly naturalized, who are under twenty-one years of age at the time of their parents being naturalized, are, if dwelling in the United States, considered as citizens of the United States. Persons born out of the limits and jurisdiction of the United States, whose fathers were or shall be citizens at the time of their birth, are, by an act of Congress, declared to be citizens of the United States; but the right of citizenship thus acquired, cannot descend to persons whose fathers never resided in the United States. Any woman who might lawfully be naturalized under the existing laws, who is married to a citizen, shall be deemed and taken to be a citizen. If an alien dies after his declaration of intention, but before he is actually naturalized, his widow and children shall be considered as citizens of the United States, and shall be entitled to all the privileges as such, upon taking the oath prescribed by law.

§ 244. Aliens, in applying to become citizens, are obliged to renounce any hereditary title or order of nobility which they may have possessed. or may become entitled to, in the country from which they have emigrated.

§ 245 This clause also invests Congress with the powei to establish uniform rules on the subject of bankruptcy.

Bankruptcy and insolvency both arise from inability on the part of a debtor to pay his debts. But there is a difference between a bankrupt law and an insolvent law. The former applies to merchants and traders, and discharges the bankrupt from all responsibility for his debts, so that the property acquired by him after his bankruptcy cannot be seized by a former creditor. An insolvent law merely protects the person of the debtor, leaving any property he may acquire afterward, liable to be seized for the old debt.

§ 246. During the Confederation, the power to establish laws on the subject of bankruptcy was vested in the several States. By the Constitution it is transferred to Congress, because it is closely connected with the regulation of commerce, and because the bankrupts themselves, and their property, may be in different States. If the States were permitted to legislate on the subject at the same time with Congress, much confusion and injustice would ensue from the differences in their enactments.

§ 247. But it has been held that the power of Congress is not exclusive, and that when it is not actually exercised by the national legislature, the States may pass bankrupt laws. Those laws, however, cannot discharge persons from contracts made prior to their passage, and they only extend to contracts made within the State between citizens of the same State. When a general bankrupt law is passed by Congress, this right of the States is suspended, and the State laws become inoperative.

§ 248. Congress exercised the power granted in this clause, by the passage of a bankrupt law, April 4, 1800, which was repealed December 19, 1803. A second bankrupt law was passed August 19, 1841, and repealed March

3, 1843. At present there is no national bankrupt law in force.

[Clause 5.] "To coin Money, regulate the Value thereof, and of foreign Coin, and fix the Standard of Weights and Measures."

§ 249. The power to coin money, and fix the standard of weights and measures, was vested in the Congress by the Articles of Confederation. The same power is conferred upon Congress by the Constitution, with the additional right to regulate the value of foreign coin. These powers are granted to Congress for the convenience of commerce, in order that uniform regulations may exist in all the States. Money is coined at the mint of the United States.

§ 250. The officers of the mint are, the director, who has the control and management of the mint, the superintendence of the persons employed therein, and the general regulation of the business of the branches; the treasurer, who keeps all moneys and accounts of the mint, and has charge of all bullion and coin in the mint; the assayer, who assays all metals used in coinage; the melter and refiner, who executes all operations which are necessary, in order to form ingots of standard silver and gold, suitable for the chief coiner, who forms the coins, according to the law, from the silver and gold ingots and the copper planchets, legally delivered to him for the purpose; the engraver, who prepares and engraves the legal devices and inscriptions, and the dies used in the coinage of the mint.

§ 251. Prior to the establishment of a mint under the Constitution, there was no national institution in which coins were struck by the United States. In 1792, a mint establishment for the United States was authorized by Congress for the purpose of national coinage, to be carried on at the seat of government for the time being The seat of government at that time was Philadelphia; but since its removal to Washington, the mint has been continued at Philadelphia in virtue of special acts of Congress.

§ 252. It is lawful for any person to take to the mint uncoined gold or silver, in order to have it coined, and the metal so brought is there assayed and coined as speedily as may be after the receipt thereof, and, if of the standard of the United States, free of expense to the person by whom it has been taken. But the treasurer of the mint is not obliged to receive, for the purpose of refining and coining, any deposite of less value than one hundred dollars, nor any metal so base as to be unsuitable for minting.

§ 253. Although the mint of the United States is located at Philadelphia, branch mints have been established at Charlotte, North Carolina; at Dahlonega, Georgia; at New Orleans, Louisiana; at San Francisco, California; and an assay, melting, and refining office at New York.

§ 254. Congress has passed several acts declaring the value at which foreign coins shall be estimated, but has not, as yet, enacted any law fixing the standard of weights and measures. The States have legislated for themselves upon that subject, or have continued in use the standards existing at the time of the adoption of the federal Constitution. The weights and measures used in the States are generally the same as those of England.

[Clause 6.] "To provide for the Punishment of counterfeiting the Securities and current Coin of the United States."

§ 255. This power is necessary, in order to carry into effect successfully the provisions of the preceding clause, since it would be vain to coin money without having authority to punish those who counterfeit it. Congress has passed many severe laws against those who falsify, lighten, or counterfeit the coin of the United States; and any officer of the mint who shall fraudulently debase the fineness or diminish the weight of any of the gold or silver coins of the United States, is liable to heavy fine and imprisonment.

[Clause 7.] "To establish Post Offices and post Roads."

§ 256. Posts appear to have been established for the first time in modern Europe in 1479, by Louis XI. of France. They were originally intended to serve merely for the conveyance of public despatches and of persons travelling by authority of government. Subsequently, however, private individuals were allowed to avail themselves of them for forwarding letters and despatches. The post-office was not established in England till the seventeenth century. Postmasters had, indeed, existed in more ancient times, but their business was confined to the furnishing of post-horses to persons who were desirous of travelling expeditiously, and to the despatching of extraordinary packets upon special occasions.

§ 257. In 1635, Charles I. erected a letter-office for England and Scotland; but it extended only to a few of the principal roads, and did not succeed. During the civil wars, Edward Prideaux, attorney-general for the commonwealth, instituted a post-office for the weekly conveyance of letters to all parts of the kingdom. In 1657, the post-office was established nearly on its present footing.

§ 258. The regularity and precision necessary to the satisfactory workings of a post-office in the United States, could scarcely be obtained otherwise than by the agency of the general government, for the mails would have to be conveyed through the various States, each independent of the other, and each, therefore, having the power to interpose difficulties leading to delay and obstruction.

§ 259. The authority on this subject, granted to Congress by the Articles of Confederation, (Art. 9,) did not include the establishing of post-roads, but extended only to the establishing and regulating of post-offices from one State to another, (leaving the post-offices within a State to the control of the State,) and it was confined to the exacting of such postage as might be requisite to defray expenses.

§ 260. The mails are carried by private individuals, in pursuance of contracts made with them by the Postmaster-General in behalf of the government. He advertises in certain newspapers that he will receive proposals, and whoever proposes to carry the mail for the least sum, upon giving satisfactory security, receives the contract. A report of all such contracts is made annually to Congress.

§ 261. The post-office establishment of the United States is under the direction of the Postmaster-General, who is authorized by act of Congress to establish post-offices, appoint certain of the postmasters, provide for the carriage of the mail on post-roads, and superintend and direct all the business of the post-office department. He and all other persons employed in the general post-office, and in the care, custody, and conveyance of the mail, are required, previous to entering upon the discharge of their duties, to take and subscribe an oath or affirmation faithfully to perform all the duties required of them, and abstain from every thing forbidden by the laws in relation to the post-office and post-roads. A heavy penalty is imposed on any postmaster who shall unlawfully detain in his office any letter or paper, or give a preference to any letter or paper over another by forwarding the one and retaining the other.

§ 262. By an act of Congress of June 22, 1854, the Postmaster-General may allow to the deputy postmasters throughout the United States the following rates of commissions, to be paid to them on the amount of postages received at their respective offices in each quarter of the year, and in due proportion for any period less than a quarter, viz.: on a sum received not exceeding $100, sixty per cent.; but any postmaster at whose office the mail is to arrive regularly between the hours of nine o'clock at night and five o'clock in the morning, may be allowed seventy per cent. on the first $100; on a sum over $100, and not exceeding $400, fifty per cent.; over $400, and not exceeding $2400, forty per cent.; over $2400, fifteen per cent. On the amount of postages on letters or packets received at a distributing office for distribution, twelve and a half per cent.

But by an act of March 3, 1825, all allowances, commissions, and emoluments are not to exceed $2000 for a year.

§ 263. The deputy postmasters for post-offices at which the commissions amount to one thousand dollars or upwards, are appointed by the President, with the advice and consent of the Senate, for the term of four years, unless sooner removed by the President. Other postmasters are appointed by the Postmaster-General.

§ 264. Certain officers connected with the government have the privilege of franking, which is the right to send and receive letters or packages by mail without paying postage thereon. This privilege is possessed by the President, ex-presidents, and the widows of deceased ex-presidents; by members of Congress and delegates from the territories, and by the Vice-President, the secretary of the Senate, and clerk of the House of Representatives, during their official terms.

§ 265. The heads of the executive departments and commissioners of the different offices and bureaus are also authorized to send and receive free all letters and packages upon official business, but not their private letters or papers. Deputy postmasters may send free all letters and packages relating exclusively to the business of their offices; and those whose compensation did not exceed $200 for the year ending June 30, 1846, may also send and receive free all letters on their own private business.

§ 266. Acts of Congress, except in a few cases, prohibit the conveyance by private expresses, of letters or other mailable matter (except newspapers, magazines, periodicals, or pamphlets) from one place to another in the United States, between which the mail is regularly transported.

§ 267. Congress has, in some instances, exercised its power of actually making post-roads, but it has generally selected and established as post-roads those roads which are already in use throughout the country. Waters on which steamboats regularly pass from port to port, the navigable canals of the several States, and all railroads in the United States, are also declared to be post-roads.

[Clause 8.] "To promote the progress of Science and useful Arts, by securing for limited Times to Authors and Inventors the exclusive Right to their respective Writings and Discoveries."

§ 268. This power was not granted to Congress by the Articles of Confederation. It is vested in Congress by the Constitution, because the laws enacted by that body will operate uniformly throughout the whole country; if vested in the States, they might establish different systems, which, by coming into conflict, and thus occasioning difficulties, would defeat the result intended to be attained.

§ 269. The object of the clause is to promote the progress of science and useful arts. The means to be employed, are the securing for limited times to authors and inventors, the exclusive right to their writings and discoveries. A similar provision exists in England by act of Parliament, and extends to those who introduce from abroad new inventions and discoveries into England, provided they are new within the realm. This clause of the Constitution is not applicable to those who introduce new discoveries into the United States from abroad; it protects none but the first and original inventors and discoverers.

§ 270. Letters patent are granted by the United States to the inventors or discoverers of any new and useful art, machine, manufacture, or composition of matter, or any new and useful improvement on any art, machine, manufacture, or composition of matter, not known or used by others before the applicant's discovery or invention thereof, and which has not been in public use, or on sale, with the consent or allowance of the applicant, for more than two years prior to the application for a patent.

§ 271. There is attached to the department of the interior, an office denominated the patent-office, the chief officer of which is called the commissioner of patents, who is to receive applications for patents, and to superintend or perform all things respecting the granting and issuing of patents, according to the various acts of Congress. There are engaged in the patent-office a number of clerks called examiners, whose duty it is to investigate the originality and novelty of every invention for which a patent is solicited.

§ 272. The patent is an official document issued from the patent-office in the name of the United States, signed by the secretary of the interior and by the commissioner of patents, and sealed with the seal of the patent-office. It contains the title of the invention or discovery, and grants to the applicant and his heirs or assigns, for the term of fourteen years, the full and exclusive right and liberty of making, using, and vending to others to be used, the invention or discovery claimed.

§ 273. There is annexed to the patent a full description of the invention by the inventor, called the specification, together with drawings where the nature of the case admits of drawings. The specification must set forth a particular description of the invention or discovery, and the manner and process of making the same, in such full, clear, and exact terms as to enable any person skilled in the art or science to which it relates, to make and use it.

§ 274. The applicant must fully explain in his specification the principles of his invention, and particularly specify and point out the part, improvement, or combination claimed by him as new. He must also furnish a model, together with drawings in all cases which admit of them, and make oath that he verily believes he is the original and first inventor of that which he seeks to patent.

§ 275. Upon the receipt of the application, specification, drawings, and model, the commissioner causes an examination of the invention or discovery to be made by one of the examiners attached to the patent-office, and if upon such examination the application appears to be well-founded, he issues a patent; if not, he rejects the application. The cost of a patent to a citizen of the United States is thirty dollars. Patentees are required to stamp on each article offered for sale, the date of the patent.

§ 276. In cases where the invention is new and useful, and is valuable and important to the public, and the inventor has not been adequately remunerated, notwithstanding he has used diligence in introducing his invention into use, the commissioner of patents is authorized, at the expiration of the fourteen years for which the patent originally issued, to extend it for an additional period of seven years.

§ 277. The authors of books, maps, charts, and musical compositions, and the inventors and designers of prints, cuts, and engravings, being citizens of the United States or residents therein, are entitled to the exclusive right of printing, publishing, and selling them, for the term of twenty-eight years. If the author be living, and a citizen of the United States, or a resident therein, at the end of that term, or if he shall have died and left a widow or children living, he or they are entitled to a renewal of the same exclusive right for the further period of fourteen years. This exclusive privilege is termed a copyright.

§ 278. The author or proprietor, in order to obtain a copyright, must, before publication, deposit a printed copy of the title of the book, map, or engraving, etc., in the office of the clerk of the district court of the United States in the district wherein such author or proprietor shall reside; and then within three months after publishing the book or other work, he must deliver a copy of it to the clerk of the court, who is required to transmit it to the Secretary of State, to be preserved in his office. The author must also, within the same period, deliver one copy to the

Smithsonian Institute at Washington, and one to the Library of Congress.

§ 279. The person to whom the copyright is granted is required to cause to be inserted in every copy of each edition published, during the duration of the right, on the title-page, or the page immediately following, if it be a book, or if a map, chart, musical composition, print, cut, or engraving, on the face thereof, the following words, viz.: "Entered according to act of Congress in the year ——, by —— ——, in the clerk's office of the district court of ———." This is to be done in order to give notice of the copyright, so that persons may not violate it from ignorance of its existence.

§ 280. An author has a right over his unpublished compositions. By an act of Congress it is provided that any person who shall print or publish any manuscript whatever without the consent of the author or legal proprietor first obtained, (if such author or proprietor be a citizen of the United States or resident therein,) shall be liable to suffer and pay to the author or proprietor all damages occasioned by such injury; and such publication of any manuscript may be restrained by a court of the United States.

[Clause 9.] "To constitute Tribunals inferior to the supreme Court."

§ 281. This clause will be considered when we come to a subsequent part of the Constitution which treats of the judiciary.

[Clause 10.] "To define and punish Piracies and Felonies committed on the high Seas, and Offences against the Law of Nations."

§ 282. By the Articles of Confederation, (Art. 9,) Congress had the power of appointing courts for the trial of piracies and felonies committed on the high seas. The Constitution confers upon Congress the right not only of punishing, but of defining such piracies and felonies. It also gives to Congress power to define and punish offences against the law of nations.

§ 283. Under this clause Congress has, in different acts, enumerated various offences on the high seas which shall be treated as piracies and felonies. Piracy, by the law of nations, is robbery on the high seas, done in the spirit and intention of universal hostility. For felony, see § 157. The high seas include the unenclosed waters of the ocean which are outside of land, and also the waters on the sea-coast which are beyond the boundaries of low-water mark. Pirates have been always regarded as the enemies of the human race, and every nation has a right to attack and kill them without any declaration of war.

§ 284. Unless the acts which are declared to be piracy by the laws of the United States amount to piracy by the law of nations, they are piracy only when committed by a citizen of the United States, and jurisdiction over such acts belongs exclusively to the tribunals of the United States. A robbery committed at sea on board of a foreign vessel belonging at the time to subjects of a foreign State, is within the jurisdiction of such foreign State, and could not, therefore, be treated as piracy by the courts of the United States, under our acts of Congress, though it would be so treated if committed on board of an American vessel.

§ 285. Among the various offences on the high seas which Congress has declared shall be treated as piracies, are, murder or robbery on the high seas, or in any river, haven, or bay, out of the jurisdiction of any particular

State, or any offence which, if committed within the body of a county, would, by the laws of the United States, be punishable with death.

§ 286. It has further been enacted that, if any captain or mariner shall piratically run away with a vessel, or any goods or merchandise of the value of fifty dollars, or shall yield up the vessel voluntarily to pirates; or if any seaman shall by force endeavour to hinder his commander from defending the ship or goods, or shall make revolt in the ship, he shall be deemed a pirate and a felon.

§ 287. By another act it is provided that, if any person upon the high seas, or in any bay or river where the tide ebbs and flows, commits the crime of robbery in and upon any vessel, or the lading thereof, or the crew, he shall be adjudged a pirate. So if any person engaged in any piratical enterprise, or belonging to the crew of any piratical vessel, shall land and commit robbery on shore, he shall also be adjudged a pirate. The slave-trade has likewise been declared piracy.

§ 288. By the law of nations is to be understood, in a general sense, those principles of justice and those usages, which define the rights and prescribe the duties of nations in their intercourse with each other, whether in peace or war. Violations of passports, infringements of the rights of ambassadors, disregard of treaties, and piracy, may be mentioned as illustrations of offences against the law of nations. The definition and punishment of such offences is vested in Congress, because that body represents the whole country in its national relations.

[Clause 11.] "To declare War, grant Letters of Marque and Reprisal, and make Rules concerning Captures on Land and Water."

§ 289. In England, the right to declare war and conclude treaties of peace, is a prerogative of the king. Here, the right to declare war is vested in the representative department of the government, and the right to make treaties is granted to the President, by and with the advice of the Senate. By the Articles of Confederation, (Art. 9,) Congress, with the assent of nine States, could declare war.

§ 290. By "letters of marque and reprisal" are meant commissions granted by the government to a private individual, to seize and take the property of a foreign State, or of its citizens or subjects, as a reparation for an injury committed by such State, or its citizens or subjects, for which it has refused satisfaction. Such letters are often issued to save a resort to a declaration of war. Reprisal means a taking in return; marque means the passing of the boundaries of a country for the purpose of such taking.

§ 291. The right to make rules concerning captures on land and water, is intrusted to Congress, because it is connected with the right to declare war, and is incident to the control of the army and navy.

§ 292. Capture is the taking of property by one belligerent from another. In general, all vessels belonging to the enemy may be captured, whether they be public vessels of war, or merchant vessels belonging to individuals. The vessel or goods captured at sea are called a prize; goods taken from a public enemy on land are called booty.

§ 293. The general practice of nations is to distribute captured property among the captors, as a reward for their bravery. Where a prize is taken at sea, it must be brought into some port, in order that a competent court may inquire into the facts. It is necessary, before a title can vest in the captors, that the ship should be judicially condemned as prize, by a prize court belonging to the country of the captor.

§ 294. By the articles of war established by Congress, the proceeds of all ships and vessels, and the goods taken on board of them, which shall be adjudged good prize, shall, when such ships or vessels are of equal or superior force to the vessel making the capture, be the sole property of the captors; and when of inferior force, shall be divided equally between the United States, and the officers and men making the capture.

§ 295. In the United States, the district courts of the United States, having admiralty jurisdiction, are the only courts authorized to try the question of prize or no prize. The decree of a prize court of competent jurisdiction is binding, not only upon the immediate parties, but upon all others, because all who have an interest may appear and assert their rights.

[Clause 12.] "To raise and support Armies, but no Appropriation of Money to that Use shall be for a longer Term than two Years."

§ 296. Under the Confederation, Congress did not possess this power; it could only make requisitions upon each State for its quota, or share, in proportion to the number of its white inhabitants. The legislature of each State appointed the regimental officers, raised the men, clothed, armed, and equipped them at the expense of the United States. (Art. 9, sec. 5.) This system was found to be wholly insufficient. The States were tardy in furnishing their supplies of men, which led to numerous difficulties in carrying on the Revolutionary war.

§ 297. The Constitution, on the contrary, grants to Congress the right to raise armies directly from among the people of the States, without any requisition upon the States themselves, and without any restriction upon the size of the armies. As large standing armies are dangerous to a nation in time of peace, and as they cannot be maintained without appropriations of money for their support, it is provided that no appropriation of money to the support of the military, shall be for a longer period than two years, though Congress may disband the army within that period, or vote supplies for even a less term. In England it is the usage of Parliament to vote the supplies annually, and such has been the practice of Congress under the Constitution.

§ 298. All enlistments in the army are voluntary, and they are required to be for the term of five years. The President has discretionary authority to discharge before the term of service has expired, but he has no power to vary the contract of enlistment, because that is fixed by act of Congress.

§ 299. The officers, non-commissioned officers, musicians and privates in the army, are required to swear or affirm "that they will bear true faith and allegiance to the United States of America, and that they will serve them honestly and faithfully against their enemies or opposers whomsoever, and that they will obey the orders of the President of the United States, and the orders of the officers appointed over them, according to the rules and articles of war."

[Clause 13.] "To provide and maintain a Navy."

§ 300. A navy is necessary to protect our commerce, navigation, and fisheries,

In consequence of repeated hostilities upon our commerce in the Mediterranean by the Barbary powers, commencing in 1784, the House of Representatives, in 1794, resolved "that a naval force, adequate to the protection of the commerce of the United States against the Algerine corsairs ought to be provided." This was the origin of our navy. In 1797, three frigates, built in pursuance of the above resolution, were completed, and were named the Constitution, the United States, and the Constellation. They were the first three vessels commissioned for our service, and constituted the whole of our naval force.

§ 301. By an act of Congress passed July 16, 1798, and the several additions it has received, navy hospitals have been established for the relief of sick and disabled seamen. It is made the duty of the master or owner of every ship or vessel of the United States arriving from a foreign port, before the ship or vessel shall be admitted to an entry, to render to the collector of the port where such vessel enters, a true account of the number of seamen employed on board the vessel since she was last entered at any port in the United States, and to pay to the collector, at the rate of twenty cents a month, (called hospital money,) for every seaman so employed, which sum he is authorized to retain out of the wages of the seamen.

§ 302. Masters of vessels enrolled or licensed for carrying on the coasting trade, are subject to similar provisions; and the same deduction, for the same purposes, is made from the pay of the officers, seamen, and marines of the navy of the United States.

§ 303. Out of the fund so collected, together with additional appropriations by Congress, hospitals, or other accommodations, have been established, with provision for the lodging, support, and comfort of sick and disabled seamen, or arrangements are made for that purpose with institutions already existing. In smaller ports, where there are no hospitals, the collectors of the port provide for invalid seamen, according to instructions from the Treasury department; one permanent naval asylum for disabled and decrepid navy officers, seamen, and marines, has also been established at Philadelphia.

§ 304. By an act of August 31, 1852, Congress authorized the secretary of the interior, under the direction of the President, to erect in the neighbourhood of Washington, an asylum for the insane of the army and navy of the United States, and of the District of Columbia.

§ 305. Besides the ordinary pay, clothing, and rations prescribed by law for military and naval services, the general government has also rewarded seamen and soldiers by annual payments of a sum of money, termed pensions, and also by grants of land. These rewards are of different kinds, depending upon numerous acts of Congress, but they have been arranged under three general heads, as follows:

§ 306. (1.) Invalid pensions: that is, pensions to such as have been disabled in the discharge of their duty, whether in the army or the navy.

§ 307. (2.) Gratuitous pensions: which include those granted to all the surviving officers and soldiers of the Revolutionary war; those granted by special acts of Congress to individuals for distinguished services; and the pensions granted to the widows and orphans of invalids and of persons slain in battle, or who have died of disabilities incurred in the army or navy.

§ 308. (3.) Bounty lands: by which is meant grants of a certain number of acres of the public lands (according to rank, length of service, &c.) to the soldiers engaged in the war with Mexico, in the late war with Great Britain, for services in the various Indian wars from the year 1790, and in the Revolutionary war.

[Clause 14.] "To make Rules for the Government and Regulation of the Land and naval Forces."

§ 309. This power naturally flows from the authority to raise armies and to maintain a navy, and is necessary in order to carry that authority into full effect, and to secure regularity and obedience in that branch of the public service. Accordingly numerous articles and rules have been established from time to time by Congress, and by the secretary of war, and the secretary of the navy, under the direction of the President, for the government of the army and navy in all their details.

[Clause 15.] "To provide for calling forth the Militia to execute the Laws of the Union, suppress Insurrections and repel Invasions."

§ 310. In the Articles of Confederation there was no provision similar to the above, which was one of the causes of the weakness of the Confederacy, inasmuch as it could not protect each State from internal violence and rebellion. This power is necessary in order to secure the common defence. It gives to Congress the right to call forth the militia of the States to execute the laws of the Union, suppress insurrection, and repel invasion. By militia is meant the military forces organized and supported by the respective States. Congress, by an act passed in 1795, authorized the President to call forth the militia of the States in cases of invasion, or danger of invasion, from any foreign nation, or from Indian tribes.

§ 311. The President, under the authority granted by the act above mentioned, is the judge whether it is necessary in any case to call forth the militia. He may either require the governor of a State to call forth the militia of the State, or he may himself send his orders directly to the officers of the militia. The army and navy of the United States are under the control of the President, as commander-in-chief, but the authority to call forth the militia is vested in Congress by the Constitution, and the President cannot call them forth except by authority of an act of Congress, such, for instance, as that above mentioned.

§ 312. By a subsequent act, in all cases where it is lawful for the President to call forth the militia to suppress insurrection or enforce the laws, either of the United States or of an individual State, he is authorized to employ for the same purposes, such part of the land or naval force of the United States as shall be judged necessary.

[Clause 16.] "To provide for organizing, arming, and disciplining, the Militia, and for governing such Part of them as may be employed in the Service of the United States, reserving to the States respectively, the Appointment of the Officers, and the Authority of training the Militia according to the Discipline prescribed by Congress."

§ 313. This power is necessary in order to secure uniformity in the organization and discipline of the militia. It is vested in Congress because one State could not control the militia of another State. The States appoint all the officers, but the militia are trained according to the regulation and discipline prescribed by act of Congress. In 1820 Congress enacted that the system of discipline and field exercise observed by the regular army should be also observed by the militia. The States train and discipline the militia when they are not in the actual service of the United States.

[Clause 17.] "To exercise exclusive Legislation in all Cases whatsoever, over such District (not exceeding ten Miles square) as may, by Cession of particular States, and the Acceptance of Congress, become the Seat of the Government of the United States, and to exercise like Authority over all Places purchased by the Consent of the Legislature of the State in which the Same shall be, for the Erection of Forts, Magazines, Arsenals, Dock-Yards, and other needful Buildings."

§ 314. The principal object of the first part of this clause was to provide a permanent and secure location for the seat of government, which should not be within the bounds of a particular State, the inhabitants of which might insult or terrify Congress, or interrupt its proceedings, or even prevent its assembling, while Congress at the same time would be without the ready means of protecting itself, or be dependent upon the favour of a State for such means.

§ 315. In the year 1800, the seat of the national government was removed to the city of Washington, in the District of Columbia, a tract ten miles square, which had been ceded to the United States by the States of Maryland and Virginia. The portion derived from Virginia was, in 1846, ceded back to that State, and the District is now confined to the Maryland side of the Potomac river.

§ 316. The seat of government had previously been established at the following places: at Philadelphia, (Pa.,) commencing September 5, 1774, and May 10, 1775; at Baltimore, December 20, 1776; at Philadelphia, March 4, 1777; at Lancaster, (Pa.) September 27, 1777; at York, (Pa.) September 30, 1777; at Philadelphia, July 2, 1778; at Princeton, (N. J.) June 30, 1783; at Annapolis, November 26, 1783; at Trenton, November 1, 1784; at New York city, January 11, 1785.

§ 317. The inhabitants of the District of Columbia are not regarded as citizens of any State, and cannot, therefore, send representatives to Congress, or vote for President or Vice-President. They are liable, however, to be taxed by Congress, because the power "to lay and collect taxes" is a general one, without limitation of place; and their local affairs are regulated by Congress. The cities of Washington and Georgetown govern themselves in pursuance of charters granted by Congress.

§ 318. Congress cannot take property within a State for the erection of forts, magazines, arsenals, and other public buildings, without first purchasing it; nor can such property be purchased from a citizen of a State without the consent of the legislature of the State within which it is situated.

§ 319. The jurisdiction of Congress over places purchased by the general government, with the consent of a State, is exclusive. The State cannot punish for offences committed there; nor can its officers, within those places, execute writs or legal processes, either civil or criminal, unless the right to do so is reserved by the State. Such offences are to be tried and punished by the courts and officers of the United States.

§ 320. But if the place has not been ceded by a State, or purchased by the United States with the consent of the legislature of the State in which it is situate, the jurisdiction of the State is not excluded, but remains in full force, subject, however, to the rightful exercise of the powers of the national government.

[Clause 18.] "To make all Laws which shall be necessary and proper for carrying into Execution the foregoing Powers, and all other Powers vested by this Constitution in the Government of the United States, or in any Department or Officer thereof."

§ 321. This clause does not in terms grant any new power, or enlarge or diminish any of the powers elsewhere granted. It simply authorizes Congress to make use of such particular means as may be necessary or proper, in order to execute the general powers conferred by the Constitution upon the federal government or any department or officer thereof.

§ 322. By the Articles of Confederation, (Art. 2,) each State retained every power and right not expressly delegated to the United States. The Constitution, however, has not only conferred upon Congress certain express powers, but has also conferred such other incidental powers (without actually naming them) as may be necessary or proper for carrying into execution the powers expressly granted.

CHAPTER IX.

RESTRICTIONS UPON CONGRESS.

SECTION 9.

THIS section enumerates certain restrictions upon the powers of Congress.

[Clause 1.] "The Migration or Importation of such Persons as any of the States now existing shall think proper to admit, shall not be prohibited by the Congress prior to the Year one thousand eight hundred and eight, but a Tax or Duty may be imposed on such Importation, not exceeding ten dollars for each Person."

§ 323. One of the main objects of this clause was to enable Congress to put an end to the introduction of slaves into the United States from abroad, after the year 1808, and to restrain their importation until then, by a tax not exceeding ten dollars for each person; but the clause includes within its language the migration of other persons as well as the importation of slaves.

§ 324. On the 1st of January, 1808, an act of Congress went into effect, which imposed heavy penalties upon persons engaged in the slave-trade; and in 1820 another act declared the slave trade to be piracy, and punishable with death.

§ 325. The restriction in this clause is applicable only

to the migration or importation of the slaves or other persons. It, therefore, left Congress at liberty to legislate on the subject of the slave-trade when prosecuted out of the limits of the United States by citizens of the United States. In the exercise of this power, Congress, by an act passed March 22, 1794, forbade citizens and other persons from fitting out any vessel in any place within the United States, for the purpose of carrying on any traffic in slaves to any foreign country.

§ 326. Many other acts have been passed on the subject, the object of which is the entire suppression of the slave-trade by American citizens, and by any and all others in American vessels.

[Clause 2.] "The Privilege of the Writ of Habeas Corpus shall not be suspended, unless when in Cases of Rebellion or Invasion the public Safety may require it."

§ 327. Writ is a legal term, and means in general a command in writing, under seal, in the name of a king, judge, or other magistrate, directed to a public officer or private individual, requiring him to do something in relation to a suit or other legal proceeding.

§ 328. The writ of habeas corpus mentioned in the above clause is a writ directed to a person charged with detaining another unlawfully in his custody, commanding him to produce the body of the prisoner, and to declare the reason of his detention. It is "a great and efficacious writ," intended to secure personal liberty, and provide a means of redress for all manner of illegal imprisonment and unlawful restraint of the person.

§ 329. The courts of the United States issue this writ in cases falling within their jurisdiction, upon the written application of any person who alleges that he is deprived of his liberty contrary to law, or upon the application of others in behalf of such person. The writ is directed to him who has the prisoner in custody, commanding him to produce the body of the prisoner, together with the cause of his detention, before the judge by whose allowance the writ is issued.

§ 330. The prisoner must be produced, in obedience to the writ, and then the judge examines the whole matter, and if the imprisonment is illegal, he discharges the party from custody; if legal, he remands him again into custody.

§ 331. This clause provides for the suspension of the writ of habeas corpus only in cases of rebellion or invasion, when the public safety requires it; but Congress has never suspended the writ since the Constitution went into operation.

[Clause 3.] "No Bill of Attainder or ex post facto Law shall be passed."

§ 332. Bills of attainder are acts of a legislature which inflict the punishment of death upon persons supposed to be guilty of great offences, without a trial had before a judicial tribunal according to law. Such bills have frequently been passed by the British Parliament in former times, during seasons of violent political excitement, by which the accused have unjustly been deprived of life, without a trial, and upon insufficient or illegal evidence, and even without an opportunity to answer the charge.

§ 333. Ex post facto laws are such as are passed after the act to which they refer has been committed. This clause has been considered as applying only to criminal acts, or to laws for penalties and punishments. Laws which make an act a crime, and punishable as such, which was not a crime when done, or which render an act punishable in a more aggravated manner than that in which it was punishable when done, or which make the crime greater than it was when committed, or require different or less testimony to convict for the offence than was required when the act was done, are instances of ex post facto laws. Such laws are prohibited, because they are clearly unjust and arbitrary.

[Clause 4.] "No Capitation, or other direct, Tax shall be laid, unless in Proportion to the Census or enumeration herein before directed to be taken."

§ 334. We have already considered the nature of capitation and other direct taxes, and the rule of apportionment according to the census, by which they are to be imposed. See § 78 and § 190.

[Clause 5.] "No Tax or Duty shall be laid on Articles exported from any State."

§ 335. The articles exported from the different States are so various in their nature, that if a tax were imposed on any single article of export, the burden would fall almost altogether upon the particular State or States exporting that article, and the States exporting other articles would be comparatively untaxed. It is to prevent such an unequal distribution of taxes or duties, that Congress is prohibited from laying them on articles exported from any State.

[Clause 6.] "No Preference shall be given by any Regulation of Commerce or Revenue to the Ports of one State over those of another: nor shall Vessels bound to, or from, one State, be obliged to enter, clear, or pay Duties in another."

§ 336. The declaration that no preference shall be given by any regulation of commerce or revenue, to the ports of one State over those of another, is intended to secure fairness and equality, in this respect, to all the States, so that one shall not enjoy any privileges above another.

§ 337. If vessels bound to, or from one State, could be compelled to enter, clear, or pay duties in another, it is easy to see that a single State would have an opportunity of imposing obstacles and restrictions upon the general commerce of the States, which would be of the most vexatious and ruinous character. Such an unjust proceeding is prevented by the prohibition in this clause.

[Clause 7.] "No Money shall be drawn from the Treasury, but in Consequence of Appropriations made by Law; and a regular Statement and Account of the Receipts and Expenditures of all public Money shall be published from time to time.

§ 338. This clause prevents any money from being drawn from the Treasury of the United States, by any person, even the President of the United States, without an appropriation made by Congress. The money in the Treasury belongs to the whole people, and it is therefore proper that it should not be expended except by a vote of the representatives of the people. The accounts of the Treasury, showing all the receipts and expenditures of the government, are kept under the direction of the Secretary of the Treasury, who makes a full annual report thereof to the President, which he transmits to Congress along with his annual message.

§ 339. As no money can be drawn from the Treasury except in consequence of an appropriation made by law, neither the Secretary of the Treasury or any other person is authorized to draw money from the Treasury, even to pay the debts of the United States, unless authorized by law to do so.

The government of the United States cannot be sued by persons who have claims against it. Their only mode of redress, is to obtain an act of Congress appropriating money from the Treasury to pay their claims.

[Clause 8.] "No Title of Nobility shall be granted by the United States: And no Person holding any Office of Profit or Trust under them, shall, without the Consent of the Congress, accept of any present, Emolument, Office, or Title, of any kind whatever, from any King, Prince, or foreign State."

§ 340. The political equality of all the citizens is a fundamental principle in our government. Titles of nobility by the United States are prohibited, because they create ranks and lead to distinctions in society, which are contrary to a spirit of equality.

§ 341. The latter part of the clause is intended to prevent foreign kings, princes, or States, from obtaining an influence in our government, and tempting our officers from their fidelity, by means of presents, emoluments, offices, or titles. Such gifts cannot be received by a person holding an office of profit or trust under the United States, without the consent of Congress. The prohibition does not extend to citizens who hold offices of profit or trust under a State, although such was the case with the corresponding prohibition in the Articles of Confederation, (art. 6, sec. 1.)

§ 342. Gifts from foreign princes are sometimes sent to

the President. Although this clause of the Constitution prohibits him from appropriating them to his own use, it has not been deemed courteous to decline them; and they have been deposited in the public offices, or sold by order of Congress. Sometimes other presents are made, by direction of Congress, in return.

CHAPTER X.

RESTRICTIONS UPON THE STATES.

SECTION 10.

THIS section enumerates certain restrictions upon the powers of the States.

SECTION 10. [Clause 1.] "No State shall enter into any Treaty, Alliance, or Confederation; grant Letters of Marque and Reprisal; coin Money; emit Bills of Credit; make any Thing but gold and silver Coin a Tender in Payment of Debts; pass any Bill of Attainder, ex post facto Law, or Law impairing the Obligation of Contracts, or grant any Title of Nobility.

§ 343. For the several States to enter into treaties, alliances, and confederations, would interfere with those made by the general government, because the States might make treaties different from, or contrary to, those made by the general government. Besides, if foreign powers could form alliances with a State, they might obtain an influence which would be dangerous in time of peace, and still more so in war. The treaty-making power is therefore taken from the States, and by a subsequent section of the Constitution is vested in the President and Senate.

§ 344. By the Articles of Confederation, (art. 6, sec. 5,) the States could issue letters of marque and reprisal against countries with which the United States had declared war. Under the Constitution the power to issue letters of marque and reprisal is vested solely in Congress in all cases. If the States could exercise it, a single State might involve the whole country in war, as the granting of letters of marque and reprisal is a hostile measure which generally leads to a war. It should, therefore, be exercised only by the national legislature, which has the exclusive power of declaring war. (See art. I., sec. 8, clause 11.) For definition of letters of marque see § 290.

§ 345. By the Articles of Confederation, (art. 9, sec. 5,) the States could coin money, subject, as to its alloy and value, to the regulation of Congress. The Constitution (art. I., sec. 8, clause 5) vests in Congress the power to coin money for reasons already mentioned, (§ 249.) If this power were shared by the States, it would conflict with its exercise by Congress; it is, therefore, declared by this clause that no State shall coin money.

§ 346. By "bills of credit" is meant paper or bills intended to circulate among the people, and to be paid and received as money. The States cannot issue such bills. During the Revolutionary war bills of credit were issued by Congress, and are well known as "continental money." They were issued to the amount of about $350,000,000, and gradually depreciated in value till they became worthless, occasioning great loss throughout the country. The object of this provision was to prevent a repetition of such evils, by restraining the States from creating a paper currency. The prohibition does not extend to bills of credit issued by individuals, either singly or collectively, so long as they are not issued upon the authority of a State, and upon a pledge of its faith and credit.

§ 347. The states are also prohibited from making any thing but gold and silver coin a tender in payment of debts. No State can, therefore, compel a creditor to receive payment of his debt in bank notes, or merchandise, or any thing but gold and silver coin. The object of this restriction, together with that relating to bills of credit, and to the coining of money, was to provide a fixed and uniform currency throughout the United States.

§ 348. We have seen already (§ 332) that Congress is prohibited from passing bills of attainder or ex post facto laws; this clause, for similar reasons, extends the same prohibition to the several States.

§ 349. The States are also prohibited from passing laws impairing the obligations of contracts. This is a very important provision, and has occasioned much discussion. A contract is an agreement to do, or not to do, a particular thing. By the obligation of a contract is here meant that duty of performing it which is recognised and enforced by the laws. If the law is so changed that the means of legally enforcing this duty are materially impaired, the obligation of the contract is no longer the same.

§ 350. Laws impairing the obligation of contracts are, for instance, such as change the intention of the parties to the contract; or affect its validity, construction, duration, or effect; or deviate from its terms by changing the time of its performance; or impose new conditions, or alter those agreed upon; or declare the contract invalid, or alter, or release it.

§ 351. A change merely in the form or manner of the remedy upon the contract, or in the legal proceedings by which it is enforced, provided an effectual remedy of some sort is left remaining, is not considered to impair the obligation of the contract, as it simply gives a different mode of obtaining redress. But to take away all modes of obtaining redress, would impair and destroy the obligation of the contract.

§ 352. A law discharging the person of a bankrupt or insolvent debtor, or his future property, from liability for his debts, is a law impairing the obligation of contracts, and therefore void, if the debt was contracted before the passage of the law; but it would be otherwise if the debt were contracted after the passage of the law.

§ 353. This prohibition embraces all contracts, whether executed or to be executed; whether between private individuals, or a State and individuals, or between corporations, or between the States themselves.

§ 354. Charters of incorporation granted to private persons by a State Legislature, have been regarded as contracts between the corporations and the States, and they cannot, therefore, be altered, repealed, or impaired by the legislature, without the consent of the incorporated body, unless the power to do so is reserved in the original act of incorporation. For instance, the legislature of New Hampshire once passed an act changing the original charter of the Dartmouth College, and transferring the rights of trustees under it, to other trustees appointed by the new act; the Supreme Court of the United States, however, decided that the act of the legislature infringed this clause of the Constitution, and was therefore void. But the charters for public corporations, created for public purposes only, such as cities and boroughs, may be repealed and changed by the legislature, making compensation for any private rights which are thereby destroyed.

§ 355. Retrospective or retroactive laws, are those which operate upon controversies, suits, or facts, which existed before their passage. The Constitution does not prohibit the States from passing such laws, though they are generally unjust, unless they amount to ex post facto laws, or impair the obligation of contracts.

§ 356. We have seen that the United States cannot grant any title of nobility, (§ 340.) The clause we are now considering extends the same prohibition to the several States. Titles of nobility create distinctions of ranks and an aristocracy, which are contrary in their nature to that political equality of all the citizens, which our free institutions are designed to establish.

[Clause 2.] "No State shall, without the consent of the Congress, lay any Imposts or Duties on Imports or Exports, except what may be absolutely necessary for executing its inspection Laws: and the net Produce of all Duties and Imposts, laid by any State on Imports or Exports, shall be for the Use of the Treasury of the United States; and all such Laws shall be subject to the Revision and Controul of the Congress."

§ 357. The right to lay and collect taxes, duties, imposts, and excises has been conferred upon Congress, (Art. I. sec. 8, clause 1;) and it has been declared that all duties, imposts, and excises shall be uniform throughout the United States. This uniformity could scarcely be maintained, if each of the States was at liberty, irrespective of Congress, to impose such duties on imports or exports as it thought proper.

§ 358. It is, therefore, provided that no State shall, without the consent of Congress, lay any imposts or duties on imports or exports, except what may be absolutely necessary for executing its inspection laws; and the net produce of all duties and imposts laid by any State on imports or exports, shall be for the use of the Treasury of the United States, and all such laws shall be subject to the revision and control of Congress.

§ 359. This clause, nevertheless, leaves to the States the right to enact and enforce inspection laws. By inspection laws are meant laws requiring certain articles of commerce to be examined, and their quality, soundness, or healthfulness to be ascertained by officers called inspectors. The object of these laws is not to raise a revenue, but to protect the public from fraud and imposition, and to ascertain the character of the merchandise, so that it shall be suitable for exportation abroad or for domestic use.

§ 360. The legislature of Maryland, in 1821, passed an act requiring every importer of goods by wholesale, bale, or package, and every person selling the same by wholesale, bale, or package, to take out a license and pay for it, with certain penalties in case of refusal. The Supreme Court of the United States decided that the act was a violation of the clause we are now considering, and therefore unconstitutional and void.

§ 361. To tax the importer, or to tax the goods in the hands of the importer, was considered by the court to be in effect a tax on imports. If a tax could be levied in that form by a State, it might be levied to such a burdensome extent as to restrain importation, and thus diminish the revenue of the general government from imports, so far as it was drawn from importations into that particular State.

§ 362. But when the importer has so acted upon the

goods imported, that they have become incorporated and mixed up with the mass of property in the country, they then lose their distinctive character as imports, and are subject to be taxed by a State. While, however, they reremain the property of the importer, in his warehouse, in the original form or packages in which they were imported, a tax upon them is a duty on imports, and, as such, is prohibited by this clause.

[Clause 3.] "No State shall, without the Consent of Congress, lay any Duty of Tonnage, keep Troops, or Ships of War in time of Peace, enter into any Agreement or Compact with another State, or with a foreign Power, or engage in War, unless actually invaded, or in such imminent Danger as will not admit of Delay."

§ 363. We have already considered the nature of tonnage duties, (§ 197,) and have seen that Congress has power to lay such duties as a part of its general authority to lay and collect taxes, duties, imposts, and excises. It is also in some measure connected with the regulation of commerce, which is likewise intrusted to Congress. This clause does not absolutely prohibit the States from laying a duty on tonnage, but declares that they shall not do so without the consent of Congress, in order that Congress may have supervision and control of the whole subject.

§ 364. The States are also prohibited from keeping troops, or ships of war, in time of peace, except with consent of Congress. The power to declare war, raise and support armies and navies, and provide for the common defence, is vested in Congress, whose authority, extending over all the States, can produce uniformity in the movements, organization, and discipline of the army and navy.

But, as it may happen to be necessary in time of peace that the States should keep ships or troops, they are authorized to do so with the consent of Congress. In time of war, the consent of Congress is not made necessary.

§ 365. Another restriction is, that no State shall, without the consent of Congress, enter into any agreement or compact with another State, or with a foreign power. Otherwise, some of the States might possibly form combinations of a political character among themselves, or with foreign powers, which would seriously embarrass the general government or endanger the whole Union.

§ 366. Nor can a State, without the consent of Congress, engage in war, unless it be actually invaded, or is in such imminent danger as will not admit of delay. The power to declare war is vested in the national representatives. Great evils would result to the other States if a single State could declare war whenever it was disposed to do so. The Articles of Confederation contained a provision nearly similar to the above. (Art. 6, sec. 1.)

CHAPTER XI.

THE EXECUTIVE POWER.

ARTICLE II.

ARTICLE I. as we have seen, treats of the legislative department; we now enter upon Article II., which treats of the executive department.

SECTION 1. [Clause 1.] "The executive Power shall be vested in a President of the United States of America. He shall hold his Office during the Term of four Years, and, together with the Vice President, chosen for the same Term, be elected, as follows."

§ 367. By the Articles of Confederation, the executive power was vested in the Congress while it was sitting, and, during the recess, it was delegated, under certain restrictions, to what was called "a committee of the States," consisting of one delegate from each State, (Art. 9 and 10.) There was no single individual in whom the executive power was vested, and this was considered one of the most serious practical defects of the confederate government.

§ 368. In some countries the executive power is in the hands of several persons, who exercise it jointly, with equal authority and rank. This division of power is apt to lead to a difference of opinion, and to dissension, rivalry, and jealousy between the different magistrates who exercise the power, which occasion delay, unsteadiness, and weakness of action in the government. To prevent these evils, as well as to secure other advantages, the Constitution intrusts the executive power to a single individual, whose title is the President of the United States of America.

§ 369. When the Constitution was framed, there was much difference of opinion as to the length of time for which the President should hold his office. If the period is too short, the government will be constantly changing hands; one administration will be succeeded by another, before its plans and policy have had a fair trial, and before it has had sufficient time to acquire knowledge from experience; thus there would be no stability in public affairs.

§ 370. Four years, the period finally agreed upon, is intermediate between two years, the period for which representatives are chosen, and six years, the period for which senators are chosen; so that, in one presidential term, the House of Representatives may be twice wholly changed, and two-thirds of the Senate may be changed.

§ 371. The term of four years, for which the President and Vice-President are chosen, commences on the fourth day of March next succeeding the day on which the votes of the electors are given, which last-mentioned day, according to an act of Congress, is the first Wednesday in December in every fourth year succeeding the presidential election; and the term expires at the end of the third day of March in the fourth year thereafter.

There is nothing in the Constitution to limit the number of terms for which a President may be successively re-elected; but as George Washington, the first President, declined to be a candidate again at the close of his second term of office, his example has become a precedent by which subsequent Presidents have guided themselves, and no one of them, therefore, has sought to be elected for a third term.

§ 372. The office of Vice-President was created in order that there might be some person to succeed the President in case of his removal from office, or of his death, or resignation, or his inability to discharge his duties; and also because it would furnish a presiding officer to the Senate who would be the most likely to be impartial, inasmuch as he is elected by the whole country, and does not represent a particular State.

[Clause 2.] "Each State shall appoint, in such Manner as the Legislature thereof may direct, a Number of Electors, equal to the whole Number of Senators and Representatives to which the State may be entitled in the Congress: but no Senator or Representative, or Person holding an Office of Trust or Profit under the United States, shall be appointed an Elector."

§ 373. This clause provides the manner in which the President and Vice-President are to be chosen. They are not chosen by the people directly, but by a body of electors, who are sometimes called "the electoral college." The framers of the Constitution believed that a small number of men, selected for that particular purpose on account of their wisdom, patriotism, and virtue, meeting separately in their respective States, would not be liable to be influenced by the excitements of a popular election, or by intrigue or corruption, would be independent in their action, well qualified to examine deliberately the merits of the candidates, and therefore likely to make a wise selection.

§ 374. It was also thought that the selection of electors

by whom the immediate choice of a President and Vice-President is to be made, would not lead to the tumults and disorders which the history of other countries shows us are apt to attend the election of high executive officers.

§ 375. In many respects, the object which the framers of the Constitution sought to obtain by the system of electors has hitherto failed to be accomplished. In actual practice, the electors are chosen for the express purpose of voting for particular candidates, to do which they are sometimes even pledged beforehand; they are expected to cast their votes for those candidates only, and not to exercise any freedom of choice themselves. It may, nevertheless, sometimes happen that the selection must be really made by the electors, as, for instance, in case of the death of one or more of the candidates before the election takes place.

§ 376. Each State is entitled to a number of electors equal to the whole number of its senators and representatives in Congress, in order that it may have about the same influence in the choice of President and Vice-President that it has in the national affairs transacted in Congress. The appointment of electors is to be made in such manner as the legislature of each State shall direct.

§ 377. Senators, representatives, and persons holding offices of trust or profit under the United States, are excluded from being electors. Senators and representatives are frequently brought into close relations with the President and Vice-President in office, and might on that account be less independent and impartial, or become subject to their influence and control, in case they were candidates for re-election.

§ 378. If there is no choice by the electors, the election will devolve upon the Senate and House of Representatives; and if members of the Senate and House have previously voted as electors, they will be less likely to be free and unbiassed in their choice as senators or representatives. Persons holding offices of trust and profit under the United States are also excluded from the electoral college, lest their official station might give them an improper influence upon the electors. The object of the provision is to prevent any interference or agency on the part of the general government in the selection of President and Vice-President.

[Clause 3.] "The Electors shall meet in their respective States, and vote by Ballot for two Persons, of whom one at least shall not be an inhabitant of the same State with themselves. And they shall make a List of all the Persons voted for, and of the Number of Votes for each; which List they shall sign and certify, and transmit sealed to the Seat of the Government of the United States, directed to the President of the Senate. The President of the Senate shall, in the Presence of the Senate and House of Representatives, open all the Certificates, and the Votes shall then be counted. The Person having the greatest Number of Votes shall be the President, if such Number be a Majority of the whole Number of Electors appointed; and if there be more than one who have such Majority and have an equal number of Votes, then the House of Representatives shall immediately chuse by Ballot one of them for President; and if no Person have a Majority, then from the five highest on the List the said House shall in like Manner chuse the President. But in chusing the

President, the Votes shall be taken by States, the Representation from each State having one Vote; a Quorum for this Purpose shall consist of a Member or Members from two thirds of the States, and a Majority of all the States shall be necessary to a Choice. In every Case, after the Choice of the President, the Person having the greatest Number of Votes of the Electors shall be the Vice President. But if there should remain two or more who have equal Votes, the Senate shall chuse from them by Ballot the Vice President."

§ 379. This clause prescribes the mode in which the electors shall proceed to vote for President and Vice-President. It has been supplied by an amended clause, as we shall see presently, but many of the original features are retained. Each electoral college, acting by itself, meets in its own State; there is, therefore, less opportunity for concert of action, intrigue, or bargaining, among the electors of the several States. Under the original clause they did not separately designate one person for President, and another person for Vice-President, but voted by the same ticket for two persons, one of whom at least, it was provided, should not be an inhabitant of the same State with themselves; such a provision prevents the President and Vice-President from being inhabitants of the same State.

§ 380. They then made out a list of all the persons voted for, and of the number of votes for each, which list, after being signed and certified by them, they transmitted, sealed, to the seat of government of the United States, directed to the President of the Senate.

§ 381. The President of the Senate, in the presence of

the Senate and House of Representatives, opened all the certificates, and the votes were then counted. The person who had the greatest number of votes was declared to be the President, provided the number of votes received by him was greater than a majority of the whole number of electors.

§ 382. If there were more than one who had such majority, and had an equal number of votes, then the House of Representatives was required immediately to choose, by ballot, one of them for President; and if no person had a majority of the whole number of electors, then from the five highest persons on the list, the House of Representatives was in like manner to choose the President. The election of President in these cases devolves upon the House of Representatives, because that is the branch of Congress which more immediately represents the people.

§ 383. In choosing the President in the House of Representatives, the vote is taken by States, the entire delegation from each State having one vote; this is intended to give to each State an equal voice in the selection. A majority of all the States is necessary to a choice, and a quorum, for the purpose of an election, consists of a member, or of members, from two-thirds of the States.

§ 384. In every case after the choice of a President, the person having the greatest number of the votes of the electors, according to the original clause, became the Vice-President. But if there were then two or more who had an equal number of votes, it devolved upon the Senate to choose from them, by ballot, the Vice-President. The choice of the Vice-President is thus given to the Senate, chiefly because he is the presiding officer in that body.

§ 385. At the election of the fourth President, the electoral votes for Thomas Jefferson and Aaron Burr were equal, and each received the votes of a majority of the whole number of electors. There was, therefore, no election by the people. Accordingly, the House of Representatives, in pursuance of this clause, as it originally stood, proceeded to choose a President. On the first ballot, eight States voted for Thomas Jefferson, six States for Aaron Burr, and the votes of two States were divided. There were then sixteen States in the Union.

§ 386. The balloting continued nearly a week, and thirty-five ballots were had, with the same result as the first. The contest was carried on with violent party spirit. Finally, on the thirty-sixth ballot, Thomas Jefferson received the votes of a majority of the States, and was declared President; Aaron Burr, having the next highest number of votes, became Vice-President.

§ 387. To prevent the occurrence of such a state of things again, Congress, on the 12th of December, 1803, proposed to the legislatures of the States an amendment to this part of the Constitution, which was adopted by three-fourths of the States, and was proclaimed by the President as a part of the Constitution, September 25, 1804, and therefore takes the place of the original clause we have just been considering. This is the twelfth of the series of amendments to the Constitution, and is as follows:—

"The Electors shall meet in their respective states, and vote by ballot for President and Vice President, one of whom, at least, shall not be an inhabitant of the same state with themselves; they shall name in their ballots the person voted for as President, and in distinct ballots the person voted for as Vice-President, and they shall make distinct lists of all persons voted for as President, and of all persons voted for as Vice-President, and of the number of votes for each, which lists they shall sign and certify, and transmit sealed to the seat of the government of the United States, directed to the President of the Senate;— The President of the Senate shall, in presence of the Senate and House of Representatives, open all the certificates and the votes shall then be counted;—The person having the greatest number of votes for President, shall be the President, if such number be a majority of the whole number of Electors appointed; and if no person have such majority, then from the persons having the highest numbers not exceeding three on the list of those voted for as President, the House of Representatives shall choose immediately, by ballot, the President. But in choosing the President, the votes shall be taken by states, the representation from each state having one vote; a quorum for this purpose shall consist of a member or members from two-thirds of the states, and a majority of all the states shall be necessary to a choice. And if the House of Representatives shall not choose a President whenever the right of choice shall devolve upon them, before the fourth day of March next following, then the Vice-President shall act as President, as in the case of the death or other constitutional disability of the President.—The person having the greatest number of votes as Vice-President, shall be the Vice-President, if such number be a majority of the whole number of Electors appointed, and if no person have a majority, then from the two highest numbers on the list, the Senate shall choose the Vice-President; a quorum for the purpose shall consist of two-thirds of the whole number of Senators, and a majority of the whole number shall be necessary to a choice. But no person constitutionally ineligible to the office of President shall be eligible to that of Vice-President of the United States."

§ 388. The amendment, as will be seen by comparison, retains many of the features of the original clause. It still leaves with Congress the right to elect a President and Vice-President, where there is no election by the people; but it changes the mode of procedure. The principal alterations it effects are the following: The electors, instead of voting generally for two persons, are to vote for one person for President and one person for Vice-President in distinct ballots, and separate lists of the persons voted for as President and as Vice President are to be sent to the seat of government.

§ 389. If no person have a majority, the House of Representatives are to elect a President from the three highest persons on the list of those voted for as President, instead of the five highest, as in the original article. This was intended to exclude from the chance of election by the House of Representatives, those persons who had received but a small number of electoral votes.

§ 390. If the House of Representatives, whenever the choice of a President shall devolve upon them, shall fail to choose a President before the fourth day of March next following, then the Vice-President shall act as President, as in case of the death or other constitutional disability of the President. There was no provision similar to this in the original article.

§ 391. As the Constitution at first stood, a Vice-President could not be designated until after the President had been elected by the House of Representatives. The amendment allows the Senate to proceed at once and choose a Vice-President from the two highest numbers on the list of persons voted for as Vice-President; two-thirds of the senators constitute a quorum for this purpose, and a majority of the whole number is necessary to a choice. The votes of the Senate in choosing a Vice-President are not taken by States, as the votes of the House are in choosing a President, but each Senator has one vote.

§ 392. It is also declared by the amendment, that a person who is constitutionally ineligible to the office of President, shall be also ineligible to that of Vice-President. This is because the Vice-President may be called on to act as President.

§ 393. Since the adoption of this amendment, there has been one election of President by the House of Representatives. At the election for the tenth Presidential term, commencing March 4, 1825, John C. Calhoun was chosen Vice-President, but there was no election of President by the electors. It therefore devolved on the House of Representatives to choose a President from the three highest on the list of candidates for the Presidency, who were Andrew Jackson, John Quincy Adams, and William H. Crawford. John Quincy Adams received a majority of the votes of the States, and was consequently declared elected by the House.

[Clause 4.] "The Congress may determine the Time of chusing the Electors, and the Day on which they shall give their Votes; which Day shall be the same throughout the United States."

§ 394. In virtue of the power given by this clause, Congress passed an act, March 1, 1792, requiring electors to be elected in each State within thirty-four days preceding the first Wednesday in December, in every fourth year succeeding the last Presidential election, which electors shall be equal to the number of senators and representatives to which the several States may by law be entitled at the time when the President and Vice-President to be chosen shall come into office; for instance, a State entitled to ten representatives, and having two senators, appoints twelve electors.

§ 395. The electors are required by the act above mentioned to meet and give their votes on the first Wednesday in December, at such place in the State as shall be directed by the legislature thereof. They usually meet at the capital of the State. Their votes are thus given on the same day throughout the United States. The electors are further required to make and sign three certificates of all the votes given by them, and to appoint a person to take charge of and deliver one of the certificates to the President of the Senate at the seat of the national government, before the first Wednesday in January, then next ensuing.

§ 396. If there should then be no President of the Senate at the seat of government, the certificate is to be deposited with the Secretary of State, to be delivered by him as soon as may be, to the President of the Senate. Another one of the certificates is to be sent by the Post-office to the President of the Senate at the seat of government. The remaining certificate is to be delivered to the judge of the district court of the United States for the district in which the electors are assembled.

§ 397. The executive authority of each State is also directed by the act to make out and certify three lists of the names of the electors of such State, and the electors are to annex one of those lists to each of the lists of their votes.

§ 398 If a list of votes shall not have been received at the seat of government on or before the first Wednesday in January, then the Secretary of State shall send a special messenger to the district judge in whose custody a list has been lodged, who shall immediately transmit his list to the seat of government.

§ 399. On the second Wednesday in February succeeding the meeting of the electors, the certificates shall be opened by the President of the Senate, in the presence of the Senate and the House of Representatives, the votes counted, and the persons who shall fill the office of President and of Vice-President ascertained and declared agreeably to the Constitution.

§ 400. The act above mentioned fixes no day for choosing the electors. It only requires them to be chosen within thirty-four days preceding the first Wednesday in December. But by a later act passed in 1845, Congress declared that the electors shall be appointed in each State on the Tuesday next after the first Monday of November of the year in which they are to be appointed; also that each State may provide by law for filling vacancies in its college of electors, when such college meets to give its electoral votes; and that when any State shall have held an election for the purpose of choosing electors, and shall fail to make a choice on the day above mentioned, the electors may be appointed on a subsequent day, in such manner as the State may by law provide.

[Clause 5.] "No person except a natural born Citizen, or a Citizen of the United States, at the time of the Adoption of this Constitution, shall be eligible to the Office of President; neither shall any person be eligible to that Office who shall not have attained to the Age of thirty-five Years, and been fourteen Years a Resident within the United States."

§ 401. The qualifications of the President consist of these four particulars:

(1.) He must be a natural born citizen of the United States.

(2.) Or if not a natural born citizen, he must have been a citizen of the United States at the adoption of the Constitution.

(3.) He must be at least thirty-five years of age.

(4.) He must have been fourteen years a resident of the United States.

§ 402. It is very proper that aliens or foreigners should be excluded from the office of President, because it is the highest and most responsible office under the Constitution. At the time, however, of the adoption of the Constitution, many of the citizens in the States were natives of Europe, and had emigrated to this country and been naturalized in the various States. They had helped to win our independence, and some of them were among the most distinguished and valuable of the patriots of the Revolution. It seemed unjust and ungrateful to exclude such persons from the office of President, and it was, therefore, in order to meet their case, provided that those who had been citizens of the United States at the time of the adoption of the Constitution should be eligible to the office of President, although they were not natural born citizens.

§ 403. It is required that the President shall be thirty-five years of age at the time of his election, because at that period of life it is probable his character will be formed, his qualifications ascertained, and his mind improved by experience and knowledge.

§ 404. A previous residence of fourteen years in the United States, is also required in order that the people may have an opportunity of ascertaining his fitness for the office, and that he may become familiar with our institutions. The residence required by the Constitution does not preclude a temporary sojourn in foreign countries; it seems designed to prohibit a permanent settlement abroad, with the intention of remaining abroad.

[Clause 6.] "In Case of the Removal of the President from Office, or of his Death, Resignation, or Inability to discharge the Powers and Duties of the said office, the same shall devolve on the Vice-President, and the Congress may by Law provide for the Case of Removal, Death, Resignation, or Inability, both of the President and Vice-President, declaring what Officer shall then act as President, and such Officer shall act accordingly, until the Disability be removed, or a President shall be elected."

§ 405. The Constitution by this clause declares that in case of the death, removal, resignation, or inability of the President, the duties of his office shall devolve upon the Vice-President. When the Vice-President succeeds to the duties of the President, he continues to discharge them until the close of the term for which the President was elected, unless it be only a temporary disability of the

President, which is sooner removed. Congress is further authorized to provide for the case of the removal, death, resignation, or inability, both of the President and Vice-President.

§ 406. Accordingly Congress, in 1792, enacted that in case of the removal, death, resignation, or inability both of the President and Vice-President, the President of the Senate, *pro tempore*, and in case there shall be no President of the Senate, the Speaker of the House of Representatives, shall act as President, until the disability be removed, or a President shall be elected.

§ 407. It is customary for the Vice-President of the United States, who is the President of the Senate, to withdraw from the Senate a short time previous to the close of every session, so that the Senate may elect a President *pro tempore*. Then if the office of President of the United States, and that of Vice-President should both become vacant during the recess of Congress, the President *pro tempore* of the Senate would act as President of the United States; and if there were no President *pro tempore* of the Senate, then the Speaker of the House of Representatives would act.

§ 408. Should such a vacancy occur while there was no President of the Senate *pro tempore*, and during the recess of Congress, after the expiration of one Congress and before the assembling of another, while, therefore, there would be no Speaker of the House of Representatives, then it would seem that no person is designated to act as President.

§ 409. Congress, by the same act, declared that when ever the office of President and of Vice-President shall both become vacant, the Secretary of State shall notify the executive of every State, and that electors of President and Vice-

President shall be chosen, as above mentioned, within thirty-four days preceding the first Wednesday in the ensuing December; provided that there shall be a space of two months between the date of the notice and the first Wednesday of December; but if there shall not be such space of two months, and if the Presidential term shall not expire on the third day of the ensuing March, then the electors shall be appointed within thirty-four days preceding the first Wednesday of December in the following year. The proceedings and duties of the electors are the same as in the case of a regular election.

[Clause 7.] "The President shall, at stated Times, receive for his Services, a Compensation, which shall neither be encreased nor diminished during the Period for which he shall have been elected, and he shall not receive within that Period any other Emolument from the United States, or any of them."

§ 410. The President would scarcely be independent of Congress, if that body had the power to deprive him of his salary, and thus control his means of support. On the other hand, if his salary could be increased during his term of office, he might be tempted from his duty by the prospect of obtaining such increase.

§ 411. The salary of the President is, by an act of Congress passed in 1793, fixed at the rate of $25,000 a year, together with the use of the Presidential mansion and its furniture. The salary of the Vice-President is at the rate of $8,000 a year.

[Clause 8.] "Before he enter on the execution of his Office, he shall take the following Oath or Affirmation:—

'I do solemnly swear (or affirm) that I will faithfully

'execute the Office of President of the United States, and 'will to the best of my Ability, preserve, protect and de- 'fend the Constitution of the United States.'"

§ 412. The object of this clause was to insure faithfulness on the part of the President, by means of the solemnity and sanction of an oath. It is his sworn duty to preserve, protect, and defend the Constitution of the United States to the best of his ability.

SECTION. 2. [Clause 1.] "The President shall be Commander in Chief of the Army and Navy of the United States, and of the Militia of the several States, when called into the actual Service of the United States; he may require the Opinion, in writing, of the principal Officer in each of the executive Departments, upon any Subject relating to the Duties of their respective Offices, and he shall have Power to grant Reprieves and Pardons for Offences against the United States, except in Cases of Impeachment."

§ 413. Experience has shown that in time of war, activity, energy, promptness, and unity, in the operations of an army or navy, are more likely to be attained when the commanding power is in the hands of a single person than when it is distributed among several persons. If, then, such power is to be vested in any single magistrate, it seems proper that it should be intrusted to the highest executive officer of the government.

§ 414. The President is the commander-in-chief of the army and navy in time of peace as well as of war; but he has no right to command the militia of the several States except when they are called into the actual service of the United States. (See art. I., sec. 8, clause 15.)

§ 415. The President is also authorized to require the opinion in writing, of the principal officer in each of the executive departments, upon any subject relating to the duties of their respective offices; at the same time he is under no obligation to adopt such opinion. He cannot require the opinion of the judges of the Supreme Court of the United States, as they can constitutionally be called on to decide only such questions as come regularly before them according to law.

§ 416. The President is authorized to grant reprieves and pardons for offences against the United States, except in cases of impeachment. A reprieve is a suspension or delay of the execution of a sentence in a criminal case, for a limited time. A pardon is a discharge of the offender from all the punishment which the law inflicts on his offence. The pardoning power also includes the remission of fines, penalties, and forfeitures under the various laws of the United States.

§ 417. Impeachment is generally employed against high officers of government for matters relating to the discharge of their official duties. The judgment does not extend farther than to removal from office and disqualification from holding office thereafter, and cannot be pronounced unless two-thirds of the Senate concur. The power to pardon in such cases, is withheld from the President, because the object of impeachment is to disgrace rather than to punish, and because the President might sometimes be inclined to favour and protect persons occupying important stations in the government, and appointed, perhaps, by himself.

[Clause 2.] "He shall have Power, by and with the Advice and Consent of the Senate, to make Treaties, provided two-thirds of the Senators present concur; and he shall nominate, and by and with the Advice and Consent of the Senate, shall appoint Ambassadors, other public Ministers and Consuls, Judges of the supreme Court, and all other Officers of the United States, whose Appointments are not herein otherwise provided for, and which shall be established by Law: but the Congress may by Law vest the Appointment of such inferior Officers, as they think proper, in the President alone, in the Courts of Law, or in the Heads of Departments."

§ 418. A treaty is an agreement between two or more independent nations. The subjects of treaties are generally peace, war, alliance, boundaries, territory, commerce, navigation, and payment of debts.

§ 419. Treaties are usually formed by agents or ministers, appointed by the governments who are parties to the treaty. Sometimes these agents or ministers are intrusted with full authority to sign and conclude the treaty; but more generally they transmit it, or the preliminary articles of the proposed treaty, to their respective governments, to be either ratified or rejected; by the usage of nations, the treaty is not finally binding until it is ratified.

§ 420. In practice, a treaty is first concluded under the direction of the President. He then lays it, with all the official documents respecting its negotiation, before the Senate, where it is discussed in executive session, with closed doors. The Senate may ratify it, or refuse to consent to it, or ratify some articles in it and reject others, or they may recommend additional articles. Amendments to the treaty in the Senate, as well as its final ratification, require a vote of two-thirds.

§ 421. If the Senate make any alterations in the proposed treaty, it does not become the law of the land until the alterations are approved by the President, and by the government with which the treaty is made.

§ 422. By this clause the appointing power is vested in the President, by and with the advice and consent of the Senate. This appointing power extends to ambassadors and other public ministers, consuls, judges of the Supreme Court, and all other officers of the United States whose appointments are not otherwise provided for by the Constitution. But Congress is authorized to vest by law the appointment of such inferior officers as they may think proper, in the President alone, or in the courts of law, or in the heads of departments.

§ 423. A rule of the Senate provides that, when nominations shall be made in writing by the President to the Senate, a future day shall be assigned, unless the Senate unanimously direct otherwise, for taking them into consideration. Another rule requires that all information or remarks concerning the character or qualifications of any person nominated by the President, shall be kept secret.

§ 424. If the nomination of the President is approved by a majority of the Senate, the nominee may be appointed and commissioned by the President. Although the Senate can reject a nomination made by the President, they cannot nominate or appoint another person instead of the one rejected; the President must then make another nomination.

It was thought that the President would be more likely

to nominate suitable persons for office, if their character and qualifications were to be subject to the examination of the Senate.

§ 425. To constitute a full appointment under this clause, it is necessary—

(1.) That the President should nominate in writing to the Senate, the person proposed to be appointed.

(2.) That the Senate should advise and consent that the nominee be appointed.

(3.) That, in pursuance of such advice and consent, the appointment should be actually made.

§ 426. The nomination is not an appointment; nor is that nomination, followed by the consent of the Senate, sufficient of itself to confer an office upon a citizen under the Constitution. The President may still, in his discretion, withhold the appointment from the nominee. The appointment is not complete, and the nominee has no legal rights, as an officer, conferred upon him until a commission has been signed by the President.

§ 427. The commission is a formal certificate of the appointment, signed by the President, and sealed by the Secretary of State with the seal of the United States, which is delivered to the person appointed. Actual delivery of the commission, after it has been signed by the President, is not absolutely necessary; nor, if lost or destroyed, would the appointment be void. The salary is paid from the date of the appointment, and not from the time the commission is received.

§ 428. Although the power of appointment is vested in the President and Senate, the power of removal has, since the Congress of 1789, which after thorough discussion sustained the right, been exercised by the President alone; the practical result of this construction of the Constitution is that offices in general are held during the pleasure of the President, unless the Constitution, or the law by which they are created, provides otherwise.

§ 429. Some of the reasons which led to this construction of the Constitution were, that the President is intrusted with the supreme executive power, and is bound to carry the laws into operation, which he can do only by means of officers responsible to him; also, that it might frequently be necessary to make removals when Congress was not in session, and the consent of the Senate, if necessary, could not for that reason be obtained.

§ 430. The power of the President to remove an officer from the public service, extends to all officers in the army and navy, as well as to civil officers.

§ 431. An important branch of the appointing power, expressly vested in the President jointly with the Senate, is that which relates to ambassadors, other public ministers, and consuls. Public ministers are sent abroad by a sovereign State to transact public business in behalf of their country with a foreign government.

§ 432. In strictness, no State is obliged to send ministers to, or receive them from, another State; the practice in this respect arises from long usage, and the courtesy of nations in their intercourse with each other. Every independent State, however, has the right to send public ministers to, and receive them from, any other sovereign State with which it desires to maintain friendly relations.

§ 433. There are, according to the practice of nations, three grades of public ministers, or diplomatic agents:

(1.) Cardinals, papal legates, or nuncios, and ministers sent with the character of ambassadors. These represent the State, or the person of the sovereign, by whom they are sent, in the highest and most eminent degree, not only in the particular affairs with which they are charged, but on all occasions. Ambassadors are divided into ordinary and extraordinary; the former are employed in permanent missions, the latter, in special and extraordinary negotiations.

§ 434. (2.) Envoys, envoys extraordinary, ministers plenipotentiary.

(3.) Ministers, ministers resident, *chargés d'affaires.*

The ministers of the second and third classes are destitute of the representative character, strictly so called, and represent their State or sovereign only for the affairs with which they are charged, either in behalf of the government or its subjects.

§ 435. Consuls are commercial agents of a government, appointed to reside in a foreign country to protect the commercial interests of their government. Although consuls are, to some extent, under the special protection of the law of nations, yet they are not considered as public ministers or diplomatic agents; they cannot enter upon their duties until they have been confirmed by the sovereign in whose dominions they are about to reside. A vice-consul is one who acts in the place of a consul.

§ 436. The duties of our consuls relate chiefly to the commerce of the United States, and to the masters of ships, mariners, and other citizens of the United States. They have authority to receive protests or declarations which captains, crews, passengers, merchants, and others may make, relating to American commerce; they are required, when the laws of the country permit it, to administer on the estate of American citizens dying within their consulate and leaving no legal representatives; to take charge of stranded American vessels in the absence of the master or owners; to settle disputes between the masters of vessels and the seamen ; to provide for destitute seamen, and send them to the United States at the public expense. They may also grant passports to American citizens abroad.

§ 437. The diplomatic and consular systems of the United States were remodelled by an act of Congress, approved March 1, 1855. By that act certain countries are designated, in which the United States are to be represented by an envoy extraordinary and minister plenipotentiary, together with a secretary of legation. Consuls are appointed to reside, during their continuance in office, in the principal cities and ports throughout the world, and consuls and commercial agents, in the less important localities, receiving a fixed annual compensation for their services. The consuls at certain of the more important places are not permitted to transact business in their own name, or through the agency of others ; but consuls and commercial agents at other places are not thus restricted. By this act, none but citizens of the United States can be appointed as diplomatic or consular agents.

§ 438. The persons and household goods of foreign ambassadors or public ministers, are, by the law of nations, exempt from arrest or seizure ; nor are ambassadors responsible to the civil or criminal laws of the country to which they are sent. As they are the representatives of their governments, and are deputed for the purposes of negotiation and friendly intercourse, they are exempt from all molestation. If they insult the government to which they are sent, or violate its laws, the government may refuse to treat with them, or application may be made to their own government for their recall, or they may be dismissed and required to depart within a reasonable time.

§ 439. But consuls, as above stated, are regarded merely

as commercial agents, and are not, by the law of nations, entitled to the privileges of public ministers; they are generally subject, in civil and criminal cases, to the laws of the country where they reside.

§ 440. Congress passed an act, April 30, 1790, declaring that all writs and processes issued out of any court of the United States, or of a particular State, or by any judge or justice, whereby any ambassador or other public minister of any foreign prince or State, or any servant of any such ambassador or minister, may be arrested, or his goods and chattels seized, shall be deemed utterly void. But to entitle the servants of an ambassador to the protection of this act, the names of such servants should be first registered in the office of the Secretary of State, and further publicity given to them in a manner pointed out in the act.

[Clause 3.] "The President shall have Power to fill up Vacancies that may happen during the Recess of the Senate, by granting Commissions which shall expire at the End of their next Session."

§ 441. This clause refers to vacancies in offices under the Constitution and laws of the United States. Vacancies may happen from death, resignation, promotion, or removal. The power of temporary appointment is given to the President alone, because the consent of the Senate cannot be obtained when it is not in session. But the appointment by the President in such case expires at the end of the next session of the Senate.

§ 442. Sometimes offices are created by law while the Senate is in session, and are not filled at the time. The President cannot appoint to those offices after the adjournment of the Senate, without special authority is given to him, because in such case the vacancy does not happen during the recess.

§ 443. But if a vacancy occur before the session of the Senate, and the President fills it by an appointment, which, by the clause we are now considering, expires at the end of the next session, and the President during the session should nominate a person for the office, and the nomination is not acted upon, or approved by the Senate, then it has been the practice of the government to consider that, after the adjournment of the Senate, a vacancy has again happened in the office during a recess of the Senate, so that the President may proceed to make another appointment until the end of the following session of the Senate. If this were not done, the office would be unoccupied, and public business might suffer.

"SECTION 3. He shall from time to time give to the Congress Information of the State of the Union, and recommend to their Consideration such Measures as he shall judge necessary and expedient; he may, on extraordinary Occasions, convene both Houses, or either of them, and in Case of Disagreement between them, with Respect to the time of Adjournment, he may adjourn them to such Time as he shall think proper; he shall receive Ambassadors and other public Ministers; he shall take Care that the Laws be faithfully executed, and shall Commission all the officers of the United States."

§ 444. From the first part of this clause has originated the practice of the President to send a written message concerning public affairs to Congress, annually, and special messages at other times. The first two Presidents, Washington and Adams, used to meet both Houses of Congress in person, and deliver addresses to them concerning national affairs. This practice was discontinued by Mr. Jefferson, upon the occasion of his first annual message, and written messages have taken the place of such speeches. Congress is not obliged to adopt the recommendations made by the President, but may take such action therein as in its judgment it shall deem proper.

§ 445. The power to call together both Houses, or either House, of Congress, on extraordinary occasions, is given to the President, because circumstances may arise during the recess in which he might require their advice and assistance. It is under the power thus given, that special sessions of Congress have sometimes been called by the President.

§ 446. When the two Houses of Congress cannot, themselves, agree upon the time to which they shall adjourn, the President is authorized to adjourn them to such time as he may think proper.

§ 447. The President is authorized to receive ambassadors and other public ministers, because he is the chief magistrate of the country, and is at the head of the government. Consuls are not mentioned in this clause by name, but they have been considered as included within the general language employed. Foreign ministers must present their credentials to the President, which must receive his allowance, or exequatur, as it is called, before they can perform any official act.

§ 448. By the clause we are now considering it is made the duty of the President to "take care that the laws are faithfully executed;" that is, the laws of the United States. This duty is properly charged upon him because he is the chief executive officer of the government. As commander in-chief of the army and navy, he has ample means of enforcing the observance of the laws.

§ 449. It belongs to the executive department to execute every law which Congress has the constitutional authority to enact. But if the President should mistake the meaning of an act of Congress, and in consequence of such mistake should give instructions not warranted by the act, any injured party might recover damages against the officer acting under those instructions, which, although given by the President, would furnish no justification or excuse.

§ 450. The President commissions all the officers of the United States, because the appointing power is vested in him, jointly with the Senate. The commissions of the public officers appointed by the President, are signed by him, and have the great seal of the United States affixed thereto. (See § 427.)

"SECTION 4. The President, Vice-President and all civil Officers of the United States, shall be removed from Office on Impeachment for, and Conviction of, Treason, Bribery, or other high Crimes and Misdemeanors."

§ 451. The power of impeachment does not extend to all citizens, but only to the President, the Vice-President, and all civil officers of the United States. By civil officers of the United States, are meant all officers who hold appointments, either of an executive or a judicial character, under the general government. But officers in the army or navy are not considered as civil officers, and are not, therefore, liable to impeachment; they are subject, however, to the discipline of the army and navy, to trial by a court-martial, and to dismission from the service by the President.

§ 452. The words "crimes" and "misdemeanors" have

nearly the same signification, but in common usage the word "crimes" is intended to denote offences of a more serious character, while "misdemeanors" denotes those of less consequence. Bribery, as used here, is the giving of money or reward to, or its receipt by, a person in office, as a compensation for acting contrary to his duty.

§ 453. It has generally been considered that members of the Senate and House of Representatives are not liable to impeachment, inasmuch as they hold their appointment under the State, or from the people they represent, and not from the national government.

We have already described the proceedings in impeachment; see § 114.

§ 454. In England the king is not constitutionally answerable for any of his official misconduct. It is presumed that he acts always by the advice of his ministers, and they are, therefore, held personally responsible for all political measures adopted during their administration. It is for this reason that the ministers resign as soon as they find that a majority of Parliament is against them. But in the United States, the President is, by the Constitution, answerable himself for his own official misconduct, and is, as we have just seen, liable to impeachment for treason, bribery, or other high crime or misdemeanor.

§ 455. The President, in all cases where his official authority and duty are not brought in question, is merely a private citizen, subject to the usual duties and obligations of a citizen. Therefore, if his testimony is necessary in any case for the purposes of justice, he may be subpœnaed into court and examined as a witness, and may be required to produce papers just as any other citizen, unless the papers relate to State affairs, which should not be disclosed.

§ 456. The following is a list of the Presidents and Vice-Presidents for each Presidential term of four years:—

Term.	President.	Vice-President.
1st, From March 4, 1789, to March 4, 1793.	George Washington, Va.	John Adams, Mass.
2d, March 4, 1793, to March 4, 1797.	George Washington, Va.	John Adams, Mass.
3d, March 4, 1797, to March 4, 1801.	John Adams, Mass.	Thomas Jefferson, Va.
4th, March 4, 1801, to March 4, 1805.	Thomas Jefferson, Va.	Aaron Burr, N. Y.
5th, March 4, 1805, to March 4, 1809.	Thomas Jefferson, Va.	George Clinton, N. Y.
6th, March 4, 1809, to March 4, 1813.	James Madison, Va.	George Clinton, N. Y.
7th, March 4, 1813, to March 4, 1817.	James Madison, Va.	Elbridge Gerry, Mass.
8th, March 4, 1817, to March 4, 1821.	James Monroe, Va.	Daniel D. Tompkins, N. Y.
9th, March 4, 1821, to March 4, 1825.	James Monroe, Va.	Daniel D. Tompkins, N. Y.
10th, March 4, 1825, to March 4, 1829.	John Quincy Adams, Mass.	John C. Calhoun, S. C.
11th, March 4, 1829, to March 4, 1833.	Andrew Jackson, Tenn.	John C. Calhoun, S. C.
12th, March 4, 1833, to March 4, 1837.	Andrew Jackson, Tenn.	Martin Van Buren, N. Y.
13th, March 4, 1837, to March 4, 1841.	Martin Van Buren, N. Y.	Richard M. Johnson, Ky.
14th, March 4, 1841, to March 4, 1845.	William Henry Harrison, Ohio, President for one month; died April 4, 1841. John Tyler, acting President 3 years, 11 m.	John Tyler, Va., Vice-President for one month; office vacant for residue of term.
15th, March 4, 1845, to March 4, 1849.	James K. Polk, Tenn.	George M. Dallas, Pa.
16th, March 4, 1849, to March 4, 1853.	Zachary Taylor, La., President 1 year, 4 m.; died July 9, 1850. Millard Fillmore acting President 2 years, 8 months.	Millard Fillmore, N. Y., Vice-President 1 year, 4 months; office vacant for residue of term.
17th, March 4, 1853, to March 4, 1857.	Franklin Pierce, N. H.	William R. King, Ala., Vice-President for 1 month, 14 days; died April 18, 1853, office vacant.

CHAPTER XII

THE EXECUTIVE DEPARTMENTS.

§ 457. THE executive and administrative business of the government is not all managed directly by the President himself, but has, by various acts of Congress, been distributed among several executive departments, viz.:

(1.) Department of State.
(2.) Department of the Navy.
(3.) Department of War.
(4.) Department of Treasury.
(5.) Post-office Department.
(6.) Department of the Interior.

§ 458. The heads of these departments, together with the Attorney General of the United States, are appointed by the President, with the advice and consent of the Senate, and they constitute what is termed the cabinet, with whom the President consults confidentially upon public affairs. The Vice-President of the United States is not a member of the cabinet.

§ 459. They are the constitutional advisers of the President, and he is authorized by the Constitution (Art. II. sec. 2, clause 1) to "require the opinion in writing of the principal officer in each of the executive departments upon any subject relating to the duties of their respective offices." These officers are again recognised by the Constitution in the clause which vests the appointment of certain inferior officers "in the heads of departments," (Art. II. sec. 2, clause 2.) The number, organization, and duties of these departments, are left to be determined by Congress.

§ 460. The chief officer, or head, in each of the departments is, as above stated, nominated by the President and approved by the Senate; but he may be removed at the will of the President alone, and is responsible to him. If a vacancy happens during the recess of Congress, the President may appoint an officer pro tempore to fill the place till the next meeting of Congress.

In some of these great departments there are established subordinate departments, termed bureaus, to which certain subjects of business are assigned.

§ 461. Each of the departments has an official seal; so also have some of the bureaus; copies of their records, authenticated by certificate and the official seal, are, by act of Congress, made evidence equally with the original record or paper; the heads of the departments are authorized by law to appoint the clerks, (except some of the principal clerks, who are appointed by the President,) by virtue of the clause in the Constitution, as above mentioned, authorizing certain appointments to be vested in the heads of departments; and they perform generally such other duties appertaining to their office as may be required of them by the President or by Congress.

§ 462. No contract in behalf of the United States can be made by the heads of departments, except under a law or appropriation authorizing it, so that they cannot involve the government in responsibility for the payment of money, beyond the amount appropriated by Congress.

§ 463. The Secretary of State performs such duties as are enjoined on or intrusted to him by the President, agreeably to the Constitution, relative to the correspondence with and instructions to the public ministers, consuls, and diplomatic agents of the United States; or to negotiations with foreign States; or to memorials or applications to our own government from foreigners or the public ministers of foreign States; and generally to all matters relating to our foreign affairs. His salary is $8000 a year.

§ 464. The Department of State was organized in the year 1789, by the first Congress which assembled under the Constitution, and was termed the Department of Foreign Affairs, and the duties assigned to it related to the foreign affairs of the government. At a subsequent period in the same year, the name was changed to that of the Department of State, and it was then made the duty of the Secretary to receive, keep, and promulgate the laws enacted by Congress, and to have the charge of the seal of the United States, and affix it to the commissions of all civil officers of the United States lawfully appointed by the President, as well where the consent of the Senate was necessary to the appointment as where it was not. Passports to American citizens visiting foreign countries, are granted by the Secretary of State.

§ 465. After laws have been passed by Congress, they are enrolled on parchment, the sheets of which are of uniform size, and are signed by the Speaker of the House of Representatives and the President of the Senate; they are then sent to the President of the United States for his approval. If approved by him, he signs them, and, after notifying Congress that he has thus approved and signed them, he deposits the originals in the office of the Secretary of State, where they are bound together in volumes and preserved.

§ 466. In the Department of State, in addition to the Secretary, there are employed an assistant Secretary of

State, who is appointed by the President; a chief clerk a claims clerk, a translator, and numerous subordinate clerks. There is also established within this department a diplomatic bureau, a consular bureau, and a domestic bureau.

§ 467. The following is a list of the Secretaries of State, from the organization of the government to the present time:—

THOMAS JEFFERSON, of Virginia. Appointed 26th September, 1789. Resigned.

EDMUND RANDOLPH, of Virginia. Appointed 2d January, 1794. Resigned.

TIMOTHY PICKERING, of Pennsylvania. Appointed 10th December, 1795. Removed.

JOHN MARSHALL, of Virginia. Appointed 13th May, 1800. Appointed Chief Justice of the Supreme Court 31st January, 1801.

JAMES MADISON, of Virginia. Appointed 5th March, 1801. Became President 4th March, 1809.

ROBERT SMITH, of Maryland. Appointed 6th March, 1809. Resigned.

JAMES MONROE, of Virginia. Appointed 2d April, 1811, in recess of Senate. Nomination confirmed and appointed 25th November, 1811. Appointed Secretary of War 27th September, 1814.

JAMES MONROE, of Virginia. Appointed 28th February, 1815. Became President of the United States 4th March, 1817.

JOHN QUINCY ADAMS, of Massachusetts. Appointed 5th March, 1817. Became President of the United States 4th March, 1825.

HENRY CLAY, of Kentucky. Appointed 7th March, 1825. Resigned.

MARTIN VAN BUREN, of New York Appointed 6th March, 1829. Resigned.

EDWARD LIVINGSTON, of Louisiana. Appointed 24th May, 1831, in recess of Senate. Nomination confirmed and appointed 12th January, 1832.

LOUIS MCLANE, of Delaware. Appointed 29th May, 1833, in recess of Senate. Resigned.

JOHN FORSYTH, of Georgia. Appointed 27th June 1834.

DANIEL WEBSTER, of Massachusetts. Appointed 5th March, 1841. Resigned.

ABEL P. UPSHUR, of Virginia. Appointed 24th July, 1843, in recess of the Senate. Nomination confirmed and appointed 2d January, 1844.

JOHN C. CALHOUN, of South Carolina. Appointed 6th March, 1844.

JAMES BUCHANAN, of Pennsylvania. Appointed 5th March, 1845.

JOHN M. CLAYTON, of Delaware. Appointed 7th March, 1849. Resigned.

DANIEL WEBSTER, of Massachusetts. Appointed 20th July, 1850.

EDWARD EVERETT, of Massachusetts. Appointed 9th December, 1852.

WILLIAM L. MARCY, of New York. Appointed March 7, 1853.

§ 468. The Secretary of War performs such duties as are intrusted to him by the President relative to military commissions, or to the land forces or warlike stores of the United States, and to other military affairs of the United States. The Secretary of War does not compose a part of the army of the United States, and is not required to perform military service in the field. His duties are such as may be performed at the seat of government and in the war office. To his department belong the direction and government of the army; the purchase and preservation of the arms and munitions of war; and the erection of all fortifications. His salary is $8000 a year.

§ 469. The Secretary of War is assisted by a chief clerk and by other clerks. Connected with this department there is a quartermaster's department, the chief officer of which is termed the quartermaster-general; an engineer department, the principal officer of which is termed the chief engineer; a bureau of topographical engineers, the chief officer of which is termed the colonel of topographical engineers; an ordnance department, the chief officer of which is termed the colonel of ordnance; a subsistence department, the chief officer of which is termed the commissary-general; a pay department, the chief officer of which is termed the paymaster-general; and a medical department, the chief officer of which is termed the surgeon-general.

§ 470. The supervision of the national armories at Springfield and at Harper's Ferry, where arms are manufactured, and of the arsenals and depots, where arms are deposited, also belongs to the Secretary of War. Prior to the creation of the Department of the Interior, to which those matters were then transferred, the Department of War had jurisdiction of Indian affairs, and the granting of pensions and land for military services.

In addition to the arms manufactured at the national armories above mentioned, the government procures arms from individuals, according to contracts made with the War Department.

§ 471. The United States and territories are divided geographically into five military divisions, as follows:

(1.) Department of the East. Head-quarters at Baltimore.

(2.) Department of the West. The country west of the Mississippi river, and east of the Rocky Mountains, except the departments of Texas and New Mexico. Head-quarters at St. Louis.

(3.) Department of Texas. The State of Texas, except the country north of the thirty-third degree of north latitude. Head-quarters at Corpus Christi, Texas.

(4.) Department of New Mexico. The territory of New Mexico, except the country west of the one hundred and tenth degree of west longitude. Head-quarters at Albuquerque.

(5.) Department of the Pacific. The country west of the Rocky Mountains, except the territory of Utah and the department of New Mexico. Head-quarters at San Francisco.

The head-quarters of the army are in the city of New York.

In each of these different departments forts and military posts are established, where troops are stationed.

SECRETARIES OF WAR.

HENRY KNOX, of Massachusetts. Appointed 12th September, 1789. Resigned.

TIMOTHY PICKERING, of Pennsylvania. Appointed 2d January, 1795. Appointed Secretary of State 10th December, 1795.

JOHN MCHENRY, of Maryland. Appointed 27th January, 1796. Resigned.

SAMUEL DEXTER, of Massachusetts. Appointed 13th May, 1800. Appointed Secretary of the Treasury 31st December, 1800.

ROGER GRISWOLD, of Connecticut. Appointed 3d February, 1801.

HENRY DEARBORN, of Massachusetts. Appointed 5th March, 1801.

WILLIAM EUSTIS, of Massachusetts. Appointed 7th March, 1809. Resigned.

JOHN ARMSTRONG, of New York. Appointed 13th January, 1813. Resigned.

JAMES MONROE, of Virginia. (Secretary of State.) Appointed 27th September, 1814. Appointed Secretary of State 28th February, 1815.

WILLIAM H. CRAWFORD, of Georgia. Appointed 3d March, 1815. Appointed Secretary of the Treasury 22d October, 1816.

GEORGE GRAHAM, of Virginia. Appointed 7th April, 1817, in recess of the Senate.

JOHN C. CALHOUN, of South Carolina. Appointed 8th October, 1817, in recess of the Senate. Nomination confirmed and appointed 15th December, 1817.

JAMES BARBOUR, of Virginia. Appointed 7th March, 1825.

PETER B. PORTER, of New York. Appointed 26th May, 1828.

JOHN H. EATON, of Tennessee. Appointed 9th March, 1829. Resigned.

LEWIS CASS, of Ohio. Appointed 1st August, 1831, in recess of the Senate. Nomination confirmed and appointed 30th December, 1831.

BENJAMIN F. BUTLER, of New York. Appointed 3d March, 1837.

JOEL R. POINSETT, of South Carolina. Appointed 7th March, 1837.

JOHN BELL, of Tennessee. Appointed 5th March, 1841. Resigned.

JOHN C. SPENCER, of New York. Appointed 12th October, 1841, in the recess of the Senate. Nomination confirmed and appointed 20th December, 1841.

JAMES M. PORTER, of Pennsylvania. Appointed 8th March, 1843, in recess of the Senate.

WILLIAM WILKINS, of Pennsylvania. Appointed 15th February, 1844.

WILLIAM L. MARCY, of New York. Appointed 5th March, 1845.

GEORGE W. CRAWFORD, of Georgia. Appointed 7th of March, 1849 Resigned.

CHARLES M. CONRAD, of Louisiana. Appointed 15th August, 1850

JEFFERSON DAVIS, of Mississippi. Appointed March 7, 1853.

§472. The Department of Treasury was organized in 1789. The duty of the Secretary of the Treasury is to prepare plans for the improvement and management of the revenue, and for the support of public credit; to make and report estimates of the public revenue and the public expenditures; to superintend the collection of the revenue of the United States; to grant warrants for money to be issued from the Treasury, and generally to perform all such services relative to the finances of the government as he shall be directed to perform. His salary is $8000 a year. All accounts of the government are finally settled at the Treasury Department.

§473. In pursuance of an act of May 10, 1800, the Secretary of the Treasury prepares and lays before Congress, at the commencement of every session, a report on the subject of finance, containing estimates of the public revenue and public expenditures, and plans for increasing the revenues, for the purpose of giving information to Congress in adopting modes of raising money to meet the public expenditures.

§474. The Secretary of the Treasury employs an assistant secretary, a chief clerk, and a large number of other clerks. In this department there are various bureaus, among which the business is distributed permanently and upon a regular system. There is a first comptroller, and a second comptroller; a first auditor, second auditor, third auditor, fourth auditor, fifth auditor, and sixth auditor.

§475. There is in this department a treasurer, and an assistant treasurer in Boston, New York, Philadelphia, St. Louis, and Charleston; also a commissioner of customs, and a solicitor of the treasury, a law-officer whose duty it is to attend to the collection of debts due to the government, to the management of suits in the local courts of the United States, and the instruction of district attorneys and marshals in relation thereto.

§476. All claims due to the United States, after a failure or refusal to pay, are put in suit in the district where the parties or some of them reside, and, except post-office suits, are placed upon the books of the solicitor of the treasury, and are collected under his direction.

§477. Accounts with the United States are received, examined, and settled by the proper auditors, and the settlements by them are then revised by one of the comptrollers. The decision of the comptroller upon all questions of law as well as of fact, in matters of account within the limits of his duty, is final, unless redress is granted by Congress. The auditors of the public accounts are authorized to administer oaths or affirmations to witnesses in any case in which they may deem it necessary for the due examination of accounts, and false swearing as to any matter concerning the expenditure of public money, or in support of any claim against the United States, is, by an act of Congress, made perjury.

§478. The coast-survey, the revenue-cutter service, (§218,) and the mint of the United States, with its branches, are all attached to this department. The light-houses of the United States were formerly under the control of the fifth auditor of the treasury; but by an act passed August 31, 1852, the "Light-house Board of the United States" was established.

§ 479. This board consists of two officers of the navy, of high rank, one officer of the corps of engineers of the army, one officer of the corps of topographical engineers of the army, two civilians of high scientific attainments, with an officer of the navy, and an officer of engineers of the army, as secretaries. The Secretary of the Treasury is, by virtue of his office, president of the board, and the board is attached to his department, and is under his superintendence.

§ 480. The duties of the Light-house Board relate to the construction, illumination, inspection, and supervision of light-houses, light-vessels, beacons, buoys, and sea-marks, and to rebuilding them, and keeping them in repair. The Atlantic, Gulf, Pacific, and Lake coasts of the United States, are divided into light-house districts, and the President of the United States assigns to each district an officer of the army or navy, as light-house inspector, under the orders of the board.

§ 481. List of Secretaries of the Treasury:—

ALEXANDER HAMILTON, of New York. Appointed 11th September, 1789. Resigned.

OLIVER WOLCOTT, Jr., of Connecticut. Appointed 3d February, 1795 Resigned.

SAMUEL DEXTER, of Massachusetts, (Secretary of War.) Appointed 31st December, 1800.

ALBERT GALLATIN, of Pennsylvania. Appointed 14th May, 1801, in recess of Senate. Nomination confirmed and appointed 26th January, 1802.

GEORGE W. CAMPBELL, of Tennessee. Appointed 9th February, 1814 Resigned.

Alexander James Dallas, of Pennsylvania, appointed 6th October, 1814.

William H. Crawford, of Georgia. Appointed 22d October, 1816. in recess of the Senate. Nomination confirmed and appointed 5th March, 1817.

Richard Rush, of Pennsylvania. Appointed 7th March, 1825.

Samuel D. Ingham, of Pennsylvania. Appointed 6th March, 1829. Resigned.

Louis McLane, of Delaware. Appointed 8th August, 1831, in recess of the Senate. Nomination confirmed and appointed 13th January, 1832.

William J. Duane, of Pennsylvania. Appointed 29th May, 1833, in recess of the Senate.

Roger B. Taney, of Maryland. Appointed 23d September, 1833, in recess of the Senate.

Levi Woodbury, of New Hampshire. Appointed 27th June, 1834.

Thomas Ewing, of Ohio. Appointed 5th March, 1841. Resigned.

Walter Forward, of Pennsylvania. Appointed 13th September, 1841.

John C. Spencer, of New York. Appointed 3d March, 1843.

George M. Bibb, of Kentucky. Appointed 15th June, 1844.

Robert J. Walker, of Mississippi. Appointed 5th March, 1845.

William Morris Meredith, of Pennsylvania. Appointed 7th March, 1849. Resigned.

Thomas Corwin, of Ohio. Appointed 20th June, 1850.

James Guthrie, of Kentucky. Appointed March 7th, 1853.

§482. The Department of the Navy was organized by act of Congress, April 30, 1798. The Secretary of the Navy executes all such orders as he shall receive from the President, relative to procuring naval stores and materials, and the construction, equipment, and employment of vessels of war, as well as all other matters connected with the naval establishment of the United States. His salary is $8000. Prior to the organization of the Navy Department, all matters and things relative to the naval force of the United States were confided to the Secretary of the War Department.

§483. By act of Congress of August 31, 1842, reorganizing the navy department, the following bureaus were created within that department, among which its various duties are assigned and distributed by the Secretary.

(1.) A bureau of navy-yards and docks.

(2.) A bureau of construction, equipment, and repair.

(3.) A bureau of provisions and clothing.

(4.) A bureau of ordnance and hydrography.

(5.) A bureau of medicine and surgery.

§ 484. The first officer in each of these bureaus is termed the chief of the bureau, and is appointed by the President; the clerks in the bureaus are appointed by the Secretary of the Navy. All the duties of the bureaus are performed under the authority of the Secretary of the Navy, and their orders and decisions are considered as emanating from him, and have force and effect as such.

§ 485. The following is a list of the Secretaries of the Navy:—

George Cabot, of Massachusetts. Appointed 3d May, 1798.

Benjamin Stoddert, of Maryland. Appointed 21st May, 1798. Resigned.

Robert Smith, of Maryland. Appointed 15th July, 1801, in recess of the Senate. Nomination confirmed and appointed 26th January, 1802. Appointed Attorney-General 2d March, 1805.

Jacob Crowninshield, of Massachusetts. Appointed 2d March, 1805.

Paul Hamilton, of South Carolina. Appointed 7th March, 1809 Resigned.

William Jones, of Pennsylvania. Appointed 12th January, 181? Resigned.

Benjamin W. Crowninshield, of Massachusetts. Appointed 17th December, 1814.

Smith Thompson, of New York. Appointed 9th November, 1818, in recess of the Senate. Nomination confirmed and appointed 30th November, 1818. Resigned.

John Rodgers. Appointed 1st September, 1823, in recess of the Senate.

Samuel L Southard, of New Jersey. Appointed 16th September

1823, in recess of the Senate. Nomination confirmed and appointed 9th December, 1823.

JOHN BRANCH, of North Carolina. Appointed 9th March, 1829. Resigned.

LEVI WOODBURY, of New Hampshire. Appointed 23d May, 1831, in recess of the Senate. Nomination confirmed and appointed 27th December, 1831. Resigned.

MAHLON DICKERSON, of New Jersey. Appointed 30th June, 1834. Resigned.

JAMES K. PAULDING, of New York. Appointed 20th June, 1838.

GEORGE E. BADGER, of North Carolina. Appointed 5th March, 1841. Resigned.

ABEL P. UPSHUR, of Virginia. Appointed 13th September, 1841.

DAVID HENSHAW, of Massachusetts. Appointed 24th July, 1843, in recess of the Senate, and served until 15th January, 1844.

THOMAS W. GILMER, of Virginia. Nomination confirmed and appointed 15th February, 1844.

JOHN Y. MASON, of Virginia. Appointed 14th March, 1844. Appointed Attorney-General 5th March, 1845.

GEORGE BANCROFT, of Massachusetts. Appointed 10th March, 1845. Resigned.

JOHN Y. MASON, of Virginia. Appointed 9th September, 1846, in recess of the Senate. Nomination confirmed and appointed 17th December, 1846.

WILLIAM BALLARD PRESTON, of Virginia. Appointed 7th March, 1849. Resigned.

WILLIAM A. GRAHAM, of North Carolina. Appointed 20th July, 1850. Resigned.

JOHN P. KENNEDY, of Maryland. Appointed 22d July, 1852.

JAMES C. DOBBIN, of North Carolina. Appointed March 7th 1853.

§ 486. The Post-Office Department, under the Constitution, was established September 22, 1789. A line of posts from Falmouth, in New England, to Savannah, in Georgia, with cross-posts, had been established by the Continental Congress as early as the year 1775, under the direction of a Postmaster-General. The duties of the Postmaster-General are to establish and superintend post-offices; appoint postmasters and other persons employed in the mail service; and provide for carrying the mail. His salary is $8000.

§ 487. The Postmaster-General is aided in the discharge of his duties by three Assistant Postmasters-General, appointed by himself. He has the sole appointment of all postmasters throughout the United States, whose commissions are less than $1000 a year; those whose commissions yield more than that sum, are appointed by the President, with the advice and consent of the Senate. In case of the death, resignation, or absence of the Postmaster-General, all his powers and duties devolve on the first assistant.

§ 488. Once in three months, the Postmaster-General renders to the Secretary of the Treasury a quarterly account of all the receipts and expenditures in his department, to be adjusted and settled as other public accounts, and the revenue arising from his department is paid into the Treasury of the United States. For a long period the Postmaster-General was not regarded as a member of the President's Cabinet, but in the opening of Jackson's administration the Postmaster-General was called to the same duties as a cabinet counsellor of the President, which had previously been discharged by the secretaries of the other departments.

§ 489. The Postmaster-General, and all other persons employed in the general post-office, or in the care, custody, or conveyance of the mail, are required, previous to entering upon their duties, to take and subscribe an oath, faithfully to perform the duties required of them, and to abstain from every thing forbidden by the laws in relation to the establishment of post-offices and post-roads. The deputy postmasters in the various cities, towns, and villages throughout the United States, are required to give bonds to secure the faithful discharge of their duties.

§ 490. The following is a list of the Postmasters-General:—

Samuel Osgood, of Massachusetts. Appointed 26th September, 1789. Resigned.

Timothy Pickering, of Pennsylvania. Appointed 12th August, 1791, in the recess of the Senate. Nomination confirmed and appointed 7th November, 1791. Appointed Secretary of War 2d January, 1795.

Joseph Habersham, of Georgia. Appointed 25th February, 1795. Resigned.

Gideon Granger, of Connecticut. Appointed 28th November, 1801, in recess of the Senate. Nomination confirmed and appointed 26th January, 1802.

Return Jonathan Meigs, Jr., (Governor of Ohio.) Appointed 17th March, 1814. Resigned.

John McLean, of Ohio. Appointed 26th June, 1823, in recess of the Senate. Nomination confirmed and appointed 9th December, 1823.

William T. Barry, of Kentucky. Appointed 9th March, 1829.

Amos Kendall, of Kentucky. Appointed 1st May, 1835, in the recess of the Senate. Nomination confirmed and appointed 15th March, 1836.

John M. Niles, of Connecticut. Appointed 18th May, 1840.

Francis Granger, of New York. Appointed 6th March, 1841. Resigned.

Charles A. Wickliffe, of Kentucky. Appointed 13th September, 1841. Resigned.

Cave Johnson, of Tennessee. Appointed 5th March, 1845.

Jacob Collamer, of Vermont. Appointed 7th March, 1849. Resigned.

Nathan K. Hall, of New York. Appointed 20th July, 1850. Resigned.

Samuel D. Hubbard, of Connecticut. Appointed 31st August, 1852.

James Campbell, of Pennsylvania. Appointed March 7th, 1853.

§ 491. By an act of Congress, approved March 3, 1849, a new department was created, called the Department of the Interior, to which were assigned certain matters which had previously appertained to the Department of State, of War, of Treasury, or of Navy.

§ 492. The Secretary of the Interior has supervision of

the patent office; the general land office; the accounts of officers of the courts of the United States; Indian affairs; the pension office; the census office; mines; and the public buildings. Salary $8000.

§ 493. The bureaus connected with this department are the land office, the chief officer of which is termed the Commissioner of the General Land Office; the patent office, the chief officer of which is the Commissioner of Patents; the Indian office, the chief officer of which is the Commissioner of Indian Affairs; the pension office, the chief officer of which is the Commissioner of Pensions; and the census bureau, the chief officer of which is the Superintendent of Census.

§ 494. The care of the Capitol, the President's house and grounds, and the bridges and buildings of a public character erected by Congress in the District of Columbia, belongs to this department.

§ 495. List of Secretaries of the Interior since the organization of the department:—

THOMAS EWING, of Ohio. Appointed 7th March, 1849. Resigned.

THOMAS M. T. MCKENNAN, of Pennsylvania. Appointed 15th August, 1850. Resigned.

ALEXANDER H. H. STUART, of Virginia. Appointed 12th September, 1850.

ROBERT MCCLELLAND, of Michigan. Appointed March 7th, 1853.

§ 496. An act of Congress of September 24, 1789, made provision for an Attorney-General, whose duty should be to prosecute and conduct all suits in the Supreme Court of the United States, in which the United States shall be concerned, and to give his advice and opinion upon questions of law, when required by the President, or when requested by the heads of any of the departments in matters which concern their departments. He also advises with and directs the solicitor of the treasury as to suits in which the United States are concerned, pending in the inferior courts of the United States, and he directs and prosecutes appeals to the Supreme Court of the United States, in suits involving title to land in the new territories acquired by the United States.

§ 497. He also examines the title to all lands purchased by the United States for the purpose of erecting thereon armories, arsenals, forts, navy-yards, custom-houses, light-houses, or other public buildings; and without his certificate of the validity of the title, no public money can be expended in such purchases. It is not his duty to give official opinions to the Senate or House of Representatives. His salary is $8000.

§ 498. The act above referred to, does not declare what effect shall be attributed to the advice and opinion of the Attorney-General when given to the President, or the head of a department; but it is believed that the practice of the government has almost invariably been to follow it.

§ 499. The following is a list of the Attorneys-General of the United States:—

EDMUND RANDOLPH, of Virginia. Appointed 26th September, 1789. Appointed Secretary of State 2d January, 1794.

WILLIAM BRADFORD, of Pennsylvania. Appointed 28th January, 1794.

CHARLES LEE, of Virginia. Appointed 10th December, 1795.

LEVI LINCOLN, of Massachusetts. Appointed 5th March, 1801 Resigned in 1805.

ROBERT SMITH, of Maryland. Appointed 2d March, 1805.

JOHN BRECKENRIDGE, of Kentucky. Appointed 23d December, 1805.

CÆSAR A. RODNEY, of Delaware. Appointed 20th January, 1807 Resigned.

WILLIAM PINKNEY, of Maryland. Appointed 11th December, 1811.

RICHARD RUSH, of Pennsylvania. Appointed 10th February, 1814.

WILLIAM WIRT, of Virginia. Appointed 13th November, 1817, in recess of the Senate. Nomination confirmed and appointed 15th December, 1817.

JOHN MACPHERSON BERRIEN, of Georgia. Appointed 9th March, 1829. Resigned.

ROGER B. TANEY, of Maryland. Appointed 20th July, 1831, in the recess of the Senate. Nomination confirmed and appointed 27th December, 1831.

BENJAMIN F. BUTLER, of New York. Appointed 15th November, 1833, in the recess of the Senate. Nomination confirmed and appointed 24th June, 1834. Resigned.

FELIX GRUNDY, of Tennessee. Appointed 7th July, 1838. Resigned.

HENRY D. GILPIN, of Pennsylvania. Appointed 10th January, 1840.

JOHN J. CRITTENDEN, of Kentucky. Appointed 5th March, 1841. Resigned.

HUGH S. LEGARE, of South Carolina. Appointed 13th September, 1841.

JOHN NELSON, of Maryland. Appointed 1st July, 1843, in the recess of the Senate. Nomination confirmed and appointed 2d January, 1844. Resigned.

JOHN Y. MASON, of Virginia. Appointed 5th March, 1845. Resigned Appointed Secretary of the Navy 9th September, 1846.

NATHAN CLIFFORD, of Maine. Appointed 17th October, 1846, in the recess of the Senate. Nomination confirmed and appointed 23d December, 1846.

ISAAC TOUCEY, of Connecticut. Appointed 21st June, 1848.

REVERDY JOHNSON, of Maryland. Appointed 7th March, 1849. Resigned.

JOHN J. CRITTENDEN, of Kentucky. Appointed 20th July, 1850.

CALEB CUSHING, of Massachusetts. Appointed March 7, 1853.

§ 500. These departments employ a large number of clerks. By an act of March 3, 1791, every clerk and other officer appointed in any of the departments, before entering on the duties of the appointment, must take an oath or affirmation before one of the justices of the Supreme Court, or one of the judges of a district court of the United States, to support the Constitution of the United States, and well and faithfully to execute the trust committed to him.

§ 501. By an act passed March 3, 1853, and its supplements, the clerks in the Departments of the Treasury, War, Navy, the Interior, and the Post-Office, were arranged in four classes. The clerks in class number one receive an annual salary of $1200 each; those in class number two, $1400 each; those in class number three, $1600 each; those in class number four, $1800 each.

§ 502. No clerk can be appointed into either of the four classes until after he has been examined and found qualified, by a board to consist of three examiners, one of them to be the chief of the bureau or office into which he is to be appointed, and the two others to be selected by the head of the department to which the clerk is to be assigned. The same act distributed a certain number of clerks, of the different classes, among the various departments, as the whole permanent clerical force of such departments.

§ 503. Various laws have been passed by Congress for the purpose of securing, as far as possible, honesty and integrity in the persons connected with these departments of the government. Any officer of the United States, or person holding any place of trust or profit under or in connection with any executive department of the government, or under the Senate or House of Representatives, or any senator or representative, who shall act as agent or attorney for prosecuting any claim against the United States, or aid or assist in the prosecution of any claim, or receive any share of a claim for having aided in its prosecution, is, by an act of February 26, 1853, made liable to indictment, and upon conviction may be sentenced to pay a fine not exceeding $5000, or suffer imprisonment in the penitentiary not exceeding one year, or both, as the court in its discretion shall adjudge.

§ 504. The same act prohibits bribery, or the undue influencing of members of Congress, or any person holding any office of trust or profit in connection with any department of the government, or under the Senate and House of Representatives. The person giving and the person receiving the bribe, are each liable to indictment as for a high crime and misdemeanor, and upon conviction may be punished by fine or imprisonment; and the person receiving, if an officer, is also forever disqualified from holding any office of honour, trust, or profit under the United States.

§ 505. An act of Congress, passed August 23, 1842, declares that no officer in any branch of the public service, or any other person whose salary, pay, or emoluments is, or are, fixed by law or regulations, shall receive any additional pay or extra allowance or compensation whatever, for any other service or duty, unless the same shall be authorized by law, and the appropriation explicitly set forth that it is for such additional pay, extra allowance, or compensation.

CHAPTER XIII.

THE JUDICIAL POWER.

ARTICLE III.

ARTICLE I. as we have seen, treats of the legislative department, and Article II. of the executive department. We now enter upon Article III., which treats of the judicial department.

"Article III. SECTION. 1. The judicial Power of the United States, shall be vested in one supreme Court, and in such inferior Courts as the Congress may from time to time ordain and establish. The Judges, both of the supreme and inferior Courts, shall hold their Offices during good Behavior, and shall, at stated Times, receive for their Services, a Compensation which shall not be diminished during their Continuance in Office."

§ 506. Prior to the adoption of the present constitution, the people of the United States, had not any national tribunal to which they could resort for justice. The administration of justice was confined to the State courts, in which the people of other States had no participation, and over which they had no control. There was then no general court of appellate jurisdiction, by which the errors of State courts, affecting either the nation at large or the citizens of any other State, could be revised and corrected.

§ 507. When laws became necessary to secure the interests of the confederacy, under the Articles of Confederation, and to exact obedience and punish disobedience by fines or otherwise, Congress was obliged to request the State legislatures to pass and enforce such laws. This was among the evils against which the people of the United States thought proper to provide by a national judiciary. Hence one of the objects of the new Constitution is stated in the preamble, to be "to establish justice."

§ 508. The Constitution itself establishes one Supreme Court, but it leaves the establishment of inferior tribunals to Congress.

§ 509. By Art. II. sec. 2, clause 2, the President is authorized to nominate, and, by and with the consent of the Senate, appoint judges of the Supreme Court. The appointment of the judges of the inferior courts is also vested in the President by virtue of his authority to appoint all officers of the United States, whose appointments are not by the Constitution otherwise provided for.

§ 510. The judges, both of the supreme and inferior courts, hold their office, not necessarily for life, or for a definite term of years, but during good behaviour, and their compensation cannot be diminished during their continuance in office. The main object of these provisions is to make the judiciary independent of the other departments of the government, in order to insure boldness and honesty in the discharge of their duties. Nor, for the same reason, can the judges be removed from office by Congress or the President, except upon impeachment and conviction for treason, bribery, and other high crimes and misdemeanors.

§ 511. Though the salary of the judges cannot be diminished, it may be increased, during their continuance in office. If there was no power to increase their pay, according to the increase of business, during the life of the judges, it might happen that their compensation would become wholly inadequate to the additional amount of labour.

§ 512. The Supreme Court of the United States is composed of one chief justice and eight associate justices, and holds, at the city of Washington, one session annually, commencing on the first Monday of December. Any five of the justices constitute a quorum. The associates take precedence according to the date of their commissions, or, where they bear date on the same day, according to their ages.

The salary of the chief justice is $6500 a year; of each of the associate justices, $6000.

The following is a list of the chief justices of the Supreme Court of the United States:—

John Jay, of New York. Appointed 26th September, 1789. Resigned.

John Rutledge, of South Carolina. Appointed 1st July, 1795, in recess of the Senate. Rejected by the Senate 15th December, 1795.

Oliver Ellsworth, of Connecticut. Appointed 4th March, 1796. Resigned.

John Marshall, of Virginia. (Secretary of State.) Appointed 31st January, 1801.

Roger B. Taney, of Maryland. Appointed 15th March, 1836.

The following is a list of the present associate justices of the Supreme Court:—

John McLean, of Ohio. Appointed March 7, 1829.
James M. Wayne, of Georgia. Appointed January 9, 1835.
John Catron, of Tennessee. Appointed March 8, 1837.
Peter V. Daniel, of Virginia. Appointed March 3, 1841.
Samuel Nelson, of New York. Appointed February 14, 1845.
Robert C. Grier, of Pennsylvania Appointed August 4, 1846.

BENJAMIN ROBBINS CURTIS, of Massachusetts. Appointed December 20, 1851.

JOHN A. CAMPBELL, of Alabama. Appointed March 22, 1853.

§ 513. In addition to the Supreme Court, Congress, under the authority given to establish inferior courts, has established Circuit Courts and District Courts. The United States are divided into nine circuits, one circuit for each of the judges of the Supreme Court. In each of these circuits a Circuit Court is held, which is composed of the judge of the Supreme Court for that circuit, and the district judge for that district. The Circuit Court is held in each circuit twice every year.

§ 514. In addition to the division of the United States into circuits, the States are also, by act of Congress, divided into districts, and a court established in every district, called the District Court of the United States; each State generally forms one district, though some of the larger States are divided into two or more districts.

§ 515. Each court has a clerk appointed by the judge. In each district there is an officer called a marshal, who is appointed by the President and Senate for four years, but removable by the President. He attends the District and Circuit Courts, and executes within his district all their writs. He is the ministerial officer of the court, and his duties correspond generally to those of a sheriff. He gives bond with sureties for the performance of his duties. He appoints deputies, who are also officers of the court, and responsible as such. In each district there is likewise a District Attorney of the United States, who institutes suits for the United States, and conducts the prosecution and trial of all indictments.

§ 516. The fees and costs to be allowed to clerks, marshalls, and attorneys of the Circuit and District Courts of the United States, are regulated by act of Congress, and any officer wilfully or corruptly receiving other or greater fees than those allowed by the act, is liable to fine and imprisonment.

§ 517. By the original jurisdiction of a court, is meant that jurisdiction which is conferred upon a court in the first instance; appellate jurisdiction is exercised by a court to which an appeal is taken from the judgment of another court. Jurisdiction is also concurrent or exclusive. It is concurrent when it may be exercised by either one of two or more courts; it is exclusive when it can be exercised only by one court.

§ 518. The Circuit Courts have original jurisdiction of all suits of a civil nature where the matter in dispute exceeds $500 exclusive of costs, brought by the United States, or where an alien is a party, or where the suit is between a citizen of the State where the suit is brought, and a citizen of another State. It has also jurisdiction in cases arising under the revenue laws of the United States, and the laws relating to copyrights, and to patents for inventions and discoveries.

§ 519. The District Courts have jurisdiction, among other matters, of certain minor crimes and offences committed within their respective districts, or on the high seas; of admiralty and maritime cases; of seizures under the trade laws, and of penalties and forfeitures incurred under those laws.

An appeal may be taken from the District Court to the Circuit Court, where the matter in dispute, exclusive of costs, exceeds the sum or value of fifty dollars.

SECTION. 2. [Clause 1.] "The judicial Power shall extend to all Cases, in Law and Equity, arising under this

Constitution, the Laws of the United States, and Treaties made, or which shall be made, under their Authority;—to all Cases affecting Ambassadors, other public Ministers and Consuls;—to all Cases of admiralty and maritime Jurisdiction;—to Controversies to which the United States shall be a Party;—to Controversies between two or more States;—between a State and Citizens of another State;—between Citizens of different States,—between Citizens of the same State claiming Lands under Grants of different States, and between a State, or the Citizens thereof, and foreign States, Citizens or Subjects."

§ 520. This clause enumerates in detail the subjects over which the courts of the United States have jurisdiction. They are as follows:

(1.) All cases in law and equity arising under the Constitution, the laws of the United States, and treaties made, or which shall be made, under their authority.

(2.) All cases affecting ambassadors, other public ministers, and consuls.

(3.) All cases of admiralty and maritime jurisdiction.

(4.) Controversies to which the United States shall be a party.

(5.) Controversies between two or more States.

(6.) Controversies between a State and citizens of another State.

(7.) Controversies between citizens of different States.

(8.) Controversies between citizens of the same State claiming lands under grants of different States.

(9.) Controversies between a State, or the citizens thereof, and foreign States, citizens, or subjects.

§ 521. The above clause, it will be seen, extends the judicial power of the United States to controversies between a State and citizens of another State. Shortly after the adoption of the Constitution, there was much discussion whether this included suits by an individual against a State, as well as suits by a State against an individual. The Supreme Court decided that both classes of suits were equally included within the language of the Constitution.

§ 522. The States were dissatisfied with this construction of the Constitution; they were unwilling to be subjected to lawsuits by the citizens of other States, deeming it an attribute of their sovereignty as States, that they could not be sued without their consent. Accordingly an amendment to the Constitution in this respect, was proposed by the third Congress, to the legislatures of the States, and on the 8th of January, 1798, President Adams communicated to Congress, by message, that the amendment had been adopted by three-fourths of the States, and it then became a part of the Constitution.

§ 523. The amendment constitutes the eleventh in the series of amendments, and is as follows:—

"The Judicial power of the United States shall not be construed to extend to any suit in law or equity, commenced or prosecuted against one of the United States by Citizens of another State, or by Citizens or Subjects of any Foreign State."

§ 524. It provides that the judicial power of the United States shall not extend to any suit in law or equity prosecuted against one of the United States by citizens of another State, or by citizens or subjects of a foreign State.

The prohibition applies only to citizens or subjects, and does not extend to suits by a State, or by a foreign State, against one of the United States. Such suits may be maintained.

[Clause 2.] "In all Cases affecting Ambassadors, other public Ministers and Consuls, and those in which a State shall be Party, the supreme Court shall have original Jurisdiction. In all the other Cases before mentioned, the supreme Court shall have appellate Jurisdiction, both as to Law and Fact, with such Exceptions, and under such Regulations as the Congress shall make."

§ 525. In some of the cases enumerated in the preceding clause, as in those affecting ambassadors, other public ministers, and consuls, and those in which a State shall be a party, the Supreme Court has original jurisdiction, by which, as we have seen, is meant that those cases may originally, or in the first instance, be brought in the Supreme Court.

§ 526. In all the other cases, the Supreme Court has appellate jurisdiction, by which is meant, that those cases must first be brought in the Circuit Court, District Court, or such other inferior court as Congress shall establish, and may then be carried up to the Supreme Court, in order to have the judgment of the inferior court reversed if it be erroneous. But the judgment of a Circuit Court cannot be brought into the Supreme Court to be examined and reversed or affirmed, unless the matter in dispute exceeds two thousand dollars, exclusive of costs.

§ 527. A final judgment or decree in any suit in the highest court of a State, may, by act of Congress, be brought up to the Supreme Court of the United States, only in three cases:

(1.) Where the validity of a treaty, or statute of, or authority exercised under the United States, was drawn in question in the State Court, and the decision was against its validity.

(2.) Where the validity of any State authority was drawn in question, on the ground of its being contrary to the Constitution, treaties, or laws of the United States, and the decision was in favour of its validity.

(3.) Where the construction of any clause of the Constitution, or of a treaty or statute of, or commission held under the United States, was drawn in question, and the decision was against the title or right claimed under the authority of the United States.

§ 528. By an act approved February 24, 1855, Congress established a court, called the Court of Claims, consisting of three judges, appointed by the President with the advice and consent of the Senate, to hold their office during good behaviour. It is the duty of this court to hear and determine all claims founded upon any law of Congress, or upon any regulation of an executive department, or upon any contract express or implied, with the government of the United States, which may be suggested to it by a petition filed therein; and also all claims which may be referred to the court by either House of Congress. An officer, called the Solicitor for the United States, is appointed by the President, with the advice and consent of the Senate, to represent the government before the court.

§ 529. It is the duty of this court to examine all the claims presented to it, to take testimony in reference thereto, to pronounce judgment either for or against the claim, and to keep a record of its proceedings. At the commencement of each session of Congress, and at the commencement of each month during the session of Congress, the court is to report to Congress the cases upon which they shall have finally acted, stating in each the material facts which they find established by the evidence, with their opinion in the case, and the reasons upon which such opinion is founded; and where the court have determined favourably upon a claim, they, together with the testimony in each case, are to present, along with their report, a bill, which, if enacted by Congress, will carry the decision of the court into effect. The reports of the court, and the proposed bills are then acted upon by Congress when presented, or continued to the following session, and so from Congress to Congress, until finally disposed of.

§ 530. If the report of the court is adverse to the claim, and that decision is confirmed by Congress, such decision is conclusive, and the court cannot at any subsequent period consider those claims, unless such reasons are presented, as by the rules of law, in suits between individuals, would be sufficient ground for granting a new trial.

[Clause 3.] "The Trial of all Crimes, except in Cases of Impeachment, shall be by Jury; and such Trial shall be held in the State where the said Crimes shall have been committed; but when not committed within any State, the Trial shall be at such Place or Places as the Congress may by Law have directed."

§ 531. Impeachments, as we have seen, are tried by the Senate; but the trial of all other crimes is to be by jury. A jury is a body of men selected according to law, for the purpose of inquiring into, and deciding some matter of fact. The jury intended by this clause, consists of twelve citizens, duly qualified by law to serve on juries, selected and sworn to decide questions of fact submitted to them in a court of justice. The decision which they render is called a verdict.

§ 532. The provision that all trials for crimes shall be held in the State where such crimes shall have been committed, is intended to prevent the accused person from being exposed to the expense and danger of a trial at a distance from his residence, or at a place where he might not be able to procure the attendance of his witnesses.

§ 533. If the crime was not committed within a State, as, for instance, on the high seas, Congress may by law direct where the trial shall take place. Such crimes have been directed to be tried in the Circuit or the District courts.

SECTION. 3. [Clause 1.] "Treason against the United States, shall consist only in levying War against them, or in adhering to their Enemies, giving them Aid and Comfort. No Person shall be convicted of Treason unless on the Testimony of two Witnesses to the same overt Act, or on Confession in open Court.

§ 534. The Constitution here declares that treason against the United States shall consist only in two things, namely:—

(1.) In levying war against the United States.

(2.) In adhering to their enemies, giving them aid and comfort.

§ 535. Levying war is the assembling of a body of men to effect by force a treasonable object. A mere conspiracy or agreement to levy war, does not amount to levying war; there must be an actual assembling of men for a treasonable purpose, in order to constitute a levying of war. If war be actually levied, all those who perform any part, however minute, or however remote from the scene of action, and who are really leagued in the general attempt, are to be considered as traitors.

§ 536. Treason is the highest crime against a government, for it is a breach of allegiance; and history shows that in other countries, during times of great political excitement, there is a strong tendency to raise lower offences up to the grade of treason, and punish them as such. It was to prevent this that the Constitution defines particularly what shall constitute treason.

§ 537. It was the same spirit of moderation and caution which led to the other part of the clause, requiring the testimony of two witnesses to the same overt or open act, or else a confession in open court, to justify a conviction for treason. The clearest evidence of guilt is required, because the offence is one of the most serious character.

[Clause 2.] "The Congress shall have Power to declare the Punishment of Treason, but no Attainder of Treason shall work Corruption of Blood, or Forfeiture except during the Life of the Person attainted."

§ 538. An act of Congress passed in 1790, declares that the punishment of treason shall be death by hanging.

The same act provides that whoever has knowledge of the commission of treason against the United States, and shall conceal, and not, as soon as may be, disclose the same to the President of the United States, or to one of the federal judges, or to the governor or a judge of a particular State, shall, on conviction thereof, suffer an imprisonment not exceeding seven years, and be fined not exceeding one thousand dollars. A knowledge and concealment of treason, without assenting to it, is termed misprision of treason.

§ 539. When sentence of death was pronounced, especially after conviction of treason, its consequence, by the ancient law of England, was attainder, and the criminal was said, as a mark of infamy, to become attaint, signifying stained or blackened.

§ 540. Attainder led to a forfeiture of all the lands and personal property of the criminal, to the king; also to what was termed corruption of blood, which disabled the attainted person from inheriting lands from his ancestors, or retaining those he was already in possession of, or transmitting them by descent to his heirs.

§ 541. The result of such attainder and corruption of blood, was really to inflict penalties after the death of the criminal, upon his descendants, for the crime of their ancestor. The Constitution humanely limits the effect of this punishment to the offender himself during his life-time, for it declares that no attainder of treason shall work corruption of blood or forfeiture, except during the life of the person attainted.

§ 542. The clause, however, does not make attainder and corruption of blood a part of the punishment of treason; it simply enacts that Congress shall declare what the punishment of treason shall be, and limits the effect of attainder, should that be made a part of the punishment, to the life of the person attainted. Congress, by an act passed in 1790, enacted that no conviction or judgment for any capital or other offences, shall work corruption of blood, or any forfeiture of estate.

CHAPTER XIV.

MISCELLANEOUS PROVISIONS.

ARTICLE IV.

THIS article consists of several miscellaneous provisions, which do not fall appropriately within either one of the three preceding articles.

"SECTION. 1. Full Faith and Credit shall be given in each State to the public Acts, Records, and judicial Proceedings of every other State. And the Congress may by general Laws prescribe the Manner in which such Acts, Records and Proceedings shall be proved, and the Effect thereof."

§ 543. As a general rule, the courts of one country are not bound to take judicial notice of the acts, records, and proceedings of the courts of a foreign country, or to admit their validity or authority. This rule would produce much inconvenience if applied to the States composing the Union. The Constitution has, therefore, adopted a different principle, and has declared that full faith and credit shall be given in each State to the public acts, records, and judicial proceedings of every other State.

§ 544. Congress, in pursuance of the power here given to pass general laws on the subject, by an act of May 26, 1790, provided a mode by which records and judicial proceedings should be authenticated; namely, by the attestation of the clerk and the seal of the court annexed, if there be a seal, together with a certificate of the judge, chief justice, or presiding magistrate, as the case may be, that the attestation is in due form.

§ 545. Records and judicial proceedings, when thus authenticated, are to have such faith and credit given to them in every court within the United States, as they have by law or usage in the courts of the State from whence they are taken.

SECTION. 2. [Clause 1.] "The Citizens of each State shall be entitled to all Privileges and Immunities of Citizens in the several States."

§ 546. In a Union composed of many States, great difficulties would arise if the citizens of one State were treated as aliens or foreigners, in all the other States. Commercial transactions, the right to make contracts or to hold lands, and the travel, intercourse, and traffic, between the several States, would be seriously embarrassed and obstructed. It was to prevent the occurrence of such evils, that the Constitution wisely extends to the citizens of each State, the privileges and immunities of citizens in the other States.

[Clause 2.] "A Person charged in any State with Treason, Felony, or other Crime, who shall flee from Justice, and be found in another State, shall on Demand of the executive Authority of the State from which he fled, be delivered up, to be removed to the State having Jurisdiction of the Crime."

§ 547. If persons committing a crime in one State could, by fleeing into another State, avoid an arrest, justice would be often defeated and offenders go unpunished. A clause quite similar to the present existed in the Articles of Confederation, (Art. 4, § 2.)

§ 548. In 1793, Congress passed an act to regulate the proceedings when a fugitive from justice is demanded. It declares that whenever the executive authority of any State shall demand any person as a fugitive from justice, of the executive authority of any State to which such person has fled, and shall produce a copy of the indictment found, or an affidavit made before a judge or magistrate of such State, charging the person so demanded with having committed treason, felony, or other crime, certified as authentic by the chief magistrate of the State or territory whence the person so charged has fled, it shall be the duty of the executive authority to cause the fugitive to be arrested and secured, and delivered to the executive authority making the demand, or his agent.

§ 549. The ordinary form of requisition in use by the executives of the several States, comprises, first, a demand upon the governor of the State to which the fugitive is alleged to have fled, for his surrender; secondly, a power to an agent, therein named, authorizing him to keep and secure the fugitive when surrendered; thirdly, affidavits or a bill of indictment, setting forth the offence with which the fugitive is charged; fourthly, an affidavit to the effect that the defendant has fled from the justice of one State, to another; and fifthly, a certificate of authentication by the governor issuing the requisition. Thereupon the executive on whom the requisition is made generally issues his warrant for the arrest of the alleged fugitive, who is delivered over, for trial in the State where the crime was committed.

[Clause 3.] "No Person held to Service or Labour in one State, under the Laws thereof, escaping into anotner, shall, in Consequence of any Law or Regulation therein, be discharged from such Service or Labour, but shall be delivered up on Claim of the Party to whom such Service or Labour may be due."

§ 550. No such provision as the above was contained in the Articles of Confederation, and the want of it was con sidered to be a great inconvenience, especially by the States containing a numerous slave population. The preceding clause relates to fugitives from justice; the present clause relates to fugitives from service or labour.

§ 551. Under this clause the citizens of a slave-holding State are allowed to reclaim their slaves when they escape into other States. So it has been held in some cases, that masters may reclaim apprentices. Fugitives from service or from labour, are not, in consequence of any laws of the State into which they have fled, to be freed from such service or labour, but are to be delivered up on claim of the party entitled to their service or labour.

§ 552. By the general law of nations it seems that no nation is bound to recognise the condition of slavery, with respect to foreign slaves found within its territory, in opposition to its own policy and institutions. Without this clause of the Constitution, the States in which slavery does not exist, might, perhaps, have declared free, all slaves coming within their borders, and thus protected them against the claim of their masters, which at the time of the adoption of the Constitution, when there were slaves in all the States, would have been deemed great injustice.

SECTION. 3. [Clause 1.] "New States may be admitted

by the Congress into this Union; but no new State shall be formed or erected within the Jurisdiction of any other State; nor any State be formed by the Junction of two or more States, or Parts of States, without the Consent of the Legislatures of the States concerned as well as of the Congress."

§ 553. Congress, by this clause, has power to admit new States into the Union. At the adoption of the Constitution the number of original States was thirteen; since then, the power to admit new States has been exercised in the admission of eighteen new States, so that the number of States now is thirty-one.

California, the last of the new States, was admitted into the Union, September 9, 1850.

§ 554. Inasmuch as the United States guarantee to every State a republican form of government, the people asking to be admitted as a new State, have, in practice, been required, before their admission, to submit to Congress a draft of their proposed State Constitution, in order that it may be ascertained whether it is of a republican character. When any of the territories of the United States become sufficiently populous to elect a representative in Congress, they are erected into States, and admitted into the Union as such, on an equal footing with the original States.

§ 555. Congress has not only admitted new States into the Union by virtue of this clause, but it has exercised the right to acquire additional territory by purchase, and by cession or grant.

§ 556. The latter part of the clause was intended to quiet the fears which the large States might entertain, of having their territory divided, so as to form other States, without their assent; and also to allay the apprehensions which the small States might feel, of being merged into adjoining States, or of being united so as to compose larger States. No new States have as yet been formed by the junction of the whole, or of parts, of other States; but States have been admitted into the Union since the adoption of the Constitution, which have been formed from the territory of other States.

[Clause 2.] "The Congress shall have Power to dispose of and make all needful Rules and Regulations respecting the Territory or other Property belonging to the United States; and nothing in this Constitution shall be so construed as to Prejudice any Claims of the United States, or of any particular State."

§ 557. This clause gives to Congress the right to dispose of, and to regulate, the territory or other public property belonging to the United States. The care of the public property which belongs to all the people of the Union, is entrusted to Congress, because it represents all the people.

§ 558. The title of the United States to the public land may be said to be derived from three sources:—

(1.) Treaties with foreign nations, as far as they relate to the acquisition of territory or to the boundaries of the United States.

By the treaty with Great Britain in 1783, certain boundaries of the United States were defined, within which the title of the United States was recognised. By the treaty with France, April 30, 1803, the Territories of Orleans and Louisiana were acquired by the United States, which included the portion of the States of Alabama and Mississippi, south of the thirty-first degree of latitude; the whole of Louisiana, Arkansas, Missouri, Iowa, and that portion of Minnesota west of the Mississippi river, Nebraska, Kansas, and Oregon. The territory forming the State of Florida was ceded by Spain to the United States, by treaty of February 22d, 1819. California, Utah, and New Mexico, are formed out of territory ceded to the United States by Mexico, by a treaty concluded at Guadalupe Hidalgo, February 2d, 1848.

§ 559. (2.) Cessions of territory to the United States by the individual States.

The States of Ohio, Indiana, Illinois, Michigan, Wisconsin, and that part of Minnesota east of the Mississippi river, have been formed out of the North-western Territory, which was ceded and relinquished to the United States, under certain restrictions, by New York, March 1, 1781; by Virginia, March 1, 1784; by Massachusetts, April 19, 1785, and by Connecticut, September 14, 1786.

§ 560. While the Articles of Confederation were pending for adoption, several of the States refused to ratify them, unless those States which had claims to the extensive tract of country lying westward of the frontiers of the United States, and extending to, and beyond the Mississippi river, would abandon their claims in favour of the United States. That region, it was contended, being unsettled at the commencement of the Revolutionary war, was won from England, and from the native Indians, by the blood and treasure of all the States, and should therefore be a common property, to be granted out on terms beneficial to the United States.

§ 561. This subject created the most serious hindrance to the ratification of the Articles of Confederation. Congress on the 6th of September, 1780, earnestly recommended to those States who had claims to the western country, to pass such laws, and give their delegates in Congress such power, as would effectually remove this, the only obstacle to a final ratification of the Articles of Confederation.

§ 562. On the 10th of October, 1780, Congress resolved that the unappropriated lands that may be ceded or relinquished to the United States by any particular State, should be disposed of for the common benefit of the United States, and be settled and formed into distinct republican States, to become members of the Federal Union, and have the same rights of sovereignty, freedom, and independence, as other States; also that the expenses incurred by any State since the commencement of the war, in subduing any British posts, or in maintaining forts or garrisons, for the defence or acquisition of any part of the territory thus ceded or relinquished to the United States, should be reimbursed.

§ 563. It was in pursuance of this resolution that the cessions above mentioned were made by the States. Other cessions of territory were also made by South Carolina in 1787, North Carolina in 1790, and Georgia in 1802, forming parts of the States of Mississippi and Alabama.

(3.) Treaties with the Indians, so far as they relate to the extinguishment of the Indian title to the public lands. Although the United States, in consequence of the treaties and cessions above referred to, own the soil of, and exercise jurisdiction over, the lands inhabited by the Indians, yet it has been conceded that the Indians have a right of occupancy, or a possessory right, as natives. This right of occupancy, or of possession, has been, from time to time, extinguished or purchased by the United States, by treaties made with the Indian tribes.

§ 564. It is under this clause of the Constitution that Congress exercises the power to dispose of the public lands by sale or grant. All public lands, before being offered for sale, are accurately surveyed by practical surveyors, in ranges of townships, each six miles square, containing therefore 23,040 acres. Townships are subdivided by lines crossing each other at right angles, and running to the cardinal points of the compass, into thirty-six sections, each of one mile square, or 640 acres.

§ 565. The sections are numbered from one to thirty-six, beginning at the northeast corner of the township and counting alternately from east to west and west to east. The sections are again divided into quarters, each containing 160 acres. Prior to 1820, no person could purchase less than a quarter section; but in that year legal authority was given for the division of the sections into eighths, containing eighty acres; and in 1832, as a further accommodation to settlers, they were divided into sixteenths, or forty-acre lots. Certain sections or townships of land in each territory, are reserved for schools or for the establishment of a university.

§ 566. The corners of townships, sections, and quarter sections, are designated by marks established by the surveyors on the ground.

After the lands have been thus surveyed, they are proclaimed by the President for sale, and offered at public auction, at not less than a dollar and twenty-five cents per acre; and such as remain unsold at the close of such public sale, are subject to be purchased at private sale at that rate.

§ 567. By an act passed August 4, 1854, the price of the public lands was graduated and reduced in favour of those who should actually settle upon and cultivate them. Lands (with a few exceptions) which shall have been in the market for ten years or upward prior to the application to purchase, are made subject to sale to actual settlers and cultivators at the price of one dollar per acre; those which have been in the market for fifteen years or upward, may be sold at seventy-five cents per acre; for twenty years or upward, fifty cents per acre; for twenty-five years or upward, twenty-five cents per acre; for thirty years or upward, twelve and a half cents per acre. But no settler is allowed to acquire more than three hundred and twenty acres in pursuance of these provisions.

§ 568. Land offices are established in the different States and territories, under the supervision of the General Land Office, for the sale of the public lands. Each office is under the direction of two officers: a register, who receives the applications and sells the lands; and a receiver, who receives the purchase-money. These two officers act as a check upon each other. The grant for the land, issued by the United States, is termed a patent.

§ 569. The patents issue from the General Land Office, under its seal, in the name of the United States, signed by the President of the United States, (or by a secretary who is authorized by law to sign for him,) and countersigned by the Commissioner of Public Lands; they are then recorded in the land office in books kept for that purpose.

§ 570. Under this clause in the Constitution, Congress from time to time erects governments in portions of the territories of the United States. These are regularly organized territorial governments. They include a governor, judges, and other officers, appointed by the President, and a legislature elected by the people of the territory, and are allowed one delegate in the House of Representatives, who may participate in the debates, but cannot vote.

§ 571. The organized territories, after their population has sufficiently increased to entitle them to a representative in Congress according to the ratio of representation, m y apply for admission into the Union as States. But they cannot be admitted unless they establish a republican form of government, and the Constitution which they propose to adopt, must, prior to their admission, be submitted to and approved by Congress.

§ 572. There are at present seven organized territories, viz:

(1.) Oregon Territory; erected into a territory August 14, 1848.

(2.) Minnesota Territory; erected into a territory March 3, 1849.

(3.) Utah Territory; erected into a territory September 9, 1850.

(4.) New Mexico Territory; erected into a territory September 9, 1850.

(5.) Washington Territory; erected into a territory March 2, 1853.

(6.) Kansas Territory; erected into a territory May 30, 1854.

(7.) Nebraska Territory; erected into a territory May 30, 1854.

The Indian Territory is not an organized territory.

§ 573. The limits of the United States, at the treaty of peace which closed the Revolution, are estimated to have included not more than 820,680 square miles. The total area of the Union on the first of July, 1854, was, by official calculations estimated at 2,963,666 square miles. Our territory doubled itself in the first twenty years of its existence, and it has increased over threefold in less than sixty years.

We have now a territorial extent nearly ten times as large as that of Great Britain and France combined; three times as large as the whole of France, Britain, Austria,

Prussia, Spain, Portugal, Belgium, Holland, and Denmark together; one and a half times as large as the Russian empire in Europe; about one-sixth less than the area of all Europe, and of equal extent with the Roman empire, or that of Alexander, neither of which is said to have exceeded 3,000,000 square miles.

SECTION. 4. [Clause 4.] "The United States shall guarantee to every State in this Union a Republican Form of Government, and shall protect each of them against Invasion, and on Application of the Legislature, or of the Executive (when the Legislature cannot be convened) against domestic Violence."

§ 574. The Articles of Confederation contained no provision similar to the above, which was one cause of the weakness of the government under those Articles. This section contains three important particulars:

(1.) A guaranty of a republican form of government to the States.

(2.) Protection of the States against invasion.

(3.) Protection of the States against domestic violence.

§ 575. The United States guarantees to every State in the Union, a republican form of government. An outbreak or rebellion in a single State, might be strong enough not only to establish therein a monarchical or despotic form of government, but to endanger the whole Union. Without a provision like that we are now considering, the State in which such an attempt should be made would have no right to call upon the general government for protection, and the general government would have no legal right, and would be under no obligation, to interfere; whereas now the whole power of the United States, and its army and navy, may be employed to assure to each State the enjoyment of a republican form of government.

§ 576. The guaranty contained in this clause does not restrict the right of a State to alter its constitution at pleasure, but it cannot, while it remains a member of the Union, adopt any other than a republican form of government.

§ 577. The United States is also bound to protect each State from invasion. This secures to every State, the power of the general government for its protection, and it is a great advantage which the Federal Constitution affords.

§ 578. In case of violence within a State, such as riot or rebellion, the legislature of the State, if in session, or, if not in session, the governor, may upon application, obtain the aid of the United States to repress such disorder. Thus each State, under the Constitution, secures the force of the United States for its protection against invasion from without, and from domestic violence, (§ 310.)

CHAPTER XV.

MODE OF AMENDING THE CONSTITUTION—MISCELLANEOUS PROVISIONS.

ARTICLE V.

THIS article treats of the mode of making amendments to the Constitution.

"The Congress, whenever two thirds of both Houses shall deem it necessary, shall propose Amendments to this Constitution, or, on the Application of the Legislatures of two thirds of the several States, shall call a Convention for proposing Amendments, which, in either Case, shall be valid to all Intents and Purposes, as Part of this Constitution, when ratified by the Legislatures of three fourths of the several States, or by Conventions in three fourths thereof, as the one or the other Mode of Ratification may be proposed by the Congress; Provided that no Amendment which may be made prior to the Year one thousand eight hundred and eight shall in any Manner affect the first and fourth Clauses in the Ninth Section of the first Article; and that no State, without its Consent, shall be deprived of its equal Suffrage in the Senate."

§ 579. Unless some peaceable mode of altering the Con stitution be provided, there is danger that violent means would be employed to effect a change. As no form of government, particularly a new and untried one, as ours was, is likely to be perfect, it is necessary that some manner of proceeding should be established, for adopting such amendments as time and experience may render useful or necessary.

§ 580. It is the right of a free people to amend their Constitution or to alter their form of government. This right was proclaimed in the Declaration of Independence, and is recognised by all the States, many of which have, at different times altered their constitutions by the popular vote.

In his Farewell Address to the American people, George Washington declares that the "basis of our political systems is the right of the people to make and to alter their Constitutions of government. But the Constitution which at any time exists, till changed by an explicit and authentic act of the whole people, is sacredly obligatory upon all."

§ 581. Two modes are provided in which amendments to the Constitution of the United States may be proposed. They are as follows:—

(1.) By two-thirds of both Houses of Congress.

(2.) By applications to Congress from the Legislatures of two-thirds of the States, for the calling of a convention for proposing amendments.

§ 582. In either case, whether the amendments originate in Congress, or in a convention called by Congress upon the application of the legislature of two-thirds of the States, the proposed amendments, before they become valid, must be ratified by the legislatures of three-fourths of the States, or by popular conventions in three-fourths of the States, according as the one or the other mode of ratification may be proposed by Congress. In the amendments heretofore made to the Constitution, Congress has proposed a ratification by the legislatures of the States, and not by conventions

§ 583. The object of these provisions is to prevent alterations in the Constitution from being made suddenly and without due deliberation, or against the consent of a large number of States.

§ 584. It will be seen that Congress, of itself, has no power to amend or alter the Constitution, and that although an amendment may be proposed by two-thirds of both Houses of Congress, yet it cannot be adopted unless by consent of the legislatures of, or by conventions called in, three-fourths of the States. The approval of the President has not been considered necessary to amendments to the Constitution. In England, Parliament has, of itself, the legal power to alter the form of government, without regard to the expressed wish or consent of the people.

§ 585. Originally there were three provisions of the Constitution, which were placed beyond the power of alteration. The first and fourth clauses of the ninth section of the first article, were not to be affected by any amendment which might be made before the year 1808.

§ 586. The former of those clauses declares that the migration or importation of such persons as any of the States shall think proper to admit, shall not be prohibited by Congress prior to 1808; the latter provides that no capitation or other direct tax shall be laid, unless in proportion to the census.

§ 587. The slave-holding States were not to be prohibited from importing slaves prior to 1808. They were also chargeable with direct taxes in proportion to the census or enumeration. So long, therefore, as they were allowed to increase their population by the importation of slaves, they were in a corresponding proportion to be subject to direct taxation. But as the limit upon that importation expired in 1808, the clause relative to the manner of laying direct taxes has since that time been open to amendment equally with the other parts of the Constitution.

§ 588. The third restriction upon the power of amendment is, that no State shall, without its consent, be deprived of its equal suffrage in the Senate. This is a permanent restriction. The object of it is to protect the smaller States.

§ 589. Since the adoption of the Constitution there have been fifteen articles added thereto, which we will consider hereafter; but no part of the Constitution, as originally framed, has been repealed or altered, except the manner of electing the President and the Vice-President, and article III., sec. 2, clause 1, so far as it authorized, or was supposed to authorize, suits against one of the United States by a citizen of another State, or of a foreign State.

ARTICLE VI.

This article consists of additional miscellaneous provisions.

[Clause 1.] "All Debts contracted and Engagements entered into, before the Adoption of this Constitution, shall be as valid against the United States under this Constitution, as under the Confederation."

§ 590. It is a general principle of the law of nations, that States are not discharged from their obligations, and do not lose their rights, by a change in their form of government.

§ 591. Without this clause the United States would, therefore, have been liable after the adoption of the Constitution, for all the debts and engagements entered into under the Confederation. The provision was inserted expressly, doubtless from a desire to allay the fears of creditors, and to assure the world that the United States, by abolishing their old, and adopting a new form of government, did not refuse to satisfy their debts and engagements.

[Clause 2.] "This Constitution, and the Laws of the United States which shall be made in Pursuance thereof; and all Treaties made, or which shall be made, under the authority of the United States, shall be the supreme Law of the Land; and the Judges in every State shall be bound thereby, any Thing in the Constitution or Laws of any State to the Contrary notwithstanding."

§ 592. The federal government would have been wholly valueless and inoperative if its Constitution and laws were not to be obeyed by the States. Indeed it would not be a government in any proper sense, if the States were independent of it, and could legislate without regard to it.

§ 593. Not only are the Constitution and laws of the United States made the supreme law of the land, but all treaties under the authority of the United States are also a part of the supreme law of the land. Treaties are negotiated by the national government, and there should be some mode of enforcing their observance upon all the States. If the States could, at their pleasure, disregard solemn treaties, foreign nations would soon cease to make treaties with us, for there would be no assurance that our treaties would be observed. It was a serious defect of the government under the Articles of Confederation, that the States slighted the obligation of treaties.

§ 594. It is only those laws passed by Congress in pursuance of the Constitution, that become the supreme law of the land. If an act of Congress be contrary to the Constitution, it is no part of the supreme law.

§ 595. The judges of every State are bound by the Constitution, the constitutional laws, and the treaties of the United States; and every thing contrary thereto in the Constitution, laws, decisions, or proceedings of any State, or even in the Acts of Congress, is void and of no effect.

§ 596. According to law and practice in England, Parliament is supreme, and an act of Parliament once passed, becomes a part of the law of the land and demands perfect obedience. It is not always so here with an act of Congress. If it should be contrary to the Constitution of the United States, it is the right and the duty of the judiciary, to declare it void and of no effect. The reason of this is, that the written Constitution limits the powers of Congress, and if Congress may, notwithstanding, go beyond those limits, the Constitution ceases to have any binding operation in that respect.

[Clause 2.] "The Senators and Representatives before mentioned, and the Members of the several State Legislatures, and all executive and judicial Officers, both of the United States and of the several States, shall be bound by Oath or Affirmation, to support this Constitution; but no religious Test shall ever be required as a Qualification to any Office or public Trust under the United States."

§ 597. The previous clause declares that the Constitution of the United States shall be the supreme law of the land; the present clause is intended to secure its observance as such, by the solemn sanction of an oath or affirmation. Fidelity to the Constitution is a test or qualification for legislative, judicial, or executive office, under the general government and in the several States.

§ 598. Senators, representatives, executive officers, and judicial officers of the United States, are required to be bound by oath or affirmation to support the Constitution, because they are directly concerned in its execution and administration. The corresponding officers of the several States are also required to be bound in like manner, because they owe obedience to the Federal Constitution as the supreme law of the land.

§ 599. June 1, 1789, Congress passed an act declaring that the oath or affirmation required by this clause shall be administered in the following form: "*I, A. B., do solemnly swear or affirm* (as the case may be) *that I will support the Constitution of the United States.*" The act further declares the time and manner of administering the oath. At the first session of Congress, after every general election of Representatives, the oath is to be administered to the Speaker by any one member of the House of Representatives, (in practice this is done by the oldest members of the House, successively,) and then by the Speaker to all the members present, and to the clerk, previous to entering on any other business.

§ 600. The President of the Senate for the time being, also administers the oath or affirmation to each newly-elected Senator, previous to his taking his seat; and if the President of the Senate has not himself taken the oath, it is administered to him by any one of the members of the Senate.

§ 601. The members of the several State legislatures, and all the executive and judicial officers of the States, are required, before they proceed to execute the duties of their respective offices, to take the oath or affirmation, to be administered by the person who is authorized by the law of the State to administer the oath of office, and a record or certificate is to be made of it, in like manner as of the oath of office.

§ 602. All officers appointed under the authority of the United States, are required to take the oath or affirmation before entering upon their official duties.

§ 603. This clause contains the important provision that no religious test shall ever be required as a qualification to any office or public trust under the United States. This prohibition was intended to restrain the effects of sectarian bigotry and intolerance, and prevent a union of church and State, such as we find in England and in many countries on the continent of Europe.

§ 604. In England, and in some other countries, public officers, before entering on the discharge of their official duties, are required to take an oath or make a declaration in favour of the established religion of the country. Such oaths or declarations are called tests. The Constitution of the United States does not establish any particular form of religious worship, or restrain the free exercise of any form, and it therefore abolishes religious tests, as inconsistent with its principles of religious liberty.

"Article VII. The Ratification of the Conventions of nine States, shall be sufficient for the Establishment of this Constitution between the States so ratifying the Same."

§ 605. At the time of the formation of the Constitution there were thirteen States. This clause does not require that all the States should assent to the Constitution, for a single State would then have been enabled to defeat the wishes of all the others. Nor does it make a majority sufficient; but it adopts a medium course, and declares that the ratification by the conventions of nine States shall be sufficient for the establishment of the Constitution between the States thus ratifying it.

§ 606. Had the Constitution been ratified by no more than nine States, those nine States only would have composed the Union, and the remaining States would not have been members of it.

For the proceedings attending the ratification of the Constitution, see § 46.

§ 607. The final clause of the Constitution is as follows:—

> "DONE in Convention by the Unanimous Consent of the States present the Seventeenth day of September in the Year of our Lord one thousand seven hundred and Eighty seven and of the Independence of the United States of America the Twelfth. **In Witness** whereof We have hereunto subscribed our Names."

It was then signed by

G° WASHINGTON—

Presidt and deputy from Virginia,

and by thirty-eight other delegates, being one or more from each of the original thirteen States, except Rhode Island, by whom no delegate was appointed.

CHAPTER XVI.

ARTICLES IN ADDITION TO, AND AMENDMENT OF THE CONSTITUTION.

§ 608. MUCH opposition was made to the ratification of the Constitution, in the conventions called by the States. The reasons for the opposition were different in their nature, but a very general opinion was entertained, that something should be added in the nature of a Declaration of Rights, which should positively assert and establish certain rights of the people. Many of the States, although they ratified the Constitution, expressed a wish that such amendments should be adopted.

§ 609. Accordingly, at the first session of the first Congress, begun and held in the city of New York, March 4, 1789, Congress, after duly considering the fact that the conventions of a number of the States, at the time of their adopting the Constitution, expressed a desire, in order to prevent misconstruction or abuse of its powers, that further declaratory and restrictive clauses should be adopted, passed a resolution on the 25th of September, 1789, two-thirds of both houses concurring, to propose twelve articles to the legislatures of the States, as amendments to the Constitution.

§ 610. Ten of those articles having been finally ratified by the legislatures of three-fourths of the States, became amendments of the Constitution of the United States on the 15th day of December, 1791.

§ 611. These amendments, constituting the first ten of

the whole number of amendments, were ratified by the States, as follows:—

By New Jersey, 20th November, 1789.
By Maryland, 19th December, 1789.
By North Carolina, 22d December, 1789.
By South Carolina, 19th January, 1790.
By New Hampshire, 25th January, 1790.
By Delaware, 28th January, 1790.
By Pennsylvania, 10th March, 1790.
By New York, 27th March, 1790.
By Rhode Island, 15th June, 1790.
By Vermont, 3d November, 1791.
By Virginia, 15th December, 1791.

§ 612. Subsequently another amendment, the eleventh, was proposed at the first session of the third Congress, 5th March, 1794, and was declared in a message from the President of the United States to both houses of Congress, dated 8th January, 1798, to have been adopted by the constitutional number of States. The twelfth amendment was proposed at the first session of the eighth Congress, 12th December, 1803, and was adopted by the constitutional number of States in 1804.

613. We have already presented these amendments, commencing on page 48, and we are now to consider each one in its order:

"ARTICLE I. Congress shall make no law respecting an establishment of religion, or prohibiting the free exercise thereof; or abridging the freedom of speech, or of the press; or the right of the people peaceably to assemble, and to petition the Government for a redress of grievances."

§ 614. We have already seen that no religious test can ever be required as a qualification to any office or public trust under the United States, (§ 603.) The object of the present amendment is to go still further, and in general terms to restrict Congress from making any law respecting an establishment of religion, or prohibiting the free exercise thereof. One purpose sought to be effected by this provision, is to prevent the supremacy of any religious denomination in consequence of national patronage, or by authority of law, and to maintain the separation of church and State.

§ 615. At the same time the Constitution extends its protection alike to all religious denominations, and by thus allowing to every citizen the free exercise of religion according to the dictates of his conscience, secures equal religious liberty. In this way the Constitution seeks to avoid the injustice, intolerance, and other evils which have accompanied the establishment of State religions in the Old World.

§ 616. This article also prohibits Congress from making any law abridging the freedom of speech or of the press. The liberty of speech and of the press has always been considered to be the right of a free people. In many countries, however, it is narrowly restricted. Some governments prohibit the printing of books on particular subjects, unless they have been previously examined and approved by an officer of the government. Others require an author to obtain a license before he can publish. Similar restraints have been applied also to newspapers and periodicals, which are even now in some countries subjected to a censorship and to other restrictions.

§ 617. Although, by the Constitution, a man may freely speak, write, and publish his sentiments on all subjects, yet that liberty may be abused, in which case the law holds the wrong-doer responsible for such abuse. One man has no right to speak or publish false, scandalous, and malicious matter concerning another; such things constitute slanders or libels, and are punishable by law. The liberty of speech or of the press does not justify a publication of what is mischievous, immoral, or illegal. That is licentiousness, not liberty.

§ 618. By our law no man can be restrained from publishing whatever he pleases, because he is not under any obligation to submit his works to the examination of any person previous to publication, and, until publication, no one can know what the work contains. But the author and publisher are both held answerable civilly for damages done to individuals, and criminally for the public offence, if any is committed by such publication, in whatever it may consist, whether in its tendency to lead to a breach of the peace or to corrupt the public morals.

§ 619. The last clause of this article declares that Congress shall make no law abridging the right of the people peaceably to assemble and to petition the government for a redress of grievances.

§ 620. The people have a natural right to petition their rulers for a redress of grievances, and it is the object of this clause to protect the right from violation by Congress. It must, however, be exercised peaceably, lest, under pretence of assembling to discuss political subjects or to petition the government, riotous, tumultuous, and disorderly proceedings take place.

§ 621. Petitions and memorials may be addressed to the Senate or House of Representatives by any person, or any number of persons, and are presented by the presiding officer, or by a member, who makes verbally a brief state ment of their contents. They are then discussed and disposed of according to the rules and practice of the Senate or of the House, as the case may be.

"ARTICLE II. A well regulated Militia, being necessary t. the security of a free State, the right of the people to keep and bear Arms, shall not be infringed."

§ 622. If citizens are allowed to keep and bear arms, it will be likely to operate as a check upon their rulers, and restrain them from acts of tyranny and usurpation. The necessity of maintaining a large standing army is also diminished by arming and disciplining the citizens generally, so that they may be ready and qualified at any time, to defend the country in a sudden emergency.

"ARTICLE III. No Soldier shall, in time of peace be quartered in any house, without the consent of the Owner, nor in time of war, but in a manner to be prescribed by law."

§ 623. It has been a frequent practice in arbitrary governments to compel the subjects to board or lodge the soldiers of the army in time of peace. It is evident that this violates the dominion which every man should have over his own house. The above article prohibits such quartering, as it is called, of soldiers in the houses of citizens in time of peace against the consent of the owner, and provides that, if soldiers be quartered in the houses of citizens in time of War, it shall be done, not arbitrarily or capriciously, but in such manner as shall be prescribed by law.

"ARTICLE IV. The right of the people to be secure in their persons, houses, papers, and effects, against unreasonable searches and seizures, shall not be violated, and no Warrants shall issue, but upon probable cause, supported by Oath or affirmation, and particularly describing the place to be searched, and the persons or things to be seized."

§ 624. The object of this article is to protect the personal liberty and private property of the citizens from interference. It secures the persons, houses, papers, and effects of the people from all unreasonable and illegal searches and seizures.

§ 625. It was an ancient doctrine of the common law of England, and one that has been adopted in this country, that "the house of every one is to him as his castle and fortress, as well for his defence against injury and violence, as for his repose." But the house of any is not a castle or privilege but for himself, and does not extend to a person who flies to his house, or the goods of any other which are brought into his house, to prevent a lawful execution, and to escape the ordinary process of law; for the privilege of his house extends only to him and his family, and to his own proper goods, or to those which are there lawfully and without fraud.

§ 626. A search-warrant is a writ requiring the officer to whom it is addressed, to search a house or other place, for property, generally such as is alleged to be stolen, and if it be found, to bring the goods together with the person occupying the premises, who is named in the warrant, before the officer issuing it, or some other legally authorized officer.

§ 627. Warrants are mentioned in English history, and known by the name of general warrants, which authorized the officer, in general language, to search any place or to arrest any person he suspected, without describing or naming either the place or the person, and without stating any probable cause for the search. Such warrants are prohibited by this article, which provides that no warrant shall issue except upon probable cause, supported by oath or affirmation, and particularly describing the place to be searched, and the person or things to be seized.

"ARTICLE V. No person shall be held to answer for a capital, or otherwise infamous crime, unless on a presentment or indictment of a Grand Jury, except in cases arising in the land or naval forces, or in the Militia, when in actual service in time of War or public danger; nor shall any person be subject for the same offence to be twice put in jeopardy of life or limb; nor shall be compelled in any Criminal Case to be a witness against himself, nor be deprived of life, liberty, or property, without due process of law; nor shall private property be taken for public use, without just compensation."

§ 628. A grand jury is a body of men chosen in the manner prescribed by law, at every term of a court having criminal jurisdiction. In the State courts they are selected by the sheriff; in the Federal courts, by the marshal. Their number must not be less than twelve, nor greater than twenty-four. Their duty is to inquire into all crimes committed within the jurisdiction of the court in which they are attending.

§ 629. The sittings of the grand jury are private. They examine under oath the party making the charge, (who is called the prosecutor,) and his witnesses; but they do not hear any witnesses in defence. If twelve of the jurors believe that there is sufficient evidence of guilt, to require the accused to be put on trial to answer a bill of indictment for the alleged offence, which has been submitted to them by the prosecuting officer of the government, they endorse on the bill the words "a true bill," to which the foreman of the jury subscribes his name and the date. The bill is then said to be found, and is taken into court by the jury and delivered to the judge. The party charged is then held to answer, and is put on his trial in due course of law.

§ 630. If the grand jury think the accusation is not sufficiently proved, they endorse on the back of the bill "not a true bill," or "not found," or "ignoramus," meaning we are ignorant of the matter, and the bill is then said to be ignored. An indictment is founded upon the testimony of witnesses examined before the grand jurors in support of a bill; a presentment is the notice taken by a grand jury of an offence, from their own knowledge, or upon evidence brought before them where no bill of indictment has been submitted to them by the prosecuting officer.

§ 631. In the army and navy, and in the militia, when in actual service, offences are tried and punished in a different mode, by courts-martial, or otherwise, according to the order of proceeding pointed out in the articles for the government of the army and navy. Excepting in cases thus arising in the land or naval forces, or in the militia, when in actual service in time of war or public danger, it is declared by this article that no person shall be held to answer for a capital or otherwise infamous crime, unless on presentment or indictment of a grand jury. Capital crimes are those the punishment of which is death.

§ 632. The next provision in the article is, that no person shall be subject to be twice put in jeopardy of life or limb for the same offence; in other words, a party cannot be tried a second time, for the same offence of which he has already been once acquitted or convicted. Where a man, after a regular acquittal before a competent court, on a sufficient indictment, is indicted again for the same offence, the former acquittal is an effectual answer to the second indictment.

§ 633. When the jury on the first trial have been discharged, under circumstances in which there was a necessity for the act, and they consequently did not give any verdict, or where, after a verdict has been given against the person charged, he has had a new trial granted him by the court, he may still be tried a second time, for in such cases it is not considered that he has legally been put in jeopardy of life or limb.

§ 634. It is next provided that no person shall be compelled in any criminal case to be a witness against himself. Torture and other forcible means have been resorted to in some countries to obtain from criminals, confessions or admissions to be used as evidence against themselves. Such cruel and unjust proceedings are effectually prohibited by this clause. In all criminal cases the guilt of the prisoner must be proved, if proved at all, by the evidence brought forward against him. If that evidence be insufficient, he must be acquitted. The law presumes that he is innocent, until the contrary appears. His free, voluntary admissions may be given in evidence; but he cannot be compelled to testify against himself. He cannot even be questioned as to his guilt or innocence.

§ 635. The next provision is, that no person shall be

deprived of life, liberty, or property without due process of law.

This is an important provision, and of very extensive signification. It is a principle of justice that the life, liberty, and property of a citizen should be protected from all illegal interference on the part, either of other citizens, or of the rulers. Government would otherwise become impossible, and would degenerate into a mere instrument of unlimited oppression. The general meaning of the clause is, that no citizen shall be deprived of his life, his liberty, or his property, except by the regular administration of the laws of the land.

§ 636. The last clause of the article declares that private property shall not be taken for public use, without just compensation.

It is evident that there would be no security for the property of a citizen if it could be taken from him at the will of the government. On the other hand, necessity or the public good may sometimes require that private property shall yield to the general interest. Accordingly, there is a right, called the right of eminent domain, by which the government, in certain cases, may take the property of individuals for public purposes. It is by virtue of this right that highways, turnpikes, railroads, canals, bridges, and other public improvements, are authorized to be laid out through or upon the property of individuals, even against their consent.

§ 637. The reason of this is that the public interest of the whole community is considered to be superior to the private interest of a single individual. But the article we are now considering imposes an important check upon the exercise of this right, by declaring that private property cannot be taken for public use, unless just compensation is made to the owner. To take it, even for public use, without such compensation for the damages done to the owner, would be illegal and unconstitutional. The amount of compensation may be ascertained in any just mode pointed out by law; it is generally required to be determined by a jury, who may examine the premises, and must give each party an opportunity to be fully heard and to produce witnesses.

§ 638. Property taken compulsorily, in the exercise of the right of eminent domain, must be taken for public uses and service. The property of an individual cannot be taken, even under the authority of the government, for private uses, without the consent of the owner.

"Article VI. In all criminal prosecutions, the accused shall enjoy the right to a speedy and public trial, by an impartial jury of the State and district wherein the crime shall have been committed, which district shall have been previously ascertained by law, and to be informed of the nature and cause of the accusation; to be confronted with the witnesses against him; to have Compulsory process for obtaining Witnesses in his favour, and to have the Assistance of Counsel for his defence.

§ 639. The above article contains several important provisions, the object of which is to secure justice and impartiality in the trial of criminal prosecutions.

§ 640. The accused is to have a speedy and public trial, by an impartial jury of the State and district wherein the crime has been committed, which district shall have been previously ascertained by law. The trial is to be speedy, otherwise justice might be unreasonably delayed; it is to be public, for publicity is more likely to ensure fairness on the part of the court and jury.

§ 641. The impartiality of the jury is further secured by a right which the prisoner has by law, to challenge, or object to such jurors as have formed and expressed an opinion about his guilt, or are otherwise disqualified to sit as jurors. We have already seen, (§ 514,) that the States are, by act of Congress, divided into judicial districts, in each of which is established a district court for, among other purposes, the trial of criminal cases.

§ 642. The prisoner is to be informed of the nature and cause of the accusation, so that he will know what the charge is which he is to meet. The bill of indictment against him is required by the rules of law, to set forth the offence charged, and the circumstances of its commission. The witnesses against him are to be examined in his presence; he is entitled to a subpœna, or other compulsory process of the court, for obtaining witnesses in his favour, and he is allowed the assistance of legal counsel for his defence.

"ARTICLE VII. In suits at common law, where the value in controversy shall exceed twenty dollars, the right of trial by jury shall be preserved, and no fact tried by a jury, shall be otherwise re-examined in any Court of the United States, than according to the rules of the common law."

§ 643. The Constitution, as we have seen in art. III., sec. 2, clause 3, declares that the trial of all crimes, except in cases of impeachment, shall be by jury. It did not, however, contain any express provision for trial by jury in civil cases. From the silence of the Constitution on this subject, the opponents of its ratification argued that it tended to abolish the trial by jury in civil cases.

§ 644. This amendment was adopted to meet the objection. It preserves the right of trial by jury in suits at common law, (by which is meant the common law of England as adopted in this country,) where the value in controversy exceeds twenty dollars. The judicial power of the United States (by art. III., sec. 2, clause 3) extends to all cases in law and equity arising under the Constitution and laws of the United States, and to all cases of admiralty and maritime jurisdiction. It is only in the cases at law, or as it is called in this article, common law, that the right of trial by jury is preserved. In cases of equity, and of admiralty or maritime jurisdiction, the mode of trial is different, for the judge in such cases determines the facts as well as the law.

§ 645. It is also provided in this clause that no fact tried by a jury shall be otherwise re-examined in any court of the United States, than according to the rules of the common law. There are certain modes, such, among others, as motion for new trial, or writ of error, known to the common law, in which facts tried by a jury in any case can be re-examined by the court in which the cause was tried, or by another court. This article, in order to give full force and effect to the verdict of a jury, so that it may not be arbitrarily disregarded, declares that no fact which has once been tried by a jury, shall be examined again in any court of the United States, except according to the rules of the common law, such, for instance, as those mentioned above.

"ARTICLE VIII. Excessive bail shall not be required,

nor excessive fines imposed, nor cruel and unusual punishments inflicted."

§ 646. By bail is meant the security given for the release of a prisoner from custody, and his appearance at a particular day, in court, or at a certain place. A party who produces sureties, who become bound for his future appearance, is said to be admitted to bail; he is then discharged from custody, and the sureties become responsible for his appearance at the time and place named. If bail is required in a very large amount, it would be difficult, or perhaps impossible, for a citizen to obtain sureties willing to assume so great a responsibility, and the party would then be committed to prison in default of bail. In order that oppression may not be practised in this way, it is provided that excessive bail shall not be required.

§ 647. The courts are frequently authorized by law to punish offences by fines. If these fines are extravagant in amount, it may be beyond the prisoner's ability to pay them. This article, therefore, declares that excessive fines shall not be imposed; and in the same spirit of mildness it also prohibits the infliction of cruel and unusual punishments.

"ARTICLE IX. The enumeration in the Constitution, of certain rights, shall not be construed to deny or disparage others retained by the people."

§ 648. This means that, because the Constitution recites particular rights which belong to the people, it is not therefore to be inferred that the people have no other rights. The enumeration of certain rights is not to be construed as a denial or disparagement of other rights retained by the people.

"ARTICLE X. The powers not delegated to the United States by the Constitution, nor prohibited by it to the States, are reserved to the States respectively, or to the people."

§ 649. The government of the United States is one of defined and limited extent. It is created by the Constitution, and possesses only such powers as are conferred upon it by the Constitution. It can exercise no powers but those which it derives from the Constitution. The States were jealous of their own sovereignty, and were fearful that their rights would be diminished or invaded by the general government. Hence this amendment was adopted, which provides expressly that the powers which are not delegated to the United States by the Constitution, nor prohibited by it to the States, are to be considered as retained by the States or by the people.

"ARTICLE XI. The Judicial power of the United States shall not be construed to extend to any suit in law or equity, commenced or prosecuted against one of the United States by Citizens of another State, or by Citizens or Subjects of any Foreign State."

We have already spoken of this article. See § 524.

"ARTICLE XII. The Electors shall meet in their respective states, and vote by ballot for President and Vice-President, one of whom, at least, shall not be an inhabitant of the same state with themselves; they shall name in their ballots the person voted for as President, and in distinct ballots the person voted for as Vice-President, and they shall make distinct lists of all persons voted for as

President, and of all persons voted for as Vice-President, and of the number of votes for each, which lists they shall sign and certify, and transmit sealed to the seat of the government of the United States, directed to the President of the Senate;—The President of the Senate shall, in presence of the Senate and House of Representatives, open all the certificates and the votes shall then be counted;—The person having the greatest number of votes for President, shall be the President, if such number be a majority of the whole number of Electors appointed; and if no person have such majority, then from the persons having the highest numbers not exceeding three on the list of those voted for as President, the House of Representatives shall choose immediately, by ballot, the President. But in choosing the President, the votes shall be taken by states, the representation from each state having one vote; a quorum for this purpose shall consist of a member or members from two-thirds of the states, and a majority of all the states shall be necessary to a choice. And if the House of Representatives shall not choose a President whenever the right of choice shall devolve upon them, before the fourth day of March next following, then the Vice-President shall act as President, as in the case of the death or other constitutional disability of the President.—The person having the greatest number of votes as Vice-President, shall be the Vice-President, if such number be a majority of the whole number of Electors appointed, and if no person have a majority, then from the two highest numbers on the list, the Senate shall choose the Vice-President; a quorum for the purpose shall consist of two-thirds of the whole number of Senators, and a majority of the whole number shall be necessary to a choice. But no person constitutionally ineligible to the office of President shall be eligible to that of Vice-President of the United States."

This article has been considered in a former part of the work. See § 388.

"ARTICLE XIII.—SECTION 1. Neither slavery nor involuntary servitude, except as a punishment for crime whereof the party shall have been duly convicted, shall exist within the United States, or any place subject to their jurisdiction.

"SECTION 2. Congress shall have power to enforce this article by appropriate legislation."

§ 650. The object of this important amendment, as plainly expressed by its language, is forever to abolish slavery and involuntary servitude (except as a punishment for crime) within the United States and all places subject to their jurisdiction. The States by whom this amendment was ratified were, in the proclamation of the Secretary of State, declared to be Illinois, Rhode Island, Michigan, Maryland, New York, West Virginia, Maine, Kansas, Massachusetts, Pennsylvania, Virginia, Ohio, Missouri, Nevada, Indiana, Louisiana, Minnesota, Wisconsin, Vermont, Tennessee, Arkansas, Connecticut, New Hampshire, South Carolina, Alabama, North Carolina and Georgia—in all, twenty-seven States, being three-fourths of thirty-six, the whole number of States.

§ 651. The fourteenth amendment was proposed to the legislatures of the several States by a joint resolution of two-thirds of the Senate and of the House of Representatives, which was communicated to the Department of State, June

16th, 1866. A concurrent resolution of the Senate and House of Representatives, passed July 21st, 1868, declared that more than three-fourths of the States had ratified the proposed amendment, and that it had accordingly become a part of the Constitution of the United States; and the Secretary of State was directed to promulgate it as such, which was accordingly done July 28th, 1868. It is as follows:

"ARTICLE XIV.—SECTION 1. All persons born or naturalized in the United States, and subject to the jurisdiction thereof, are citizens of the United States and of the State wherein they reside. No State shall make or enforce any law which shall abridge the privileges or immunities of citizens of the United States: nor shall any State deprive any person of life, liberty, or property, without due process of law, nor deny to any person within its jurisdiction the equal protection of the laws."

§ 652. By this section the rights, privileges and immunities of citizenship are extended to all persons born or naturalized in the United States, and subject to the jurisdiction thereof, without distinction of color or race.

"SECTION 2. Representatives shall be apportioned among the several States according to their respective numbers, counting the whole number of persons in each State, excluding Indians not taxed. But when the right to vote at any election for the choice of electors for President and Vice-President of the United States, representatives in Congress, the executive or judicial officers of a State, or the members of the Legislature thereof, is denied to any of the male inhabitants of such State, being twenty-one years of age, and citizens of the United States, or in any way abridged, except for participation in rebellion or other crime, the basis of representation therein shall be reduced in the proportion which the number of such male citizens shall bear to the whole number of male citizens twenty-one years of age in such State."

§ 653. This section provides that if any State shall deny the right of voting for certain officers to any of its male citizens, being twenty-one years of age, except for crime, the basis of representation of such State in Congress shall be reduced in like proportion.

"SECTION 3. No person shall be a senator or representative in Congress, or elector of President or Vice-President, or hold any office, civil or military, under the United States, or under any State, who, having previously taken an oath as a member of Congress, or as an officer of the United States, or as a member of any State Legislature, or as an executive or judicial officer of any State, to support the Constitution of the United States, shall have engaged in insurrection or rebellion against the same, or given aid or comfort to the enemies thereof. But Congress may, by a vote of two-thirds of each House, remove such disability."

§ 654. Under this section certain persons described therein are disqualified from holding any office under the United States, or any State, unless Congress shall by a two-thirds vote remove such disability.

"SECTION 4. The validity of the public debt of the United States, authorized by law, including debts incurred for payment of pensions and bounties for services in suppressing insurrection or rebellion, shall not be questioned. But neither the United States nor any State shall assume or pay any debt or obligation incurred in aid of insurrection or rebellion against the United States, or any claim for the loss or emancipation of any slave; but all such debts, obligations and claims shall be held illegal and void."

§ 655. This enforces the validity of certain debts of the United States, and declares that debts or obligations incurred in aid of insurrection or rebellion, and claims for the loss or emancipation of slaves, are illegal and void.

"SECTION 5. Congress shall have power to enforce, by appropriate legislation, the provisions of this article."

§ 656. This section grants to Congress, in express terms, the right to pass such laws as may be appropriate for enforcing the preceding sections of the amendment.

§ 657. The fifteenth amendment was proposed to the legislatures of the several States by a joint resolution of two-thirds of the Senate and of the House of Representatives, passed in the month of February, 1869, and communicated to the Department of State on the 27th day of that month. On March 30th, 1870, the Secretary of State announced by proclamation that three-fourths of the States had ratified the amendment, and that it had become a part of the Constitution.

"ARTICLE XV.—SECTION 1. The right of the citizens of the United States to vote shall not be denied or abridged by the United States, or by any State, on account of race, color or previous condition of servitude."

§ 658. The object of this amendment is to provide that the right of citizens of the United States to vote shall not be denied or abridged by the United States, or by any State, on account of race, color, or previous condition of servitude.

"SECTION 2. The Congress shall have power to enforce this article by appropriate legislation."

APPENDIX.

I.

THE DECLARATION OF RIGHTS.

II.

THE DECLARATION OF INDEPENDENCE.

III.

THE ARTICLES OF CONFEDERATION.

IV.

WASHINGTON'S FAREWELL ADDRESS TO THE AMERICAN PEOPLE.

APPENDIX.

I.

We have already stated that the first Continental Congress, which assembled at Philadelphia September 5, 1774, adopted a Declaration of Rights. (§ 21.) The following is the document, as finally agreed upon by the Congress, October 14, 1775. It is confined to the consideration of such rights as had been infringed by acts of the British Parliament since the year 1763, for the further consideration of the general state of American rights was postponed until a subsequent day.

DECLARATION OF RIGHTS.

Whereas, since the close of the last war, the British parliament claiming a power of right, to bind the people of America by statutes in all cases whatsoever, hath, in some acts, expressly imposed taxes on them, and in others, under various pretences, but in fact for the purpose of raising a revenue, hath imposed rates and duties payable in these colonies, established a board of commissioners, with unconstitutional powers, and extended the jurisdiction of courts of admiralty, not only for collecting the said duties, but for the trial of causes merely arising within the body of a county.

And whereas, in consequence of other statutes, judges, who before held only estates at will in their offices, have been made dependant on the crown alone for their salaries, and standing armies kept in times of peace: And whereas it has lately been resolved in parliament, that by force of a statute, made in the thirty-fifth year of the reign of king Henry the eighth, colonists may be transported to England, and tried there upon accusations for treasons, and misprisions, or concealments of treasons committed in the colonies, and by a late statute, such trials have been directed in cases therein mentioned.

And whereas, in the last session of parliament, three statutes were made; one, entitled an "Act to discontinue, in such manner and for such time as are therein mentioned, the landing "and discharging, lading, or shipping of goods, wares and mer-"chandise, at the town, and within the harbour of Boston, in "the province of Massachusetts-Bay, in North-America;" another, entitled "An act for the better regulating the government of "the province of Massachusetts-Bay in New-England;" and another, entitled "An act for the impartial administration of "justice, in the cases of persons questioned for any act done by "them in the execution of the law, or for the suppression of "riots and tumults, in the province of the Massachusetts-Bay, "in New-England;" and another statute was then made, "for "making more effectual provision for the government of the pro-"vince of Quebec, &c." All which statutes are impolitic, unjust, and cruel, as well as unconstitutional, and most dangerous and destructive of American rights.

And whereas, assemblies have been frequently dissolved, contrary to the rights of the people, when they attempted to deliberate on grievances; and their dutiful, humble, loyal, and reasonable petitions to the crown for redress, have been repeatedly treated with contempt, by his majesty's ministers of state:

The good people of the several colonies of New-Hampshire Massachusetts-Bay, Rhode-Island and Providence Plantations, Connecticut, New-York, New-Jersey, Pennsylvania, New-Castle, Kent, and Sussex, on Delaware, Maryland, Virginia, North-Carolina, and South-Carolina, justly alarmed at these arbitrary proceedings of parliament and administration, have severally elected, constituted, and appointed deputies to meet, and sit in General Congress, in the city of Philadelphia, in order to obtain such establishment, as that their religion, laws, and liberties, may not be subverted. Whereupon the deputies so appointed being now assembled, in a full and free representation of these colonies, taking into their most serious consideration, the best means of attaining the ends aforesaid, do, in the first place, as Englishmen, their ancestors in like cases have usually done, for affecting and vindicating their rights and liberties, DECLARE,

That the inhabitants of the English colonies in North-America, by the immutable laws of nature, the principles of the English constitution, and the several charters or compacts, have the following RIGHTS:

*Resolved, N. C. D.** 1. That they are entitled to life, liberty, and property, and they have never ceded to any sovereign power whatever, a right to dispose of either without their consent.

Resolved, N. C. D. 2. That our ancestors, who first settled these colonies, were at the time of their emigration from the mother country, entitled to all the rights, liberties, and immunities of free and natural-born subjects, within the realm of England.

Resolved, N. C. D. 3. That by such emigration they by no means forfeited, surrendered, or lost any of those rights, but that they were, and their descendants now are, entitled to the exercise and enjoyment of all such of them, as their local and other circumstances enable them to exercise and enjoy.

Resolved, 4. That the foundation of English liberty, and of all free government, is a right in the people to participate in their legislative council: and as the English colonists are not represented, and from their local and other circumstances, cannot properly be represented in the British parliament, they are entitled to a free and exclusive power of legislation in their several provincial legislatures, where their right of representation can alone be preserved, in all cases of taxation and internal polity, subject only to the negative of their sovereign, in such manner as has been heretofore used and accustomed. But, from the necessity of the case, and a regard to the mutual interest of both countries, we cheerfully consent to the operation of such acts of the British parliament, as are bona fide, restrained to the regulation of our external commerce, for the purpose of securing the commercial advantages of the whole empire to the mother country, and the commercial benefits of its respective members; excluding every idea of taxation internal or external, for raising a revenue on the subjects in America, without their consent.

Resolved, N. C. D. 5. That the respective colonies are entitled to the common law of England, and more especially to the great and inestimable privilege of being tried by their peers of the vicinage, according to the course of that law.

Resolved, 6. That they are entitled to the benefit of such of the English statutes, as existed at the time of their colonization; and which they have, by experience, respectively found to be applicable to their several local and other circumstances.

Resolved, N. C. D. 7. That these, his majesty's colonies, are

---

* An abbreviation for *nemine contradicente;* that is, no one opposing or disagreeing.

likewise entitled to all the immunities and privileges granted and confirmed to them by royal charters, or secured by their several codes of provincial laws.

Resolved, *N. C. D.* 8. That they have a right peaceably to assemble, consider of their grievances, and petition the king; and that all prosecutions, prohibitory proclamations, and commitments for the same, are illegal.

Resolved, *N. C. D.* 9. That the keeping a standing army in these colonies, in times of peace, without the consent of the legislature of that colony, in which such army is kept, is against law.

Resolved, *N. C. D.* 10. It is indispensably necessary to good government, and rendered essential by the English constitution, that the constituent branches of the legislature be independent of each other; that, therefore, the exercise of legislative power in several colonies, by a council appointed, during pleasure, by the crown, is unconstitutional, dangerous and destructive to the freedom of American legislation.

All and each of which the aforesaid deputies, in behalf of themselves, and their constituents, do claim, demand, and insist on, as their indubitable rights and liberties; which cannot be legally taken from them, altered or abridged by any power whatever, without their own consent, by their representatives in their several provincial legislatures.

In the course of our inquiry, we find many infringements and violations of the foregoing rights, which from an ardent desire, that harmony and mutual intercourse of affection and interest may be restored, we pass over for the present, and proceed to state such acts and measures as have been adopted since the last war, which demonstrate a system formed to enslave America.

Resolved, *N. C. D.* That the following acts of parliament are infringements and violations of the rights of the colonists; and that the repeal of them is essentially necessary, in order to restore harmony between Great Britain and the American colonies, viz.

The several acts of 4 Geo. III. ch. 15, and ch. 34.—5 Geo. III. ch. 25.—6 Geo. III. ch. 52.—7 Geo. III. ch. 41, and ch. 46.—8 Geo. III. ch. 22, which impose duties for the purpose of raising a revenue in America, extend the power of the admiralty courts beyond their ancient limits, deprive the American subject of trial by jury, authorize the judges' certificate to indemnify the prosecutor from damages, that he might otherwise be liable to, requiring oppressive security from a claimant of ships and goods seized, before he shall be allowed to defend his property, and are subversive of American rights.

Also 12 Geo. III. ch. 24, entitled "An act for the better "securing his majesty's dock-yards, magazines, ships, ammuni "tion, and stores," which declares a new offence in America, and deprives the American subject of a constitutional trial by jury of the vicinage, by authorizing the trial of any person, charged with the committing any offence described in the said act, out of the realm, to be indicted and tried for the same in any shire or county within the realm.

Also the three acts passed in the last session of parliament, for stopping the port and blocking up the harbour of Boston, for altering the charter and government of Massachusetts-Bay, and that which is entitled "An act for the better administration of "justice," &c.

Also the act passed in the same session for establishing the Roman Catholic religion, in the province of Quebec, abolishing the equitable system of English laws, and erecting a tyranny there, to the great danger, (from so total a dissimilarity of religion, law and government) of the neighbouring British colonies, by the assistance of whose blood and treasure the said country was conquered from France.

Also the act passed in the same session, for the better providing suitable quarters for officers and soldiers in his majesty's service, in North-America.

Also, that the keeping a standing army in several of these colonies, in time of peace, without the consent of the legislature of that colony, in which such army is kept, is against law.

To these grievous acts and measures, Americans cannot submit, but in hopes their fellow subjects in Great-Britain will, on a revision of them, restore us to that state, in which both countries found happiness and prosperity, we have for the present, only resolved to pursue the following peaceable measures: 1. To enter into a non-importation, non-consumption, and non-exportation agreement or association. 2. To prepare an address to the people of Great-Britain, and a memorial to the inhabitants of British America: and 3. To prepare a loyal address to his majesty, agreeable to resolutions already entered into.

II.

THE DECLARATION OF INDEPENDENCE, ADOPTED BY CONGRESS JULY 4, 1776.

A DECLARATION BY THE REPRESENTATIVES OF THE UNITED STATES OF AMERICA, IN CONGRESS ASSEMBLED.

WHEN, in the course of human events, it becomes necessary for one people to dissolve the political bands which have connected them with another, and to assume, among the powers of the earth, the separate and equal station to which the laws of nature and of nature's God entitle them, a decent respect to the opinions of mankind requires that they should declare the causes which impel them to the separation.

We hold these truths to be self-evident, that all men are created equal; that they are endowed by their Creator with certain unalienable rights; that among these, are life, liberty, and the pursuit of happiness. That, to secure these rights, governments are instituted among men, deriving their just powers from the consent of the governed; that, whenever any form of government becomes destructive of these ends, it is the right of the people to alter or to abolish it, and to institute a new government, laying its foundation on such principles, and organizing its powers in such form, as to them shall seem most likely to effect their safety and happiness. Prudence, indeed, will dictate that governments long established, should not be changed for light and transient causes; and, accordingly, all experience hath shown, that mankind are more disposed to suffer, while evils are sufferable, than to right themselves by abolishing the forms to which they are accustomed. But, when a long train of abuses and usurpations, pursuing invariably the same object, evinces a design to reduce them under absolute despotism, it is their right, it is their duty, to throw off such government, and to provide new guards for their future security. Such has been the patient sufferance of these colonies, and such is now the necessity which constrains them to alter their former systems of government. The history of the present king of Great Britain is a history of repeated injuries and usurpations, all having, in direct object, the establishment of an absolute tyranny over these States. To prove this, let facts be submitted to a candid world:

He has refused his assent to laws the most wholesome and necessary for the public good.

He has forbidden his Governors to pass laws of immediate and pressing importance, unless suspended in their operation till his assent should be obtained; and, when so suspended, he has utterly neglected to attend to them.

He has refused to pass other laws for the accommodation of large districts of people, unless those people would relinquish the right of representation in the legislature; a right inestimable to them, and formidable to tyrants only.

He has called together legislative bodies at places unusual, uncomfortable, and distant from the depository of their public records, for the sole purpose of fatiguing them into compliance with his measures.

He has dissolved representative houses repeatedly, for opposing, with manly firmness, his invasions on the rights of the people.

He has refused, for a long time after such dissolutions, to cause others to be elected; whereby the legislative powers, incapable of annihilation, have returned to the people at large for their exercise; the State remaining, in the mean time, exposed to all the danger of invasion from without, and convulsions within.

He has endeavoured to prevent the population of these States; for that purpose, obstructing the laws for naturalization of foreigners; refusing to pass others to encourage their migration hither, and raising the conditions of new appropriations of lands.

He has obstructed the administration of justice, by refusing his assent to laws for establishing judiciary powers.

He has made judges dependent on his will alone, for the tenure of their offices, and the amount and payment of their salaries.

He has erected a multitude of new offices, and sent hither swarms of officers to harass our people, and eat out their substance

He has kept among us, in times of peace, standing armies, without the consent of our legislature.

He has affected to render the military independent of, and superior to, the civil power.

He has combined, with others, to subject us to a jurisdiction foreign to our constitution, and unacknowledged by our laws; giving his assent to their acts of pretended legislation:

For quartering large bodies of armed troops among us:

For protecting them, by a mock trial, from punishment, for

any murders which they should commit on the inhabitants of these States:

For cutting off our trade with all parts of the world:

For imposing taxes on us without our consent:

For depriving us, in many cases, of the benefits of trial by jury:

For transporting us beyond seas to be tried for pretended offences:

For abolishing the free system of English laws in a neighbouring province, establishing therein an arbitrary government, and enlarging its boundaries, so as to render it at once an example and fit instrument for introducing the same absolute rule into these colonies:

For taking away our charters, abolishing our most valuable laws, and altering, fundamentally, the powers of our governments:

For suspending our own legislatures, and declaring themselves invested with power to legislate for us in all cases whatsoever.

He has abdicated government here, by declaring us out of his protection, and waging war against us.

He has plundered our seas, ravaged our coasts, burnt our towns, and destroyed the lives of our people.

He is, at this time, transporting large armies of foreign mercenaries to complete the works of death, desolation, and tyranny. already begun, with circumstances of cruelty and perfidy scarcely paralleled in the most barbarous ages, and totally unworthy the head of a civilized nation.

He has constrained our fellow-citizens, taken captive on the high seas, to bear arms against their country, to become the executioners of their friends and brethren, or to fall themselves by their hands.

He has excited domestic insurrections amongst us, and has endeavoured to bring on the inhabitants of our frontiers, the merciless Indian savages, whose known rule of warfare is an undistinguished destruction, of all ages, sexes, and conditions.

In every stage of these oppressions, we have petitioned for redress, in the most humble terms; our repeated petitions have been answered only by repeated injury. A prince, whose character is thus marked by every act which may define a tyrant, is unfit to be the ruler of a free people.

Nor have we been wanting in attention to our British brethren. We have warned them, from time to time, of attempts made by their legislature to extend an unwarrantable jurisdiction over us. We have reminded them of the circumstances of our emigration and settlement here. We have appealed to their native justice and magnanimity, and we have conjured them, by the ties of our common kindred, to disavow these usurpations, which would inevitably interrupt our connections and correspondence. They, too, have been deaf to the voice of justice and consanguinity. We must, therefore, acquiesce in the necessity, which denounces our separation, and hold them as we hold the rest of mankind, enemies in war, in peace, friends.

We, therefore, the representatives of the UNITED STATES OF AMERICA, in GENERAL CONGRESS assembled, appealing to the Supreme Judge of the world for the rectitude of our intentions, do, in the name, and by the authority of the good people of these colonies, solemnly publish and declare, That these United Colonies are, and of right ought to be, *free and independent States;* that they are absolved from all allegiance to the British crown, and that all political connexion between them and the state of Great Britain, is, and ought to be totally dissolved; and that, as FREE AND INDEPENDENT STATES, they have full power to levy war, conclude peace, contract alliances, establish commerce, and to do all other acts and things which INDEPENDENT STATES may of right do. And, for the support of this declaration, with a firm reliance on the protection of DIVINE PROVIDENCE, we mutually pledge to each other, our lives, our fortunes, and our sacred honor.

The foregoing declaration was, by order of Congress, engrossed, and signed by the following members:

JOHN HANCOCK.

New Hampshire.
Josiah Bartlett,
William Whipple,
Matthew Thornton.

Massachusetts Bay.
Samuel Adams,
John Adams,
Robert Treat Paine,
Elbridge Gerry.

Rhode Island.
Stephen Hopkins,
William Ellery.

Connecticut.
Roger Sherman,
Samuel Huntington,
William Williams,
Oliver Wolcott.

New York.
William Floyd,
Philip Livingston,
Francis Lewis,
Lewis Morris.

New Jersey.
Richard Stockton,

John Witherspoon,
Francis Hopkinson,
John Hart,
Abraham Clark.

Pennsylvania.

Robert Morris,
Benjamin Rush,
Benjamin Franklin,
John Morton,
George Clymer,
James Smith,
George Taylor,
James Wilson,
George Ross.

Delaware.

Cæsar Rodney,
George Read,
Thomas M'Kean.

Maryland.

Samuel Chase,
William Paca,
Thomas Stone,
Charles Carroll, of Carollton.

Virginia.

George Wythe,
Richard Henry Lee,
Thomas Jefferson,
Benjamin Harrison,
Thomas Nelson, jun.
Francis Lightfoot Lee,
Carter Braxton.

North Carolina.

William Hooper.
Joseph Hewes,
John Penn.

South Carolina.

Edward Rutledge,
Thomas Heyward, jun.
Thomas Lynch, jun.
Arthur Middleton.

Georgia.

Button Gwinnett,
Lyman Hall,
George Walton.

Copies of the foregoing Declaration were, by a resolution of Congress, sent to the several assemblies, conventions, and committees, or councils of safety, and to the several commanding officers of the continental troops; and it was also proclaimed in each of the United States, and at the head of the army.

III.

We have already spoken (§ 24) of the adoption of the Articles of Confederation. They are, at length, as follows:

ARTICLES OF CONFEDERATION AND PERPETUAL UNION BETWEEN THE STATES.

To all to whom these presents shall come, we the undersigned Delegates of the States affixed to our names, send greeting:—Whereas the Delegates of the United States of America in Congress assembled did on the 15th day of November in the Year of our Lord 1777, and in the Second Year of the Independence of America agree to certain articles of Confederation and perpetual Union between the States of New-Hampshire, Massachusetts-bay, Rhode-Island and Providence Plantations, Connecticut, New-York, New-Jersey, Pennsylvania, Delaware, Maryland, Virginia, North-Carolina, South-Carolina, and Georgia, in the words following, viz.

Articles of Confederation and Perpetual Union between the States of New Hampshire, Massachusetts-bay, Rhode Island and Providence Plantations, Connecticut, New-York, New-Jersey, Pennsylvania, Delaware, Maryland, Virginia, North-Carolina, South-Carolina, and Georgia.

Article I. The Stile of this confederacy shall be "The United States of America."

Article II. Each state retains its sovereignty, freedom and independence, and every Power, Jurisdiction and right, which is not by this confederation expressly delegated to the united states, in congress assembled.

Article III. The said states hereby severally enter into a firm league of friendship with each other, for their common defence, the security of their Liberties, and their mutual and general welfare, binding themselves to assist each other, against all force offered to, or attacks made upon them, or any of them, on account of religion, sovereignty, trade, or any other pretence whatever.

Article IV. The better to secure and perpetuate mutual friendship and intercourse among the people of the different states in this Union, the free inhabitants of each of these states, paupers, vagabonds, and fugitives from Justice excepted, shall be entitled to all privileges and immunities of free citizens in the several states; and the people of each state shall have free ingress and regress to and from any other state, and shall enjoy therein all the privileges of trade and commerce, subject to the same duties, impositions and restrictions as the inhabitants thereof respectively, provided that such restriction shall not extend so far as to prevent the removal of property imported into any state, to any other state of which the Owner is an inhabitant; provided also that no imposition, duties or restriction shall be laid by any state, on the property of the united states, or either of them.

If any person guilty of, or charged with treason, felony, or other high misdemeanor in any state, shall flee from Justice, and be found in any of the united states, he shall upon demand of the Governor or executive power, of the state from which he fled, be delivered up and removed to the state having jurisdiction of his offence.

Full faith and credit shall be given in each of these states to the records, acts and judicial proceedings of the courts and magistrates of every other state.

Article V. For the more convenient management of the general interest of the united states, delegates shall be annually appointed in such manner as the legislature of each state shall direct, to meet in congress on the first Monday in November, in every year, with a power reserved to each state,. to recal its delegates, or any of them, at any time within the year, and to send others in their stead, for the remainder of the Year.

No state shall be represented in congress by less than two, nor by more than seven members; and no person shall be capable of being a delegate for more than three years in any term of six years; nor shall any person, being a delegate, be capable of holding any office under the united states, for which he, or another for his benefit receives any salary, fees or emolument of any kind.

Each state shall maintain its own delegates in any meeting of the states, and while they act as members of the committee of the states.

In determining questions in the united states, in congress assembled, each state shall have one vote.

Freedom of speech and debate in congress shall not be impeached or questioned in any Court, or place out of congress, and the members of congress shall be protected in their persons from arrests and imprisonments, during the time of their going to and from, and attendance on congress, except for treason, felony, or breach of the peace.

ARTICLE VI. No state without the Consent of the united states in congress assembled, shall send any embassy to, or receive any embassy from, or enter into any conference, agreement, alliance or treaty with any King prince or state; nor shall any person holding any office of profit or trust under the united states, or any of them, accept of any present, emolument, office or title of any kind whatever from any king, prince, or foreign state; nor shall the united states in congress assembled, or any of them, grant any title of nobility.

No two or more states shall enter into any treaty, confederation or alliance whatever between them, without the consent of the united states in congress assembled, specifying accurately the purposes for which the same is to be entered into, and how long it shall continue.

No state shall lay any imposts or duties, which may interfere with any stipulations in treaties, entered into by the united states in congress assembled, with any king, prince, or state, in pursuance of any treaties already proposed by congress, to the courts of France and Spain.

No vessels of war shall be kept up in time of peace by any state, except such number only, as shall be deemed necessary by the united states in congress assembled, for the defence of such state, or its trade; nor shall any body of forces be kept up by any state, in time of peace, except such number only, as in the judgment of the united states, in congress assembled, shall be deemed requisite to garrison the forts necessary for the defence of such state; but every state shall always keep up a well regulated and disciplined militia, sufficiently armed and accoutred, and shall provide and have constantly ready for use, in public stores, a due number of field pieces and tents, and a proper quantity of arms, ammunition and camp equipage.

No state shall engage in any war without the consent of the united states in congress assembled, unless such state be actually invaded by enemies, or shall have received certain advice of a resolution being formed by some nation of Indians to invade such state, and the danger is so imminent as not to admit of a delay, till the united states in congress assembled can be consulted: nor shall any state grant commissions to any ships or vessels of war, nor letters of marque or reprisal, except it be after a declaration of war by the united states in congress assembled, and then only against the kingdom or state and the subjects thereof, against which war has been so declared, and under such regulations as shall be established by the united states in congress assembled, unless such state be infested by pirates, in which case vessels of war may be fitted out for that occasion, and kept so long as the danger shall continue, or until the united states in congress assembled shall determine otherwise.

ARTICLE VII. When land-forces are raised by any state for the common defence, all officers of or under the rank of colonel, shall be appointed by the legislature of each state respectively by whom such forces shall be raised, or in such manner as such state shall direct, and all vacancies shall be filled up by the state which first made the appointment.

ARTICLE VIII. All charges of war, and all other expenses that shall be incurred for the common defence or general welfare, and allowed by the united states in congress assembled, shall be defrayed out of a common treasury, which shall be supplied by the several states, in proportion to the value of all land within each state, granted to or surveyed for any Person, as such land and the buildings and improvements thereon shall be estimated according to such mode as the united states in congress assembled, shall from time to time, direct and appoint. The taxes for paying that proportion shall be laid and levied by the authority and direction of the legislatures of the several states within the time agreed upon by the united states in congress assembled.

ARTICLE IX. The united states in congress assembled, shall have the sole and exclusive right and power of determining on peace and war, except in cases mentioned in the 6th article—of sending and receiving ambassadors—entering into treaties and alliances, provided that no treaty of commerce shall be made whereby the legislative power of the respective states shall be restrained from imposing such imposts and duties on foreigners, as their own people are subjected to, or from prohibiting the exportation or importation of any species of goods or commodities whatsoever—of establishing rules for deciding in all cases, what captures on land or water shall be legal, and in what manner prizes taken by land or naval forces in the service of the united states shall be divided or appropriated—of granting letters of marque and reprisal in times of peace—appointing courts for the trial of piracies and felonies committed on the high seas and establishing courts for receiving and determining finally appeals in all cases of captures, provided that no member of congress shall be appointed a judge of any of the said courts.

The united states in congress assembled shall also be the last resort on appeal in all disputes and differences now subsisting or that hereafter may arise between two or more states concerning boundary, jurisdiction or any other cause whatever; which authority shall always be exercised in the manner following. Whenever the legislative or executive authority or lawful agent of any state in controversy with another shall present a petition to congress, stating the matter in question and praying for a hearing, notice thereof shall be given by order of congress to the legislative or executive authority of the other state in controversy, and a day assigned for the appearance of the parties by their lawful agents, who shall then be directed to appoint by joint consent, commissioners or judges to constitute a court for hearing and determining the matter in question: but if they cannot agree, congress shall name three persons out of each of the united states, and from the list of such persons each party shall alternately strike out one, the petitioners beginning, until the number shall be reduced to thirteen; and from that number not less than seven, nor more than nine names as congress shall direct, shall in the presence of congress be drawn out by lot, and the persons whose names shall be so drawn or any five of them, shall be commissioners or judges, to hear and finally determine the controversy, so always as a major part of the judges who shall hear the cause shall agree in the determination: and if either party shall neglect to attend at the day appointed, without showing reasons, which congress shall judge sufficient, or being present shall refuse to strike, the congress shall proceed to nominate three persons out of each state, and the secretary of congress shall strike in behalf of such party absent or refusing; and the judgment and sentence of the court to be appointed, in the manner before prescribed, shall be final and conclusive; and if any of the parties shall refuse to submit to the authority of such court, or to appear or defend their claim or cause, the court shall nevertheless proceed to pronounce sentence, or judgment, which shall in like manner be final and decisive, the judgment or sentence and other proceedings being in either case transmitted to congress, and lodged among the acts of congress for the security of the parties concerned: provided that every commissioner, before he sits in judgment, shall take an oath to be administered by one of the judges of the supreme or superior court of the state, where the cause shall be tried, "well and truly to hear and determine the manner in question, according to the best of his judgment, without favour, affection or hope of reward:" provided also that no state shall be deprived of territory for the benefit of the united states.

All controversies concerning the private right of soil claimed under different grants of two or more states, whose jurisdictions as they may respect such lands, and the states which passed such grants are adjusted, the said grants or either of them being at the same time claimed to have originated antecedent to such settlement of jurisdiction, shall on the petition of either party to the congress of the united states, be finally determined as near as may be in the same manner as is before prescribed for deciding disputes respecting territorial jurisdiction between different states.

The united states in congress assembled shall also have the sole and exclusive right and power of regulating the alloy and value of coin struck by their own authority, or by that of the respective states—fixing the standard of weights and measures throughout the United States—regulating the trade and managing all affairs with the Indians, not members of any of the states, provided that the legislative right of any state within its own limits be not infringed or violated—establishing or regulating post-offices from one state to another, throughout all the united states, and exacting such postage on the papers passing thro' the same as may be requisite to defray the expenses of the said office—appointing all officers of the land forces, in the service of the united states, excepting regimental officers—appointing all the officers of the naval forces, and commissioning all officers whatever in the service of the united states—making rules for the government and regulation of the said land and naval forces, and directing their operations.

The united states in congress assembled shall have authority to appoint a committee, to sit in the recess of congress, to be denominated "A Committee of the States," and to consist of one delegate from each state; and to appoint such other committees and civil officers as may be necessary for managing the general affairs of the united states under their direction—to appoint one of their number to preside, provided that no person be allowed to serve in the office of president more than one year in any term of three years; to ascertain the necessary sums of Money to be raised for the service of the united states, and to appropriate and apply the same for defraying the public expenses—to borrow money, or emit bills on the credit of the united states, transmitting every half year to the respective states an account of the sums of money so borrowed or emitted,—to build and equip a navy—to agree upon the number of land forces, and to make requisitions from each state for its quota, in proportion to the number of white inhabitants in such state; which requisition shall be binding, and thereupon the legislature of each state shall appoint the regimental officers, raise the men and cloath, arm and equip them in a soldier like manner, at the expense of the united states; and the officers and men so cloathed, armed and equipped shall march to the place appointed, and within the time agreed on by the united states in congress assembled: But if the united states in congress assembled shall, on consideration of circumstances judge proper that any state should not raise men, or should raise a smaller number than its quota, and that any other state should raise a greater number of men than the quota thereof, such extra number shall be raised, officered, cloathed, armed and equipped in the same manner as the quota of such state, unless the legislature of such state shall judge that such extra number cannot be safely spared out of the same, in which case they shall raise officer, cloath, arm and equip as many of such extra number as they judge can be safely spared. And the officers and men so cloathed, armed and equipped, shall march to the place appointed, and within the time agreed on by the united states in congress assembled.

The united states in congress assembled shall never engage in a war, nor grant letters of marque and reprisal in time of peace, nor enter into any treaties or alliances, nor coin money, nor regulate the value thereof, nor ascertain the sums and expenses necessary for the defence and welfare of the united states, or any of them, nor emit bills, nor borrow money on the credit of the united states, nor appropriate money, nor agree upon the number of vessels of war, to be built or purchased, or the number of land or sea forces to be raised, nor appoint a commander in chief of the army or navy, unless nine states assent to the same: nor shall a question on any other point, except for adjourning from day to day be determined, unless by the votes of a majority of the united states in congress assembled.

The Congress of the united states shall have power to adjourn to any time within the year, and to any place within the united states, so that no period of adjournment be for a longer duration than the space of six months, and shall publish the Journal of their proceedings monthly, except such parts thereof relating to treaties, alliances or military operations, as in their judgment require secrecy; and the yeas and nays of the delegates of each state on any question shall be entered on the Journal, when it is desired by any delegate; and the delegates of a state, or any of them, at his or their request shall be furnished with a transcript of the said Journal, except such parts as are above excepted, to lay before the legislatures of the several states.

ARTICLE X. The committee of the states, or any nine of them, shall be authorized to execute, in the recess of congress, such of the powers of congress as the united states in congress assembled, by the consent of nine states, shall from time to time think expedient to vest them with; provided that no power be delegated to the said committee, for the exercise of which, by the articles of confederation, the voice of nine states in the congress of the united states assembled is requisite.

ARTICLE XI. Canada acceding to this confederation, and joining in the measures of the united states, shall be admitted into, and entitled to all the advantages of this union; but no other colony shall be admitted into the same, unless such admission be agreed to by nine states.

ARTICLE XII. All bills of credit emitted, monies borrowed and debts contracted by, or under the authority of congress, before the assembling of the united states, in pursuance of the present confederation, shall be deemed and considered as a charge against the united states, for payment and satisfaction whereof the said united states, and the public faith are hereby solemnly pledged.

ARTICLE XIII. Every state shall abide by the determinations of the united states in congress assembled, on all questions which by this confederation is submitted to them. And the Articles of this confederation shall be inviolably observed by every state, and the union shall be perpetual; nor shall any alteration at any time hereafter be made in any of them; unless such alteration be agreed to in a congress of the united states, and be afterwards confirmed by the legislatures of every state.

And Whereas it hath pleased the Great Governor of the

World to incline the hearts of the legislatures we respectively represent in congress, to approve of, and to authorize us to ratify the said articles of confederation and perpetual union. Know Ye that we the undersigned delegates, by virtue of the power and authority to us given for that purpose, do by these presents, in the name and in behalf of our respective constituents, fully and entirely ratify and confirm each and every of the said articles of confederation and perpetual union, and all and singular the matters and things therein contained: And we do furthur solemnly plight and engage the faith of our respective constituents, that they shall abide by the determinations of the united states in congress assembled, on all questions, which by the said confederation are submitted to them. And that the articles thereof shall be inviolably observed by the states we respectively represent, and that the union shall be perpetual. In witness whereof we have hereunto set our hands in Congress. Done at Philadelphia in the state of Pennsylvania the 9th day of July in the Year of our Lord, 1778, and in the 3d year of the Independence of America.

Josiah Bartlett,	John Wentworth, jun. August 8th, 1778,	On the part and behalf of the state of New Hampshire.
John Hancock, Samuel Adams, Elbridge Gerry,	Francis Dana, James Lovell, Samuel Holton,	On the part and behalf of the state of Massachusetts-Bay.
William Ellery, Henry Marchant,	John Collins,	On the part and behalf of the state of Rhode-Island and Providence Plantations.
Roger Sherman, Samuel Huntington, Oliver Wolcott,	Titus Hosmer, Andrew Adam,	On the part and behalf of the state of Connecticut.
Jas Duane, Fras Lewis,	William Duer, Gouvr Morris,	On the part and behalf of the state of New-York.
Jno Witherspoon,	Nathl Scudder,	On the part and behalf of the state of New-Jersey, November 26th, 1778.
Robt Morris, Daniel Roberdeau, Jona Bayard Smith,	William Clingan, Joseph Reed, 22d July, 1778.	On the part and behalf of the state of Pennsylvania.
Tho. M'Kean, Feb. 12, 1779, John Dickinson, May 5, 1779,	Nicholas Van Dyke,	On the part and behalf of the state of Delaware.
John Hanson, March 1st, 1781,	Daniel Carroll, March 1st, 1781,	On the part and behalf of the state of Maryland.
Richard Henry Lee, John Banister, Thomas Adams,	Jno Harvie, Francis Lightfoot Lee,	On the part and behalf of the state of Virginia.
John Penn, July 21st, 1778,	Corns Harnett, Jno Williams,	On the part and behalf of the state of North-Carolina.
Henry Laurens, William Henry Drayton, Jno Matthews,	Richd Hutson, Thos. Heyward, jun.	On the part and behalf of the state of South-Carolina.
Jno Walton, 24th July, 1778,	Edwd Telfair, Edwd Langworthy,	On the part and behalf of the state of Georgia.

IV.

FAREWELL ADDRESS OF GEORGE WASHINGTON, PRESIDENT, TO THE PEOPLE OF THE UNITED STATES, SEPTEMBER 17, 1796.

Friends and Fellow-citizens:

THE period for a new election of a citizen to administer the Executive Government of the United States being not far distant, and the time actually arrived when your thoughts must be employed in designating the person who is to be clothed with that important trust, it appears to me proper, especially as it may conduce to a more distinct expression of the public voice, that I should now apprize you of the resolution I have formed, to decline being considered among the number of those out of whom a choice is to be made.

I beg you, at the same time, to do me the justice to be assured that this resolution has not been taken without a strict regard to all the considerations appertaining to the relation which binds a dutiful citizen to his country; and that, in withdrawing the tender of service, which silence, in my situation, might imply, I am influenced by no diminution of zeal for your future interest; no deficiency of grateful respect for your past kindness; but am supported by a full conviction that the step is compatible with both.

The acceptance of, and continuance hitherto in, the office to which your suffrages have twice called me, have been a uniform sacrifice of inclination to the opinion of duty, and to a deference for what appeared to be your desire. I constantly hoped that it would have been much earlier in my power, consistently with motives which I was not at liberty to disregard, to return to that retirement from which I had been reluctantly drawn. The strength of my inclination to do this, previous to the last election, had even led to the preparation of an address to declare it to you; but mature reflection on the then perplexed and critical posture of our affairs with foreign nations, and the unanimous advice of persons entitled to my confidence, impelled me to abandon the idea.

I rejoice that the state of your concerns, external as well as internal, no longer renders the pursuit of inclination incompatible with the sentiment of duty or propriety; and am persuaded, whatever partiality may be retained for my services, that, in the present circumstances of our country, you will not disapprove my determination to retire.

The impressions with which I undertook the arduous trust were explained on the proper occasion. In the discharge of this trust, I will only say, that I have with good intentions contributed towards the organization and administration of the Government the best exertions of which a very fallible judgment was capable. Not unconscious in the outset of the inferiority of my qualifications, experience, in my own eyes—perhaps still more in the eyes of others—has strengthened the motives to diffidence of myself; and every day the increasing weight of years admonishes me, more and more, that the shade of retirement is as necessary to me as it will be welcome. Satisfied that if any circumstances have given peculiar value to my services, they were temporary, I have the consolation to believe that, while choice and prudence invite me to quit the political scene, patriotism does not forbid it.

In looking forward to the moment which is intended to terminate the career of my public life, my feelings do not permit me to suspend the deep acknowledgment of that debt of gratitude which I owe to my beloved country for the many honors it has conferred upon me; still more for the steadfast confidence with which it has supported me; and for the opportunities I have thence enjoyed of manifesting my inviolable attachment, by services faithful and persevering, though in usefulness unequal to my zeal. If benefits have resulted to our country from these services, let it always be remembered to your praise, and as an instructive example in our annals, that, under circumstances in which the passions, agitated in every direction, were liable to mislead; amidst appearances sometimes dubious, vicissitudes of fortune often discouraging; in situations in which, not unfrequently, want of success has countenanced the spirit of criticism,—the constancy of your support was the essential prop of the efforts, and a guarantee of the plans, by which they were effected. Profoundly penetrated with this idea, I shall carry it with me to my grave, as a strong incitement to unceasing vows, that Heaven may continue to you the choicest tokens of its beneficence; that our union and brotherly affection may be perpetual; that the free Constitution, which is the work of your hands, may be sacredly maintained; that its administration, in every department, may be stamped with wisdom and virtue; that, in fine, the happiness of the people of these States, under the auspices of liberty, may be made complete, by so careful a preservation and so prudent a use of this blessing as will acquire to them the glory of recommending it to the applause, the affection, and the adoption of every nation which is yet a stranger to it.

Here, perhaps, I ought to stop; but a solicitude for your welfare, which cannot end but with my life, and the apprehension of danger natural to that solicitude, urge me, on an occasion like the present, to offer to your solemn contemplation, and to recommend to your frequent review, some sentiments, which are the result of much reflection, of no inconsiderable observation, and which appear to me all-important to the permanency of your felicity as a people. These will be afforded to you with the more freedom, as you can only see in them the disinterested warnings of a parting friend, who can possibly have no personal motive to bias his counsel; nor can I forget, as an encouragement to it, your indulgent reception of my sentiments on a former and not dissimilar occasion.

Interwoven as is the love of liberty with every ligament of your hearts, no recommendation of mine is necessary to fortify or confirm the attachment.

The unity of government, which constitutes you one people, is also now dear to you. It is justly so; for it is a main pillar in the edifice of your real independence—the support of your tranquillity at home, your peace abroad, of your safety, of your prosperity, of that very liberty which you so highly prize. But as it is easy to foresee that, from different causes and from different quarters, much pains will be taken, many artifices employed, to weaken in your minds the conviction of this truth; as this is the point in your political fortress against which the batteries of internal and external enemies will be most constantly and actively (though often covertly and insidiously) directed,—it is of infinite moment that you should properly estimate the immense value of your national union to your collective and individual happiness; that you should cherish a cordial, habitual, and immovable attachment to it; accustoming yourselves to think and speak of it as of the palladium of your political safety and prosperity; watching for its preservation with jealous anxiety; discountenancing whatever may suggest even a suspicion that it can, in any event, be abandoned; and indignantly frowning upon the first dawning of every attempt to alienate any portion of our country from the rest, or to enfeeble the sacred ties which now link together the various parts.

For this you have every inducement of sympathy and interest. Citizens by birth or choice, of a common country, that country has a right to concentrate your affections. The name of *American*, which belongs to you in your national capacity, must always exalt the just pride of patriotism, more than any appellation derived from local discriminations. With slight shades of difference, you have the same religion, manners, habits, and political principles. You have, in a common cause, fought and triumphed together; the independence and liberty you possess are the work of joint counsels and joint efforts, of common dangers, sufferings, and successes.

But these considerations, however powerfully they address themselves to your sensibility, are greatly outweighed by those which apply more immediately to your interest; here every portion of our country finds the most commanding motives for carefully guarding and preserving the union of the whole.

The North, in an unrestrained intercourse with the South, protected by the equal laws of a common government, finds, in the productions of the latter, great additional resources of maritime and commercial enterprise, and precious materials of manufacturing industry. The South, in the same intercourse, benefiting by the agency of the North, sees its agriculture grow, and its commerce expand. Turning partly into its own channels the seamen of the North, it finds its particular navigation invigorated; and while it contributes, in different ways, to nourish and increase the general mass of the national navigation, it looks forward to the protection of a maritime strength to which itself is unequally adapted. The East, in like intercourse with the West, already finds, and in the progressive improvement of interior communication, by land and water, will more and more find, a valuable vent for the commodities which it brings from abroad, or manufactures at home. The West derives from the East supplies requisite to its growth and comfort; and what is perhaps of still greater consequence, it must, of necessity, owe the secure enjoyment of indispensable outlets for its own productions, to the weight, influence, and the future maritime strength of the Atlantic side of the Union, directed by an indissoluble community of interest as one nation. Any other tenure by which the West can hold this essential advantage, whether derived from its own separate strength, or from an apostate and unnatural connexion with any foreign power, must be intrinsically precarious.

While, then, every part of our country thus feels an immediate and particular interest in union, all the parts combined cannot fail to find, in the united mass of means and efforts, greater strength, greater resource, proportionably greater security from external danger, a less frequent interruption of their peace by foreign nations; and what is of inestimable value, they must derive from union an exemption from those broils and wars between themselves, which so frequently afflict neighbouring countries, not tied together by the same government; which their own rivalships alone would be sufficient to produce, but which opposite foreign alliances, attachments, and intrigues, would stimulate and imbitter. Hence, likewise, they will avoid the necessity of those over-grown military establishments, which, under any form of government, are inauspicious to liberty, and which are to be regarded as particularly hostile to republican liberty; in this sense it is that your union ought to be considered as a main prop of your liberty, and that the love of the one ought to endear to you the preservation of the other.

These considerations speak a persuasive language to every reflecting and virtuous mind, and exhibit the continuance of the Union as a primary object of patriotic desire. Is there a doubt, whether a common government can embrace so large a sphere? Let experience solve it. To listen to mere speculation, in such a case, were criminal. We are authorized to hope, that a proper organization of the whole, with the auxiliary agency of governments for the respective subdivisions, will afford a happy issue to the experiment. It is well worth a fair and full experiment. With such powerful and obvious motives to Union, affecting all parts of our country, while experience shall not have demonstrated its impracticability, there will always be reason to distrust the patriotism of those, who, in any quarter, may endeavour to weaken its bands.

In contemplating the causes which may disturb our Union, it occurs, as a matter of serious concern, that any ground should have been furnished for characterizing parties by geographical discriminations—Northern and Southern—Atlantic and Western: whence designing men may endeavour to excite a belief that there is a real difference of local interests and views. One of the expedients of party to acquire influence within particular districts, is to misrepresent the opinions and aims of other districts. You cannot shield yourselves too much against the jealousies and heart-burnings which spring from these misrepresentations; they tend to render alien to each other those who ought to be bound together by fraternal affection. The inhabitants of our western country have lately had a useful lesson on this head; they have seen in the negotiation by the Executive, and in the unanimous ratification by the Senate, of the treaty with Spain, and in the universal satisfaction at that event throughout the United States, a decisive proof how unfounded were the suspicions propagated among them, of a policy in the General Government, and in the Atlantic States, unfriendly to their interests in regard to the Mississippi: they have been witnesses to the formation of two treaties—that with Great Britain, and that with Spain, which secure to them every thing they could desire in respect to our foreign relations, towards confirming their prosperity. Will it not be their wisdom to rely for the preservation of these advantages on the Union by which they were procured? Will they not henceforth be deaf to those advisers, if such there are, who would sever them from their brethren, and connect them with aliens?

To the efficacy and permanency of your Union, a Government for the whole is indispensable. No alliance, however strict between the parts, can be an adequate substitute; they must inevitably experience the infractions and interruptions which all alliances, in all time, have experienced. Sensible of this momentous truth, you have improved upon your first essay, by the adoption of a Constitution of Government better calculated than your former for an intimate Union, and for the efficacious management of your common concerns. This government, the offspring of our own choice, uninfluenced and unawed, adopted upon full investigation and mature deliberation, completely free in its principles, in the distribution of its powers, uniting security with energy, and containing within itself a provision for its own amendment, has a just claim to your confidence and your support. Respect for its authority, compliance with its laws, acquiescence in its measures, are duties enjoined by the fundamental maxims of true liberty. The basis of our political systems, is the right of the people to make and to alter their constitutions of Government: but the Constitution which at any time exists, till changed by an explicit and authentic act of the whole people, is sacredly obligatory upon all. The very idea of the power, and the right of the people to establish Government, pre-supposes the duty of every individual to obey the established Government.

All obstructions to the execution of the laws, all combinations and associations, under whatever plausible character, with the real design to direct, control, counteract, or awe the regular deliberation and action of the constituted authorities, are destructive to this fundamental principle, and of fatal tendency. They serve to organize faction, to give it an artificial and extraordinary force, to put in the place of the delegated will of the nation, the will of a party, often a small but artful and enterprising minority of the community; and, according to the alternate triumphs of different parties, to make the public administration the mirror of the ill-concerted and incongruous projects of faction, rather than the organ of consistent and wholesome plans, digested by common counsels, and modified by mutual interests.

However combinations or associations of the above description may now and then answer popular ends, they are likely, in the course of time and things, to become potent engines, by which cunning, ambitious, and unprincipled men, will be enabled to subvert the power of the people, and to usurp for themselves the reins of Government; destroying, afterwards, the very engines which had lifted them to unjust dominion.

Towards the preservation of your Government, and the permanency of your present happy state, it is requisite, not only that you steadily discountenance irregular oppositions to its acknowledged authority, but also that you resist with care the spirit of innovation upon its principles, however specious the pretexts. One method of assault may be to effect, in the forms of the Constitution, alterations which will impair the energy of the system, and thus to undermine what cannot be directly overthrown In all the changes to which you may be invited, remember that time and habit are at least as necessary to fix the true character of governments as of other human institutions; that experience is the surest standard by which to test the real tendency of the existing constitution of a country; that facility in changes, upon the credit of mere hypothesis and opinion, exposes to perpetual change, from the endless variety of hypothesis and opinion; and remember, especially, that for the efficient management of your common interests, in a country so extensive as ours, a Government of as much vigour as is consistent with the perfect security of liberty, is indispensable. Liberty itself will find in such a Government, with powers properly distributed and adjusted, its surest guardian. It is, indeed, little else than a name, where the Government is too feeble to withstand the enterprises of faction, to confine each member of the society within the limits prescribed by the laws, and to maintain all in the secure and tranquil enjoyment of the rights of person and property.

I have already intimated to you the danger of parties in the

State, with particular reference to the founding of them on geographical discriminations. Let me now take a more comprehensive view, and warn you, in the most solemn manner, against the baneful effects of the spirit of party generally.

This spirit, unfortunately, is inseparable from our nature, having its root in the strongest passions of the human mind. It exists under different shapes, in all Governments, more or less stifled, controlled, or repressed; but in those of the popular form it is seen in its greatest rankness, and is truly their worst enemy.

The alternate domination of one faction over another, sharpened by the spirit of revenge, natural to party dissension, which, in different ages and countries, has perpetrated the most horrid enormities, is itself a frightful despotism. But this leads, at length, to a more formal and permanent despotism. The disorders and miseries which result, gradually incline the minds of men to seek security and repose in the absolute power of an individual; and, sooner or later, the chief of some prevailing faction, more able or more fortunate than his competitors, turns this disposition to the purposes of his own elevation on the ruins of public liberty.

Without looking forward to an extremity of this kind, (which, nevertheless, ought not to be entirely out of sight,) the common and continual mischiefs of the spirit of party are sufficient to make it the interest and duty of a wise people to discourage and restrain it.

It serves always to distract the public councils, and enfeeble the public administration. It agitates the community with ill-founded jealousies and false alarms; kindles the animosity of one part against another; foments, occasionally, riot and insurrection. It opens the door to foreign influence and corruption, which find a facilitated access to the Government itself, through the channels of party passions. Thus the policy and the will of one country are subjected to the policy and will of another.

There is an opinion that parties, in free countries, are useful checks upon the administration of the Government, and serve to keep alive the spirit of liberty. This, within certain limits, is probably true; and in Governments of a monarchical cast, patriotism may look with indulgence, if not with favour, upon the spirit of party. But in those of the popular character, in Governments purely elective, it is a spirit not to be encouraged. From their natural tendency, it is certain there will always be enough of that spirit for every salutary purpose. And there being constant danger of excess, the effort ought to be, by force of public opinion, to mitigate and assuage it. A fire not to be quenched, it demands a uniform vigilance to prevent its bursting into a flame, lest, instead of warming, it should consume.

It is important, likewise, that the habits of thinking, in a free country, should inspire caution in those intrusted with its administration, to confine themselves within their respective constitutional spheres, avoiding, in the exercise of the powers of one department, to encroach upon another. The spirit of encroachment tends to consolidate the powers of all the departments in one, and thus to create, whatever the form of Government, a real despotism. A just estimate of that love of power, and proneness to abuse it which predominates in the human heart, is sufficient to satisfy us of the truth of this position. The necessity of reciprocal checks in the exercise of political power, by dividing and distributing it into different depositories, and constituting each the guardian of the public weal, against invasions by the others, has been evinced by experiments, ancient and modern; some of them in our own country, and under our own eyes. To preserve them must be as necessary as to institute them. If, in the opinion of the people, the distribution or modification of the constitutional powers be, in any particular, wrong, let it be corrected by an amendment in the way which the Constitution designates. But let there be no change by usurpation; for though this, in one instance, may be the instrument of good, it is the customary weapon by which free Governments are destroyed. The precedent must always greatly overbalance, in permanent evil, any partial or transient benefit which the use can, at any time, yield.

Of all the dispositions and habits which lead to political prosperity, religion and morality are indispensable supports. In vain would that man claim the tribute of patriotism, who should labour to subvert these great pillars of human happiness, these firmest props of the duties of men and citizens. The mere politician, equally with the pious man, ought to respect and to cherish them. A volume could not trace all their connexions with private and public felicity. Let it simply be asked, where is the security for property, for reputation, for life, if the sense of religious obligation *desert* the oaths which are the instruments of investigation in courts of justice? And let us with caution indulge the supposition, that morality can be maintained without religion. Whatever may be conceded to the influence of refined education on minds of peculiar structure, reason and experience both forbid us to expect that national morality can prevail in exclusion of religious principles.

It is substantially true, that virtue or morality is a necessary spring of popular Government. The rule, indeed, extends with more or less force to every species of free Government. Who, that is a sincere friend to it, can look with indifference upon attempts to shake the foundation of the fabric?

Promote, then, as an object of primary importance, institutions for the general diffusion of knowledge. In proportion as the structure of a Government gives force to public opinion, it is essential that public opinion should be enlightened.

As a very important source of strength and security, cherish public credit. One method of preserving it is to use it as sparingly as possible; avoiding occasions of expense by cultivating peace, but remembering also that timely disbursements to prepare for danger, frequently prevent much greater disbursements to repel it; avoiding, likewise, the accumulation of debt, not only by shunning occasions of expense, but by vigorous exertions in time of peace to discharge the debts which unavoidable wars may have occasioned; not ungenerously throwing upon posterity the burden which we ourselves ought to bear. The execution of these maxims belongs to your representatives, but it is necessary that public opinion should co-operate. To facilitate to them the performance of their duty, it is essential that you should practically bear in mind, that towards the payment of debts there must be revenue; that to have revenue there must be taxes; that no taxes can be devised, which are not more or less inconvenient and unpleasant; that the intrinsic embarrassment inseparable from the selection of the proper objects, (which is always a choice of difficulties,) ought to be a decisive motive for a candid construction of the conduct of the Government in making it, and for a spirit of acquiescence in the measures for obtaining revenue, which the public exigencies may at any time dictate.

Observe good faith and justice towards all nations; cultivate peace and harmony with all; religion and morality enjoin this conduct; and can it be that good policy does not equally enjoin it? It will be worthy of a free, enlightened, and, at no distant period, a great nation, to give to mankind the magnanimous and too novel example of a people always guided by an exalted justice and benevolence. Who can doubt that, in the course of time and things, the fruits of such a plan would richly repay any temporary advantages which might be lost by a steady adherence to it? Can it be that Providence has not connected the permanent felicity of a nation with its virtue? The experiment, at least, is recommended by every sentiment which ennobles human nature. Alas! is it rendered impossible by its vices?

In the execution of such a plan, nothing is more essential than that permanent inveterate antipathies against particular nations, and passionate attachments for others, should be excluded; and that, in place of them, just and amicable feelings towards all should be cultivated. The nation which indulges towards another an habitual hatred, or an habitual fondness, is, in some degree, a slave. It is a slave to its animosity or to its affection; either of which is sufficient to lead it astray from its duty and its interest. Antipathy in one nation against another, disposes each more readily to offer insult and injury, to lay hold of slight causes of umbrage, and to be haughty and intractable, when accidental or trifling occasions of dispute occur. Hence frequent collisions, obstinate, envenomed, and bloody contests. The nation, prompted by ill will and resentment, sometimes impels to war the Government, contrary to the best calculations of policy. The government sometimes participates in the national propensity, and adopts, through passion, what reason would reject; at other times it makes the animosity of the nation subservient to projects of hostility, instigated by pride, ambition, and other sinister and pernicious motives. The peace often, sometimes perhaps the liberty, of nations has been the victim.

So, likewise a passionate attachment of one nation to another produces a variety of evils. Sympathy for the favourite nation, facilitating the illusion of an imaginary common interest, in cases where no real common interest exists, and infusing into one the enmities of the other, betrays the former into a participation in the quarrels and wars of the latter, without adequate inducement or justification. It leads also to concessions to the favourite nation of privileges denied to others, which is apt doubly to injure the nations making the concessions; by unnecessarily parting with what ought to have been retained, and by exciting jealousy, ill will, and a disposition to retaliate, in the parties from whom equal privileges are withheld; and it gives to ambitious, corrupted, or deluded citizens (who devote themselves to the favourite nation) facility to betray, or sacrifice the interest of their own country, without odium; sometimes even with popularity; gilding with the appearance of a virtuous sense of obligation, a commendable deference for public opinion, or a laudable zeal for public good, the base or foolish compliances of ambition, corruption, or infatuation.

As avenues to foreign influence in innumerable ways, such attachments are particularly alarming to the truly enlightened and independent patriot. How many opportunities do they afford to tamper with domestic factions, to practise the art of seduction, to mislead public opinion, to influence or awe the public councils! Such an attachment of a small or weak, towards a great and powerful nation, dooms the former to be the satellite of the latter.

Against the insidious wiles of foreign influence (I conjure you to believe me, fellow-citizens) the jealousy of a free people ought to be *constantly* awake; since history and experience prove that foreign influence is one of the most baneful foes of republican Government. But that jealousy, to be useful, must be impartial; else it becomes the instrument of the very influence to be avoided, instead of a defence against it. Excessive partiality for one foreign nation, and excessive dislike for another, cause those whom they actuate to see danger only on one side, and serve to veil, and even second, the arts of influence on the other. Real patriots, who may resist the intrigues of the favourite, are liable to become suspected and odious; while its tools and dupes usurp the applause and confidence of the people, to surrender their interests.

The great rule of conduct for us, in regard to foreign nations, is, in extending our commercial relations, to have with them as little political connexion as possible. So far as we have already formed engagements, let them be fulfilled with perfect good faith. Here let us stop.

Europe has a set of primary interests, which to us have none, or a very remote relation. Hence she must be engaged in frequent controversies, the causes of which are essentially foreign to our concerns. Hence, therefore, it must be unwise in us to implicate ourselves, by artificial ties, in the ordinary vicissitudes of her politics, or the ordinary combinations and collisions of her friendships or enmities.

Our detached and distant situation invites and enables us to pursue a different course. If we remain one people, under an efficient Government, the period is not far off when we may defy material injury from external annoyance; when we may take such an attitude as will cause the neutrality we may at any time resolve upon, to be scrupulously respected; when belligerent nations under the impossibility of making acquisitions upon us, will not lightly hazard the giving us provocation; when we may choose peace or war, as our interest, guided by justice, shall counsel.

Why forego the advantages of so peculiar a situation? Why quit our own to stand upon foreign ground? Why, by interweaving our destiny with that of any part of Europe, entangle our peace and prosperity in the toils of European ambition, rivalship, interest, humour, or caprice?

It is our true policy to steer clear of permanent alliances with any portion of the foreign world; so far, I mean, as we are now at liberty to do it; for let me not be misunderstood as capable of patronising infidelity to existing engagements. I hold the maxim no less applicable to public than to private affairs, that honesty is always the best policy. I repeat it, therefore, let those engagements be observed in their genuine sense. But, in my opinion, it is unnecessary, and would be unwise to extend them.

Taking care always to keep ourselves, by suitable establishments, on a respectable defensive posture, we may safely trust to temporary alliances for extraordinary emergencies.

Harmony, and a liberal intercourse with all nations, are recommended by policy, humanity, and interest. But even our commercial policy should hold an equal and impartial hand; neither seeking nor granting exclusive favours or preferences; consulting the natural course of things; diffusing and diversifying, by gentle means, the streams of commerce, but forcing nothing; establishing, with powers so disposed, in order to give trade a stable course, to define the rights of our merchants, and to enable the Government to support them, conventional rules of intercourse, the best that present circumstances and mutual opinions will permit, but temporary, and liable to be, from time to time, abandoned or varied, as experience and circumstances shall dictate; constantly keeping in view, that it is folly in one nation to look for disinterested favours from another; that it must pay, with a portion of its independence, for whatever it may accept under that character; that by such acceptance it may place itself in the condition of having given equivalents for nominal favours, and yet of being reproached with ingratitude for not giving more. There can be no greater error than to expect, or calculate upon, real favours from nation to nation. It is an illusion which experience must cure, which a just pride ought to discard.

In offering to you, my countrymen, these counsels of an old and affectionate friend, I dare not hope they will make the strong and lasting impression I could wish; that they will control the usual current of the passions, or prevent our nation from running the course which has hitherto marked the destiny of nations; but if I may even flatter myself that they may be productive of some partial benefit, some occasional good; that they may now and then recur to moderate the fury of party spirit, to warn against the mischiefs of foreign intrigues, to guard against the impostures of pretended patriotism; this hope will be a full recompense for the solicitude for your welfare by which they have been dictated.

How far, in the discharge of my official duties, I have been guided by the principles which have been delineated, the public records, and other evidences of my conduct, must witness to you and the world. To myself, the assurance of my own conscience is, that I have at least believed myself to be guided by them.

In relation to the still subsisting war in Europe, my proclamation of the 22d of April, 1793, is the index to my plan. Sanctioned by your approving voice, and by that of your Representatives in both Houses of Congress, the spirit of that measure has continually governed me, uninfluenced by any attempts to deter or divert me from it.

After deliberate examination, with the aid of the best lights I could obtain, I was well satisfied that our country, under all the circumstances of the case, had a right to take, and was bound in duty and interest to take, a neutral position. Having taken it, I determined, as far as should depend upon me, to maintain it with moderation, perseverance, and firmness.

The considerations which respect the right to hold this conduct, it is not necessary on this occasion to detail. I will only observe, that according to my understanding of the matter, that right, so far from being denied by any of the belligerent powers has been virtually admitted by all.

The duty of holding a neutral conduct may be inferred, without any thing more, from the obligation which justice and humanity impose on every nation, in cases in which it is free to act, to maintain inviolate the relations of peace and amity towards other nations.

The inducements of interest, for observing that conduct, will best be referred to your own reflections and experience. With me, a predominant motive has been to endeavour to gain time to our country to settle and mature its yet recent institutions, and to progress, without interruption, to that degree of strength and consistency which is necessary to give it, humanly speaking, the command of its own fortunes.

Though in reviewing the incidents of my administration, I

am unconscious of intentional error; I am, nevertheless, too sensible of my defects not to think it probable that I may have committed many errors. Whatever they may be, I fervently beseech the Almighty to avert or mitigate the evils to which they may tend. I shall also carry with me the hope, that my country will never cease to view them with indulgence; and that, after forty-five years of my life dedicated to its service with an upright zeal, the faults of incompetent abilities will be consigned to oblivion, as myself must soon be to the mansions of rest.

Relying on its kindness in this, as in other things, and actuated by that fervent love towards it which is so natural to a man who views in it the native soil of himself and his progenitors for several generations, I anticipate, with pleasing expectation, that retreat in which I promise myself to realize, without alloy, the sweet enjoyment of partaking, in the midst of my fellow-citizens, the benign influence of good laws under a free government—the ever favourite object of my heart—and the happy reward, as I trust, of our mutual cares, labours, and dangers.

GEORGE WASHINGTON.

United States, 17th September, 1796.

QUESTIONS FOR EXAMINATION.

CHAPTER I.

1. WHEN, and by whom, were John Cabot and his three sons commissioned to set forth on a voyage of discovery? What was done under this commission?

2. What was the origin of the title of England to North America? Upon what did that title depend? What was it called? What principle was adopted by European nations in relation to the discovery of unknown countries?

3. What restrictions were imposed upon the original inhabitants under this title? To whom could the natives grant a title?

4. What was the probable origin of the Right of Discovery?

5. Are uninhabited countries considered as belonging to any particular nation? What right does a nation acquire in the discovery of uninhabited lands? Under what conditions will its title be regarded as good by other nations? Under what conditions will its title be considered incomplete?

6. Can the titles derived from discovery be easily overthrown? Where have they become vested by successive transfers? Under what title do we hold this country? How has that title descended to us?

7. What laws govern the settlers of an uninhabited country? What laws govern them if the country be inhabited?

8. How did the North American colonists regard the occupancy and claims of the Indian tribes? What laws did they take with them to the New World? By what body were those laws ratified?

9. What did the charters under which the colonies were settled expressly declare? What colony alone was excepted? Did the acts of Parliament always affect the colonies?

10. Name the thirteen original colonies? Into how many classes have these colonies been divided? In reference to what? Name the three divisions or classes.

11. By whom was a governor appointed under the provincial governments? What rank did he hold? How did he rule? Who established courts and raised military forces? What power had the governor with regard to legislative assemblies? What kind of laws did they make? Name the provincial colonies.

12. What did the king grant to the proprietary governments? What powers did the proprietaries possess? How many proprietary governments were there at the time of the Revolution? Name them and their proprietors. What proprietary governments became provincial or royal before the Revolution?

13. How and in whom were the rights vested in the charter governments? By whom were the governor, council, and assembly chosen in Connecticut and

Rhode Island? How were they chosen in Massachusetts? By what charter? Name the charter governments existing at the time of the Revolution.

14. In what important particulars was there a similarity in the situation and circumstances of the colonists?

15. What induced many of the settlers of the colonies to emigrate from England? What had this excitement produced? What institutions of learning were founded? What were encouraged? Of what benefit to the colonies was their great distance from the mother country? What is meant by the law of primogeniture? In what colonies was this law abolished? What was the consequence of its abolishment? What the tendency?

16. Had the colonies any political connection with each other? Had they a right to form treaties or alliances with each other? How were they recognised by the law of nations? What rights had each colonist in every other colony?

CHAPTER II.

17. Were the colonies politically united? Did they ever unite together? For what purpose? Why did the New England colonies unite?

18. What colonies united together for the purpose of protecting themselves against the Dutch and Indians? When was this alliance formed? What was its name?

19. What colonies sent delegates to deliberate together upon the best means of defending themselves in case of a war with France? In what year did they assemble?

20. What led the colonies to form a union for their common protection? In what year did the Congress of nine colonies assemble in New York? What did they assert in their bill of rights?

21. Where did the first Continental Congress assemble? When? Who was its President? Who its secretary? What did the members style themselves? How long did they continue in session? What valuable State paper did this Congress publish?

22. When and where did the second Continental Congress meet? How long did it continue in session? How were the votes taken in these Congresses? If a colony had seven delegates, how many votes would they cast? If the delegates were equally divided, how did they vote?

23. When was the Declaration of Independence declared? What effect did it produce? In the Declaration of Independence, what were the colonies styled for the first time? What then became necessary?

24. What two important committees were appointed on the 11th of June, 1776?

25. When were the Articles of Confederation adopted by Congress? By the delegates of what States were they ratified, and when? By what States were they subsequently signed, and when? When was the ratification completed? When did Congress assemble under the Confederation?

26. For what purpose were the thirteen States formed into a league?

27. Did the States delegate all their powers to the United States? How often were delegates chosen for each State? How many for each State? How were the expenses defrayed? How were questions decided?

28. How were the expenses of the war supplied?

29. How was a committee of the States formed? What were its duties?

30. In what cases was the assent of nine States required? What questions did not require a majority of votes?

31. Was this Confederation intended to be altered?

32. When were the Articles finally ratified? Who directed the war? What were the powers of Congress? the character of the government?

33. Did the Articles answer the purpose intended? Name its principal defects.

34. What led to the formation of the present Constitution?

35. Through how many forms has the government passed? What are they?

36. Describe the Revolutionary government; the Confederate; the Constitutional.

CHAPTER III.

37. For what purpose did Virginia and Maryland appoint commissioners? When?

38. For what purpose did the legislature of Virginia make an appointment? When?

39. Where was the meeting held? When?

40. Why did they not proceed to the business?

41. What did they prepare? What was recommended?

42. What State first appointed delegates? What did the legislature of New York do? What was the resolution of Congress? When was it declared?

43. What was the consequence of these proceedings? When and where did the convention meet? When did they organize? Who was elected to preside? From what State was he a delegate?

44. What was the object of calling the convention? What did the majority determine upon?

45. What was the result of their labours? What were the difficulties in its formation?

46. What did the convention direct? What did Congress do? When?

47. When and where did the conventions assemble? What followed?

48. What resolutions did Congress adopt? Where?

49. How many electoral votes were cast? Who was elected President? How many votes did he receive? Who was Vice-President?

50. Of representatives from how many States was the first Constitutional Congress composed? When did they assemble? When did they first transact business?

51. When did Washington take the oath and deliver his inaugural address? Who administered the oath? When did Adams enter upon his duties?

52. The ratification of what States was afterwards received? When? How had those States been regarded?

53. Name the States and time of ratification.

CHAPTER IV.

55. What is a constitution?

56. Of what does it consist in some countries?

57. Can an act of Congress be contrary to the Constitution?

58. How is the constitution of England formed?

59. Recite the first paragraph of the Constitution.

60. What is a preamble?

61. How many objects had the framers of the present Constitution in view? Name them.

62. What is the object of the preamble?

63. How many great departments of government are there? Name them. What power has the legislative department? the judicial? the executive?

64. How does the Constitution recognise these departments? Of what does the first article of the Constitution treat? the second? the third? How are the legislative powers granted by the Constitution vested?

65. What States were in favour of dividing Congress into two distinct bodies?

66. Of what does the English Parliament consist? What does Congress include?

67. What are the advantages of two branches of legislative power? Repeat section 2, clause 1.

68. How are the repesentatives elected?

69. What are the qualifications for voters under the Constitution?

70. What persons are qualified to vote for members of Congress?

71. When do popular elections not represent the will of the people?

73. How often are representatives to Congress chosen? How long do members of Parliament occupy their seats? How often is there a new Congress? Repeat clause 2.

74. How are the qualifications of a representative divided?

75. Must a representative be a citizen by birth? How may a foreigner become a citizen? After how long a citizenship?

76. At the time of the adoption of the Federal Constitution, could emigrants hold office? What rendered them eligible? How long must an alien reside here before he becomes a citizen? How long before he is eligible as a representative?

77. Where must a representative reside? Must he reside in the district from which he is chosen? Would he lose his seat on removal? What amount of property is necessary? Religious belief?

78. What is a tax? How many kinds are there? Name them. How is a direct tax laid? An indirect tax? Are direct taxes often levied? How are direct taxes to be apportioned?

79. What was the basis of taxation by the Articles of Confederation? What by the Constitution?

80. How is the representative population ascertained? How are Indians included if taxed? Is the representative greater or less than the total population?

81. When the Constitution was adopted, were there slaves in all the States?

82. Are slaves included in the representative population? What was the effect in the States having the most slaves?

83. How often is the census taken?

84. Who takes the census? What officers are they?

85. How are the districts divided? What is the duty of the assistant? What is the penalty of refusing to answer?

86. What is the object of the census? What the results?

89. How many inhabitants are required for one representative? If a State should not contain that number, what is the law? Is the number of representatives the same as formerly?

90. How many delegates has each organized territory? What are the privileges of the territorial representatives? What are these territories generally called?

91. How is the entire representative population of the United States ascertained? How is the representative population of each State ascertained? What is the aggregate thus found?

92. When the apportionment is completed, what is then required?

93. How is the ratio of representation obtained? What States have a population less than the ratio? How many representatives are left? How are they assigned?

94. Why was an additional representative allowed to California? When?

95. How many modes are there in which a State may be entitled to a representative? Name them.

97. What is the law when vacancies occur in the representation? For what time are they elected?

98. How is the Speaker of the House of Representatives chosen? What is his rank?

99. What are the other officers of the House of Representatives? What are the duties of the clerk? Sergeant-at-arms? Postmaster of the House? What oath is required of the clerk? Sergeant-at-arms and door-keeper? For what does the clerk give security? What are the duties of chaplain?

CHAPTER V.

Repeat clause 1.

100. What constitutes the other branch of legislative power? How are senators elected? How many delegates does each State send to the Senate? In what respect does the Constitution resemble the old Confederation?

101. Does the Constitution prescribe the mode for electing senators? How are the senators chosen in most of the States? How in some? What is the latter mode termed?

103. If all or a majority of the States should refuse to elect senators, what would be the effect? What if one State should refuse?

Repeat clause 2.

104. What is the effect of this clause? What occurs every two years?

105. Would a State be represented in case of the death of a senator? How are vacancies filled? How long do such appointments continue? What is the rule if the vacancy occurs when the legislature is in session?

Repeat clause 3.

107. Of how many particulars do the qualifications of senator consist? Name them.

108. Why must a senator be thirty years of age? Must he be a native of the United States? What if an alien?

109. Where must he reside when elected? Why are the qualifications of a senator higher than those of a representative?

Repeat clause 4.

111. Is the presiding officer of the Senate a member of that body? What reasons are assigned for it? Why would the Vice-President be supposed to be more impartial?

Repeat clause 5.

112. How are the other officers of the Senate chosen? When has the Senate power to elect its president?

113. What is it customary for the Vice-President to do just before the close of each session? What does the Senate do then?

Repeat clause 6.

114. What body has the sole power of impeachment? What the power to try impeachments? What is the object of this provision?

115. What is an impeachment?

116. Is a judge of the Supreme Court of the United States liable to impeachment?

117. When the Senate tries an impeachment, are the senators sworn? What is an affirmation? What majority of the Senate is necessary for conviction?

118. Upon the removal of the President, where do his powers and duties devolve? Who is president of the Senate in a case of impeachment of the President of the United States.

120. What is the judgment in cases of impeachment in the United States? Suppose his offence to be punishable by law?

121. What would be the judgment of the Senate on conviction for treason? Would the person be subject to indictment in a court of law? If so, what would be the punishment? If acquitted, how would the judgment of the Senate stand?

122. What is the first step when it is proposed to impeach an officer? What is done if the report be favourable? What is then done by the Senate? What is done on the day of his appearance? What body replies? What does it declare?
123. Describe the mode of trial.

CHAPTER VI.

Repeat clause 1.
124. Why was not a general election law established? To what bodies is the regulation of elections intrusted? What power is reserved to Congress? In what cases would that power be necessary? Can Congress alter the place of choosing senators?
126. What is the provision of the act of June 25, 1842?
Repeat clause 2.
127. How does the English Parliament assemble? How often does Congress assemble? When?
128. How long does a Parliament exist under statute of George I.?
129. Does the Constitution determine the place where Congress shall meet? Under what contingencies may the President convene Congress at any place he may think proper?
Repeat clause 1, sec. 5.
131. What is the law when an election of a member of the House shall be contested?
132. How shall evidence be taken in such cases?
133. How is the passage of laws by a small number prevented?
134. What are the rules in case of absence of members from the House of Representatives?
Repeat clause 2.
135. Does the Constitution prescribe the mode of transacting business in Congress?
136. What enables Congress to maintain its usefulness and independence?
138. Has either House power to punish for a breach of its privileges, &c.?
139. When imprisonment is part of the punishment, when does it terminate?
Repeat clause 3.
140. What is the object of a journal? Who draws up the journal of the House? Who that of the Senate?
141. Are the deliberations of both Houses open to the public? What are executive sessions? What is the rule when the Senate is acting on confidential business?
142. What is the rule when the House receives confidential communications? What is the rule when the Speaker or a member has a secret communication?
143. In what cases are the proceedings of the Senate contained in manuscript records? To whom are they accessible?
144. What publications have been printed and regularly issued from the time of the organization of government? What are the rules with regard to printed copies of the journal of the House?
145. What is meant by taking the yeas and nays? How is it done? Why can they not be taken except by a vote of one-fifth of the members?
146. Can a member of Congress vote by proxy?
147. In what case is a member of the House not allowed to vote? What contract is a member of Congress forbidden to enjoy? What is the law if he enters into such contract? What is the effect if an officer of the United States enters into a public contract with a member of Congress?
Repeat clause 4.

149. Can the President put an end to a session of Congress? Can he adjourn its sittings?

150. How only can Congress separate? How often does a new Congress commence? How many sessions does a Congress generally hold? What does the Constitution require? How is the closing of one session and the commencement of another determined? What time must Congress necessarily adjourn in every second year?

Repeat clause 1, sec. 6.

151. Do the members of the English Parliament receive compensation? Are members of Congress compensated? Why?

153. Since 1817, what has been the compensation of members of Congress? Of the President of the Senate in the absence of Vice-President, and of the Speaker of the House?

154. What is the duty of the sergeant-at-arms, by the rules of the House?

155. Who has charge of the funds for the use of the Senate? What security does he give for their faithful application?

156. What personal privileges are members of Congress entitled to? What is the reason for this exemption? Do these privileges extend to the families of the members?

157. What are the limits of this privilege?

158. Is it lawful to question a member of Congress in any other place for any speech, &c.? How have the debates in Congress been published?

Repeat clause 2.

160. Can an officer under the United States be a member of Congress? Can one who holds such an office be elected? When must he resign it?

CHAPTER VII.

Repeat clause 1.

161. How are bills for raising revenue generally considered?

162. Which house has the right to originate such bills? Why?

163. What kind of body is the Senate?

Repeat clause 2.

164. How is the mode of enacting laws determined? When may bills originate? What are the exceptions?

165. How may a bill be introduced in the House?

166. How many readings must a bill receive? How many in the same day? If opposed at the first reading, what is the question? If no opposition is made, what is done next? Is the whole bill read? Why?

167. What is the practice when a bill is ordered to be engrossed?

169. What takes place after the passage of the bill in the House? What if the Senate refuse to concur? What if the Senate pass the bill with amendments?

170. What is a committee of conference? What are its duties?

171. After a bill has passed both houses, what is done?

172. By whom is the enrolled bill signed? What does the endorsement certify? To whom is it then presented?

173. Does he sign it? To what is his power confined? What is this power called?

174. What is the meaning of the word veto?

175. In England is the king's veto absolute? Is the President's veto absolute? What is the effect?

176. What is the object of the veto? What is it intended to check?

178. Are the objections of the President recorded? How is the vote upon the passage of a law required to be taken? Why is this done?

179. If a bill is passed by a vote of two-thirds of the house in which it

originated, what is the rule? What if approved by two-thirds of that house?

180. How might the President prevent or delay the passage of a bill? What is the provision to avoid such a contingency?

181. When does an act of Congress go into effect? What is the exception? Repeat the commencement of an act of Congress.

Repeat clause 3.

CHAPTER VIII.

184. WHAT are concurrent powers? Exclusive powers?

Repeat clause 1.

186. To how many purposes is the power of Congress to lay taxes limited? What are they?

187. How are duties charged? To what are they chiefly confined? Why are taxes laid upon exported articles? What is the meaning of impost? What are excises?

189. Are duties, imposts, and excises different in the several States? Are taxes uniform throughout the States? What is a capitation or poll-tax?

190. What two rules govern Congress in imposing taxes? How are capitation and other direct taxes laid? How are duties, imposts, excises, and indirect taxes generally laid?

191. Illustrate the difference between the operation of a direct tax laid according to the first rule, and an indirect tax according to the second rule.

194. How far does the power of Congress to lay and collect taxes, duties, imposts, and excises extend? Where is Congress not bound to extend a direct tax? Why are they held subject to taxation?

195. What are generally considered direct taxes?

196. Of how many kinds are duties on imposts? Name them. What is a specific duty? What is an *ad valorem* duty?

197. On what are duties laid? What is meant by tonnage?

198. Do vessels of the United States pay duty when entering the ports of the United States? In what cases are tonnage duties on foreign vessels abolished?

199. Can the States lay imposts or duties on exports or imports? What are inspection laws? Can the States lay duties on tonnage?

200. Who pays the duties charged upon imports or exports? What is the law if the imported goods are not to be used in the United States? What is this allowance called? What is debenture?

201. What is a tariff?

202. What is a bonded warehouse?

203. Where the acts of Congress impose an *ad valorem* rate of duty, how is true value of the goods ascertained upon which the duties are assessed?

204. Who are the detectors of frauds in invoices?

205. What is an invoice? How must invoices of imported goods be verified? Who is the consignor? Who the consignee?

206. Who are the appraisers? What are their duties?

207. What is done when goods are not invoiced to their true value through ignorance? What when fraud is suspected?

208. What is a manifest? What is required in the manifests of vessels belonging in whole or part to citizens of the United States?

209. Under what direction are the charges upon goods, &c. imported or exported collected? For this purpose how are the States divided? What is established in each collection district?

210. What does the collector receive? What is meant by the entry of goods?

211. What are the duties of the collector? What is the law with regard to the unloading and delivery of goods? Where is the official business of the collector transacted?

213. What other officers are appointed in some of the more important ports? What are the duties of the naval officer?

214. Who appoints the naval officer? What officer is he a check upon? What entries are continued in the naval office?

215. What are the duties of the surveyor? By whom is he appointed?

216. What are the duties of the officers of the ports if they suspect goods subject to duty to be concealed in a vessel? If concealed in any store or building?

217. What goods are liable to forfeiture? How are other violations of the revenue laws punished?

218. What are revenue cutters? For what are they used? Who are smugglers? What other laws do the revenue cutters aid in enforcing?

219. What are the privileges of vessels owned and commanded by our own citizens?

220. What is the registry of a vessel?

221. Is the owner of a vessel bound to register it? What is the law if a vessel is not registered?

222. What is required in order to obtain a register? What if the master be changed or the vessel's name altered?

223. What is the coasting trade? What is required of vessels in the coasting and fishing trades in order to be entitled to the privileges of vessels of the United States? What if they are less than twenty tons burden? How long are licenses valid?

224. How may registered vessels be enrolled and licensed? How may those enrolled and licensed be registered? What is required of vessels enrolled and licensed for the coasting trade, before proceeding on a foreign voyage?

225. What are unregistered vessels? Under what authority do they sail?

226. When are certificates of registry, enrolment, and licenses termed permanent? When temporary?

227. What is a protection certificate?

Repeat clause 2. Repeat clause 3.

229. What is commerce? How is the word used in the Constitution?

231. What power has Congress in regulating commerce? How far does the power extend?

232. Why cannot a State lay a tax on importers or imported goods?

233. What is quarantine? What is the object of compelling a vessel to perform quarantine?

234. To what other cases does the authority of Congress also extend? What is an embargo?

236. How are the Indians within a State or the territories regarded?

Repeat clause 4.

237. What is meant by naturalization?

240. How long must a foreigner reside in the United States before he can be naturalized?

241. How may an alien, being a free white person, become a citizen of the United States? What is this act called?

242. What is required at the time of his application? How long must he have resided in the United States? How long in the State or territory where he then resides? What other qualifications are necessary? How must the applicant prove his residence?

243. In what cases are children of persons duly naturalized considered as citizens of the United States? When are persons born out of the United States considered as citizens? In what cases are the widow and children of an alien considered as citizens?

244. What are aliens required to renounce on becoming citizens?

245. What is the cause of bankruptcy and insolvency? To what class of persons does a bankrupt law apply? Who does the insolvent law protect?

246. Where is the power to establish bankrupt laws vested?

248. Is there any national bankrupt law in force now?

Repeat clause 5.

249. Why are the powers to coin money and to fix the standard of weights and measures vested in Congress? Where is money coined?

250. What are the duties of the director of the mint? The treasurer? The assayer? The melter and refiner? Chief coiner? The engraver?

251. Where is the mint situated?

252. Would it be lawful for a person to take uncoined gold or silver to the mint to have it coined? Is the treasurer of the mint obliged to receive deposits of less value than one hundred dollars.

253. Where have branches of the mint been established?

254. What are the weights and measures of the States?

Repeat clause 6. Repeat clause 7.

260. How are the mails carried?

261. Under whose direction is the post-office of the United States? What power has he by act of Congress. What is required of him and others employed in the general post-office previous to entering upon the discharge of their duties? In what cases is a heavy penalty imposted on a postmaster?

263. What postmasters are appointed by the President? What by the Postmaster General?

264. What is meant by franking? By whom is this privilege possessed?

267. What are the post-roads generally selected? Of what are post-roads declared to consist?

Repeat clause 8.

269. What are the means used to promote science and arts? What class of persons does this clause protect?

270. To whom are letters-patent granted?

271. Who is the chief officer of the patent-office? What are his duties? What are the duties of the examiners?

272. What is a patent? What does it contain?

273. What is the specification? What is required in the specification?

275. What is the duty of the commissioner on the receipt of the application, &c.? What is the cost of a patent to a citizen of the United States?

276. Can a patent be extended?

277. For what term are the authors of books, &c. entitled to the exclusive right of printing, publishing, and selling them? What is this privilege termed?

278. What is required of an author or proprietor in order to obtain a copyright?

279. What is required to be inserted in every copy during the duration of the right? Why is this done?

280. Is a person entitled to print or publish a manuscript without the consent of the author?

Repeat clause 9. Repeat clause 10.

283. What is piracy? What do the high seas include?

285. What are the offences on the high seas declared by Congress to be treated as piracies?

286. In what case shall a mariner or captain be deemed a pirate and felon?

287. What has the slave-trade been declared?

288. What is understood by the law of nations? Mention some offences against the law of nations? Where is the punishment of such offences vested?

Repeat clause 11.

290. What are meant by letters of marque and reprisal? What is the meaning of reprisal? What of marque?

292. What is capture? May all vessels belonging to the enemy be captured? What is a prize? What is booty?

293. What is the general practice of nations with regard to captured property? What is the rule when a prize is taken at sea?

294. When are the proceeds of all ships and vessels considered the sole property of the captors? When of inferior force, what is the law?

295. What courts are authorized to try the question of prize or no prize?

Repeat clause 12.

297. How has Congress the right to raise armies? For how long a period shall there be an appropriation for the support of the military?

298. How long are enlistments required to be?

299. What is the oath required by the officers, &c. of the army?

Repeat clause 13.

300. Of what use is a navy? Name the first three vessels commissioned for our service.

301. What is hospital money?

302. What others are subject to the same deduction?

303. How are invalid seamen provided for in smaller ports? Where has one permanent naval asylum been established?

304. What institution did Congress authorize to be erected near Washington?

305. What are pensions?

306. What are invalid pensions?

307. What are gratuitous pensions?

308. What are bounty lands?

Repeat clause 14. Repeat clause 15.

310. For what purpose has Congress a right to call the militia of the States? What is meant by militia?

311. Who is to judge of the necessity of calling out the militia? How may the militia be called forth? Under whose control are the army and navy of the United States? How can the President call forth the militia?

Repeat clause 16.

313. Can one State control the militia of another State? How are the officers appointed? How are the militia trained? When do the States train and discipline the militia?

Repeat clause 17.

314. In what State, if any, is the seat of government?

315. Where is it? What is the name of the District?

317. Are the inhabitants of the District regarded as citizens of any State? Are they liable to taxation? How are their local affairs regulated? How are Washington and Georgetown governed?

318. How can Congress acquire property in a State? The consent of what body is required?

319. Who has the jurisdiction over places purchased by government? How are offences committed there to be tried?

Repeat clause 18.

CHAPTER IX.

REPEAT clause 1.

323. What was the main object of this clause? By the act of 1820 how is the slave-trade considered?

Repeat clause 2.

327. What is a writ?

328. What is meant by a writ of *habeas corpus?*

329. What would be done if a person alleged in writing that he was unlawfully deprived of his liberty? To whom is the writ directed?

330. What is done when the imprisoment is illegal? When legal?

Repeat clause 3.

332. What are bills of attainder?

333. What are *ex post facto* laws? Why are those laws prohibited?

Repeat clause 4. Repeat clause 5. Repeat clause 6.

336. Why is no preference given to one port over another?

Repeat clause 7.

338. What does this clause prevent? To whom does the money in the Treasury belong? Who keep the Treasury accounts? To whom does he report, and to what body is the report transmitted?

339. Can the government be sued for claims? What is the mode of redress?

Repeat clause 8.

340. What is a fundamental principle of our government? Why are titles of nobility prohibited?

341. Why is a person holding office prohibited from receiving a present from a foreign power? What is required in order that such officer may receive those gifts? To what persons does the prohibition not extend?

342. Are gifts from foreign princes ever sent to the President? What is generally done in those cases?

CHAPTER X.

REPEAT clause 1.

343. Can a State enter into a treaty? Why? Why should not foreign powers form alliances with any State? In whom is the treaty-making power vested?

344. Under the Constitution where is the power to issue letters of marque and reprisal vested? What danger might arise if this power was vested in the States?

345. Can any State coin money?

346. What is meant by bills of credit? Can the States issue such bills? What were the bills of credit issued during the Revolution called? To what amount were bills of credit then issued? What was the object of this prohibition?

347. What is the lawful tender of the States? What was the object of this restriction?

349. Can the States impair the obligations of contracts? What is a contract? What is the obligation of a contract? What would be the effect if the law was changed enforcing its fulfilment?

354. In what cases can charters granted by a State be altered or impaired? What charters may be repealed and changed?

355. What are retrospective laws?

356. Can the States grant titles of nobility?

Repeat clause 2.

358. Can a State lay duties on exports or imports?

359. Can a State enact inspection laws? What are inspection laws? What is the object of these laws?

Repeat clause 3.

363. Under what restrictions can the States lay duty on tonnage?

364. Can the States keep troops or ships of war in time of peace? What is the rule in time of war?

365. Can a State enter into compact with another State? What is the restriction? What is the utility of this law?

366. Can a State engage in war without the consent of Congress? Where is the power to declare war vested?

CHAPTER XI.

REPEAT clause 1.

368. In whom is the executive power vested?

370. How long does the President hold his office?

371. When does the term commence? When does it expire? How often may a President be re-elected? What example guides this matter?

372. Why was the office of Vice-President created?

Repeat clause 2.

373. How are the President and Vice-President chosen? What is meant by the electoral college?

376. To what number of electors is each State entitled?

377. Who are excluded from being electors?

378. What is the rule if the electors fail to make a choice?

379. Where does each electoral college meet?

383. How is the President chosen in the House of Representatives?

385. Describe the manner in which Thomas Jefferson was elected?

388. How are the electors to vote?

389. What is the rule if no one has a majority?

390. What if the choice of a President falls on the House of Representatives, and they fail?

391. How is the Vice-President elected? What proportion of senators constitute a quorum for this purpose? How are the votes of the Senate taken?

392. Can one who is ineligible to the office of President be eligible to the office of Vice-President?

393. How was John Q. Adams elected in 1825?

Repeat clause 4.

394. How many electors is each State entitled to?

395. Where are the electors required to give their votes? Where do they usually meet? What is further required of the electors?

396. What is the rule if there should then be no President of the Senate at the seat of government? What is required to be done with the other two certificates?

397. What is required of the executive authority of each State?

398. What is required to be done if a list of votes shall not have been received at the time appointed?

399. Where are the certificates to be opened? By whom? In the presence of whom?

Repeat clause 5.

401. Of how many particulars do the qualifications of President consist? Name the first; the second; the third; the fourth.

402. Why are aliens and foreigners excluded from the office of President?

403. Why should the President be thirty-five years of age?

404. Why is a previous residence of fourteen years required? Does it preclude a temporary sojourn in foreign countries?

Repeat clause 6.

405. In case of death, &c. of the President, on whom do his duties devolve?

406. In case of death, &c. of the President and Vice-President, who shall act as President? Who in case there shall be no President of the Senate *pro tempore?*

407. What does the Vice President generally do just before the close of every session?

408. In what case is there no provision made for President?

409. What is the rule when the office of President and Vice-President shall both become vacant?

Repeat clause 7.

410. Has Congress the power to deprive the President of his salary? Can his salary be increased during his term of office?

411. What is the salary of the President? Of the Vice-President?

Repeat clause 8. Repeat clause 1, sec. 2.

414. Who is commander-in-chief of the army and navy? When only can he command the militia of the several States?

415. The opinions of whom may the President require in writing? Is he bound to adopt such opinions? The opinions of whom can he not require?

416. Who is authorized to grant reprieves and pardons for offences against the United States? What cases excepted? What is a reprieve? A pardon? What does the pardoning power include?

417. Against whom is impeachment generally employed? For what? How far does the judgment extend? What portion of the Senate must concur? What is the object of impeachment?

Repeat clause 2.

418. What is a treaty? What are the subjects of treaties?

419. How are treaties usually formed? When is the treaty finally binding?

420. How is a treaty concluded in practice?

421. Can the Senate make alterations in a treaty? When does it become a law?

422. In whom is the appointing power vested? Under what restrictions? To whom does this power extend?

423. What is the rule when nominations shall be made by the President in writing? What is the rule as to remarks concerning the character, &c. of a person nominated?

424. Can the Senate reject a nomination made by the President? Can they nominate another person?

425. To constitute a full appointment there are three requisites Name the first; the second; the third.

426. What is necessary to make an appointment complete?

427. What is the commission? Is its delivery necessary? If lost, would the appointment be void? From what date is the salary received?

428. In whom is the power of removal vested?

430. How far does the power of the President to remove officers extend?

431. What are the duties of public ministers?

433. How many grades of public ministers are there? Name those of the first class. Whom do they represent? How are ambassadors divided? How are ordinary ambassadors employed? How are extraordinary?

434. Name the second class of public ministers. Name the third. How do ministers of the second and third classes represent their State or sovereign?

435. Who are consuls? Are they considered as public ministers? What is required before they can enter on their duties? Who is a vice-consul?

436. What are the duties of consuls of the United States? What have they authority to receive? What is required of them? What power have they?

437. Are consuls permitted to transact business in their own name? What is the penalty?

438. What is the law with regard to the persons and goods of foreign ambassadors? Are they responsible to the laws of the country to which they are sent? What is the law if they insult the government to which they are sent, or violate its laws?

439. Are consuls entitled to the privileges of public ministers? Are they subject to the laws of the country where they reside?

Repeat clause 3.

441. What is the law should a vacancy occur when the Senate is not in session? When does that appointment expire?

Repeat section 3.

444. What was the origin of the President's written message to Congress? What two Presidents delivered them personally? By whom was the practice

discontinued? Is Congress obliged to adopt the recommendations of the President?

445. Why has the President the power to call together both houses of Congress?

447. Who is authorized to receive public ministers? What is required of foreign ministers?

448. What laws does the President see executed? Why is this duty laid upon him?

450. Who commissions all the officers of the United States? By whom are the commissions of the public officers signed? What seal have they?

Repeat section 4.

451. To whom does the power of impeachment extend? What is meant by civil officers of the United States? Who are not considered as civil officers? Are they liable to impeachment? To what discipline are they subject?

452. What is commonly meant by crimes? By misdemeanors? What is bribery?

453. Are members of Congress liable to impeachment?

454. Is the sovereign of England answerable for official misconduct? Is the President of the United States?

455. Is the President considered as a private citizen? Except in what cases?

456. Name the Presidents, and the number of terms they were in office?

CHAPTER XII.

457. How is the executive and administrative business of the government managed? Name the executive departments?

458. By whom are the heads of the departments appointed? What do they constitute? Is the Vice-President a member of the cabinet?

459. Who are the constitutional advisers of the President?

460. By whom is the head or chief officer of a department nominated? By whom may he be removed? What is the rule if a vacancy should happen during the recess of Congress? What are bureaus?

461. How can copies of their records be made evidence?

462. Can the heads of the departments make a contract in behalf of the United States? What is the exception?

463. What are the duties of Secretary of State? What is his salary?

464. By whom are passports granted to American citizens?

465. After laws have been passed by Congress, what is done?

466. What other officers are there in the Department of State besides the Secretary?

468. What are the duties of the Secretary of War? Does he compose part of the army? What is his salary?

469. Who is the Quartermaster-general? The Chief Engineer? Colonel of Topographical Engineers? Colonel of Ordnance? Commissary-general? Paymaster-general? Surgeon-general?

470. The supervision of what armories belongs to the Secretary of War? For what purpose are these armories? In what other way does government procure arms?

471. Into how many military divisions are the United States and territories divided? Name the first; the second; the third; the fourth; the fifth. Where are the head-quarters of the army? What are established in each of these departments?

472. What is the duty of the Secretary of the Treasury? His salary? Where are the accounts of the government finally settled?

476. What are done with claims due to the United States after failure or refusal to pay?
478. What other important officers are attached to this department?
479. Of what officers does the Light-house Board consist? Who is president of the Board?
480. What are the duties of the Light-house Board?
482. What are the duties of the Secretary of the Navy?
483. What bureaus belong to the Navy Department?
484. By whom is the chief of the bureau appointed? Under whose authority are the duties of the bureaus performed?
486. What are the duties of the Postmaster-general? What is his salary?
487. By whom is he aided? By whom are they appointed? Of what postmasters has he the appointment? What postmasters are appointed by the President? Who fills the office of Postmaster-general in case of death, &c.
488. How often does the Postmaster-general render his account? To whom does he render it? When is the revenue rising from his department paid?
489. What is required of him and others employed in that department previous to entering on the duties of office? What is required of the various deputy postmasters?
491. What new department was created in 1849?
492. What are the duties of the Secretary of the Interior? His salary?
493. What are the bureaus connected with the Department of the Interior?
494. What other duties are assigned to this department?
496. What are the duties of the Attorney-general?

CHAPTER XIII.

500. PRIOR to the adoption of the Constitution, had the people of the United States any national tribunal? Where was the administration of justice confined?
507. When laws became necessary to secure the interests of the Confederacy, what did Congress do? What was one of the objects of the new Constitution?
508. What does the Constitution establish?
510. How long do the judges of the Supreme and inferior courts hold their office? Can their compensation be diminished? What is the object of these provisions? How can the judges be removed from office?
511. May their salary be increased?
512. Of what is the Supreme Court of the United States composed? How many sessions does it hold annually? How many constitute a quorum? What is the salary of the chief justice? Of each associate judge?
513. Into how many circuits are the United States divided? What kind of court is held in each? Of whom is it composed? How often is it held?
514. Into what other divisions are they divided? What are the courts held in these divisions called?
515. Who appoints the clerk of the court? What are the duties of the marshal? What other officer is there in each district?
517. What is meant by the original jurisdiction of a court? How is appellate jurisdiction exercised? When is it concurrent? When exclusive?
518. In what cases have the circuit courts original jurisdiction?
519. In what have the district courts?
520. There are nine subjects in which the courts of United States have jurisdiction. Name the first; the second; the third; the fourth; the fifth; the sixth: the seventh: the eighth; the ninth.
523. Repeat the amendment to this clause.

528. What is the name of the court established by Congress in February, 1855? Who represents the government before the court?
529. What is the duty of this court?
Repeat clause 3.
531. How are impeachments tried? What is a jury? Of what number does the jury consist? What is a verdict?
532. Where is the trial for crimes to be held?
533. Where if they are not committed within a State?
Repeat clause 1, sec. 3.
534. Of what two things does treason consist?
535. What is levying war? If war be actually levied, who are considered as traitors?
536. What is the highest crime against a government?
537. How many witnesses are necessary in order to convict for treason?
Repeat clause 2.
538. What is the punishment for treason? What is the duty of one who has knowledge of the commission of treason? What is a knowledge and concealment of treason, without assenting to it, termed?
539. What is meant by becoming attaint?
540. To what did attainder lead?

CHAPTER XIV.

543. What has the Constitution declared in regard to the public acts, &c. of the States?
544. What is the mode by which records, &c. should be authenticated?
545. How are records, &c. to be considered when thus authenticated?
Repeat clause 1, sec. 2.
546. Repeat clause 2.
548. If the executive authority of one State demand a fugitive from justice of the executive authority of another State, what is the duty of the latter?
549. What course does the executive on whom the requisition is made generally pursue?
Repeat clause 3.
551. Are the citizens of slave-holding States allowed to reclaim their slaves when they escape into other States? Are fugitives from service or labour freed when they flee into another State?
553. Has Congress the power to admit new States into the Union? What was the number of States at the adoption of the Constitution? What is the number at present?
554. What form of government does the United States guarantee to every State? When are the territories erected into States?
555. How has Congress acquired additional territory?
557. To what body is the care of the public property intrusted?
558. The title of the United States to public land is derived from three sources. Name the first.
559. Name the second source.
561. What did Congress recommend to those States who had claims to the Western country?
562. What did Congress resolve with regard to the unappropriated lands?
563. Does the United States own the soil inhabited by the Indians? What has it conceded to them? How has their right of occupancy been extinguished or purchased? What is done before the public lands are offered for sale? How are townships subdivided?

565. How are the sections numbered? How are the sections again divided For what purpose are certain sections reserved in each territory?

566. After the lands have been surveyed, what is done?

568. For what purpose were land-offices established? What is a grant for land termed?

570. What officers do territorial governments include, and by whom are they appointed?

571. What is required of the territories who apply for admission as States?

572. How many organized territories are there at present? Name them. Is the Indian Territory organized?

573. How does the extent of our country compare with England and France? How much less than the area of all Europe?

Repeat clause 4.

574. How many important particulars does this clause contain? Name them.

575. What would be the power of the United States in case of a rebellion in any State?

576. Has any State a right to alter its constitution? What form of government must it adopt?

577. Is the United States bound to protect each State from invasion?

578. When may the aid of the United States be solicited by any State?

CHAPTER XV.

580. WHAT right was proclaimed in the Declaration of Independence and recognised by the States? What does Washington declare in his Farewell Address?

581. In what two modes may amendments be proposed?

582. What is required before amendments can become valid?

584. Has Congress power to amend or alter the Constitution? Is the approval of the President necessary?

588. Can any State be deprived of equal suffrage in the Senate?

Repeat clause 1, Article VI. Repeat clause 2.

592. Why are the laws of the federal government required to be obeyed by the States?

593. What constitute the supreme law of the land? Can the States disregard treaties?

594. If an act of Congress be contrary to the Constitution, is it a supreme law of the land?

595. What are the judges of every State bound to by the Constitution?

596. What is the law if an act of Congress should be contrary to the Constitution?

598. How are senators, &c. bound to support the Constitution?

599. What is the form of the oath or affirmation? How is the oath administered to the Speaker of the House of Representatives? How to the members?

600. Who administers the oath to each newly-elected senator? Who to the President of the Senate, if he has not taken it before?

602. What is required of all officers employed under the government of the United States?

603. What other important provision does this clause contain? What was this prohibition intended to restrain?

604. Does the Constitution establish any form of religious worship?

CHAPTER XVI.

609. What resolution was adopted by the first Congress, two-thirds of both houses concurring?

610. How many of these articles were ratified?

Repeat Article I.

614. Can Congress make a law respecting the establishment of religion?

615. Does the Constitution secure religious liberty?

616. What is considered the right of a free people?

617. Can any one publish his sentiments freely? What does the liberty of speech not justify?

618. Does the law restrain a man from publishing what he pleases?

619. Have the people a right to petition government for redress?

620. In what way must it be exercised?

Repeat Article II.

622. What diminishes the necessity of maintaining a large standing army?

Repeat Article III.; Article IV.

624. What is the object of this article?

625. How far does the privilege of a person's house extend?

626. What is a search-warrant?

628. What is a grand jury? How are they selected in the State courts? In the Federal courts? What must be their number? Their duty?

629. What is said of their sittings? Who is the prosecutor? If they believe the evidence sufficient, what do they endorse on the bill? What is then said of the bill?

630. If the evidence is insufficient, what do they endorse? When is a bill ignored? How is an indictment founded? What is a presentment?

631. How are the officers in service in the army and navy tried? What are capital crimes?

632. Can a person be tried twice for the same offence?

633. Under what circumstances?

634. Must a person be witness against himself? Can he be questioned as to his guilt or innocence?

636. Can private property be taken for public use? What is the right of eminent domain? What is done by virtue of this right?

637. What reason is alleged for this law? What is the check upon the exercise of this law? How can the amount of compensation be ascertained?

638. Can property be taken by government for private uses without consent of the owner?

Repeat Article VI.

640. Why is the trial of an accused person to be speedy? Why public?

641. How is the impartiality of the jury secured?

642. Of what must the prisoner be informed?

Repeat Article VII.

644. What is meant by common law?

655. Can a fact tried by a jury be re-examined in any court of the United States? What is the exception?

Repeat Article VIII.

656. What is meant by bail? When is a person said to be admitted to bail?

Repeat Article IX.; Article X.

INDEX.

[*The figures refer to the page.*]

THE END.

www.ingramcontent.com/pod-product-compliance
Lightning Source LLC
LaVergne TN
LVHW020213110826
845151LV00003B/694